M000158753

EXCOMMUNICATION

TRI◎S

Each TRIOS book
addresses an important
theme in critical theory,
philosophy, or cultural
studies through three
extended essays written
in close collaboration by
leading scholars.

EXCOMMUNICATION

THREE INQUIRIES IN
MEDIA AND MEDIATION

ALEXANDER R.
Galloway

EUGENE
Thacker

MCKENZIE
Wark

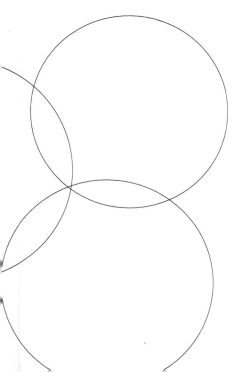

The University of Chicago Press
Chicago and London

ALEXANDER R. GALLOWAY is associate professor of media studies at New York University. He is the author of four books on digital media and critical theory, most recently, *The Interface Effect*. EUGENE THACKER is associate professor in the School of Media Studies at the New School. He is the author of many books, including *After Life*, also published by the University of Chicago Press. MCKENZIE WARK is professor of liberal studies at the New School for Social Research. His books include *A Hacker Manifesto* and *Gamer Theory*.

The University of Chicago Press, Chicago 60637
The University of Chicago Press, Ltd., London
© 2014 by The University of Chicago
All rights reserved. Published 2014.
Printed in the United States of America

23 22 21 20 19 18 17 16 15 14   1 2 3 4 5

ISBN-13: 978-0-226-92521-9 (cloth)
ISBN-13: 978-0-226-92522-6 (paper)
ISBN-13: 978-0-226-92523-3 (e-book)
DOI: 10.7208/chicago/9780226925233.001.0001

Library of Congress Cataloging-in-Publication Data

Excommunication : three inquiries in media and mediation/
Alexander R. Galloway, Eugene Thacker, McKenzie Wark.
    pages cm — (Trios)
    ISBN 978-0-226-92521-9 (cloth : alk. paper) — ISBN 978-0-226-92522-6
(pbk. : alk. paper) — ISBN 978-0-226-92523-3 (e-book)
    1. Communication—Social aspects. 2. Communication—Psychological
aspects. I. Galloway, Alexander R., 1974– Love of the middle. 2013.
II. Thacker, Eugene. Dark media. 2013. III. Wark, McKenzie, 1961– Furious
media. 2013. IV. Series: Trios (Chicago, Ill.)
    HM1166.E93 2013
    302.2—dc23

                                                           2013022635

♾ This paper meets the requirements of ANSI/NISO Z39.48-1992 (Permanence of Paper).

CONTENTS

INTRODUCTION

EXECRABLE MEDIA

Alexander R. Galloway,
Eugene Thacker, McKenzie Wark

It was otherwise a very fine conference. Except that, once again, we were put on the panel about "new media." In this case, "new media" was juxtaposed with "literary theory," although it could have been "new media *and*" pretty much anything else. New media and the novel, new media and education, new media and cultural studies, or new media and philosophy. One thing the trio of us share is a desire to cease adding "new media" to existing things. Media are transformative. They affect conditions of possibility in general. Mediation does not merely add something to the existing list of topics that scholars study. It changes the practice of study itself.

A question: do media always have to be "new" to be an object of a theory? Is it even possible to think about new media without thinking about media in general? Likewise is it possible to think about media without thinking about the *temporality* of media, about why they are labeled new or old? The moment we hear the call for new media, we offer the response of Friedrich Kittler: "What's new about new media?"[1] Much of the so-called new media are not, after all, particularly new. Writing about the phonograph, Lisa Gitelman shows how old the "new" media experience is. And in *Remediation*, Jay Bolter and Richard Grusin show how media are constantly translating old forms into new.[2] So let's have no more talk about "new media"—as if we already knew everything about old media. Instead let us try to think about media and mediation as *conceptual objects* in their own right.

What do media do? And what does it mean to ask the question? Kittler has shown, with considerable brilliance, how discourse networks have changed over three centuries: how the typewriter, the gramophone, and film have disaggregated and mechanized the component systems of sense-making, and how in turn the digital began recomposing the circuits of subject production once again.[3] His is a powerful argument for the relative autonomy of media as a conceptual object, and an indication that "the literary" might not be the only thing produced through the act of reading. In other words, Kittler is an exemplary reader of texts, but when such "texts" come in the form of diverse artifacts such as physical machines or even mathematical formulae, can such texts still be classified as literature? The literary is thus not the sole object to be found when reading. For the text may be read backward into its mediatic status, just as it may be read forward into its hermeneutic status. Each approach may find gold hidden in the cracks between the letters.

In this way, media force us to think less about things like senders and receivers, and more about questions of channels and protocols. Less about encoding and decoding, and more about context and environment. Less about writing and reading, and more about structures of interaction. These other issues do not disappear, of course, but must now be tackled within a slightly different set of considerations. To ask the media question is to invoke orders of materiality, and a certain basic familiarity with these orders of materiality is required, a certain technical fluency. For example, Matthew Kirschenbaum asks the question of when and how the word processor enters literary production. "How is writing made?" he asks, articulating what is most essentially and emblematically a media-theoretical question.[4]

So just as we detach the idea of "new" from media, let us also detach the idea of "literary" from theory. There can be no literary theory of new media other than as a subset of something more primary, namely, *media theory.* Media theory without qualification. So in parallel to Kirschenbaum lies another line of inquiry. Consider these word processing machines from another point of view. Besides producing a class of objects already designated as literature, did they, or can they, produce other things, which may or may not be literature, and which may be even more interesting than literature? The question of media theory, then, should not be "is this literature?" but rather a prior question: "is this a text"? It would therefore concern itself with how texts are extracted from media before concerning itself with how the literary is extracted from texts.

Having removed the qualifiers from new media and literary theory, we are left with media theory. But what would media entail if not the literary? It might entail *data sets*, as in Franco Moretti's "distant reading," which uses computation to study literary genres.[5] It might entail *games*, *algorithms*, or *procedures*, as Ian Bogost demonstrates in his work.[6] Or, as Lev Manovich writes, it might entail an attention not just to discrete media objects, but to media as *meta-media*.[7]

Peter Krapp constructs a prehistory of the database through an examination of index cards.[8] And Roland Barthes, we know, was an avid user of index cards, with some of his books being selections from such cards. So perhaps even the great advocate for the pleasures of the text enjoyed another kind of pleasure, the pleasure of the database, which is not so much a text as a media machine for making texts. Perhaps here the Owl of Minerva casts its shadow over the media. Perhaps media become thinkable precisely because they are passing away. Thus, in a counterintuitive sense, to engage in media theory often requires questioning whether or not there is even such a thing as a media object, at least in its more familiar iterations of text or image.

But it is not simply the object of study that has shifted. So too the practice of investigation itself modulates under the media-theoretical model. Moretti's deviation is not just the deviation of data, but of data *processing*. When Gilles Deleuze writes about complex systems, he deploys a method of writing equally complex, at times schizophrenic. Likewise, media theory requires not only a reconsideration of the object in question but also an upheaval at the level of method. In other words: not just a theory of the rhizome but a rhizomatic theory; not just a treatise on collaboration but a collaborative treatise. What would it mean to write theory that is itself algorithmic or procedural?

Kenneth Goldsmith—whose works *Day* and *Soliloquy* relentlessly interrogate the boundary between text and data—suggests we think about writing as an "uncreative writing."[9] Similarly, while masquerading as "fiction," Stewart Home's *Blood Rites of the Bourgeoisie* is a nice example of procedural writing in the way it takes spam seriously as a textual machine.[10] These are serious undertakings and we three cannot pretend to emulate them in this book, even as we have each attempted to do so at other times and in other media. For writing this book, three was already a crowd.

What, then, are the key works of media? What are works that identify key phase shifts or points of transition? Just as we speak of *The Magic Mountain*, or "The Call of Cthulhu," or *Fear and Trembling* as literary objects, shall we not speak of things like the *King James Bible*, the *Oxford English Dictionary*, or *Wikipedia* as media objects?[11] Indeed, what if we took *Wikipedia* to be the great media work of our time? And if so, what kind of history will help us grasp and anticipate such a claim? The Fluxus movement, for example, might loom large, not just within art history but within media history—indeed it is within Fluxus that a concept of *intermedia* was thought and practiced.[12] Christiane Paul has already explored the extension of those methods into the realm of media art practice in the late twentieth century.[13] On the theory side too, our roster of precursors might change. Perhaps the Situationists, for example, should figure more significantly in any history of critical media theory and practice, more significantly than our old friends in the "linguistic turn."[14]

The story of media theory in the twentieth century has still yet to be written. Lydia Liu's account of the relation between psychoanalysis and information theory is exemplary in this regard, as is Timothy Campbell's study of Marconi's wireless technology and Marinetti's poetics.[15] The past starts to appear differently when media and theory are thought together.

But then so too does the question of media practice. It may turn out that many of our more interesting theorists were also practitioners in peculiar ways. It is generally thought that, between the two of them, Theodor Adorno was a better theorist than Max Horkheimer. But who was the better practitioner? Was it not an act of genius to take the results of a survey of attitudes on authoritarianism among the German working class as evidence not only for a theory but also for moving the Institute's money out of Germany?[16] Was not Horkheimer's brilliance that of contriving a bubble that could form the medium of critical theory in exile? Today we might live in less interesting times. But nevertheless we are still confronted with serious questions of media practice. For what is the humanities academy made of today, if not media? What is the academy if not an assemblage of media, some necessary and worth preserving, while others merely the lingering mannerisms of a dead era? Rita Raley has picked this up with regard to the media of the counter-public sphere (as Alexander Kluge called it), while Kathleen Fitzpatrick has done the same for the humanities academy.[17]

Of course the more institutions change, the more they stay the same. Lisa Nakamura shows how questions of race play out in contemporary media, and Beth Coleman shows how the avatar may be a way of conceptualizing how contemporary discourse networks produce subjectivity in new ways.[18] But then, like them, the three of us live in what the Situationists helpfully called the *overdeveloped* world, and our media experience is hardly typical. For example, Brian Larkin shows how video circulates in Nigeria as a distinctive infrastructure for a media economy and culture.[19]

An awareness of how media networks operate in the present can alert one to how they might have worked in the past, even as they are often forgotten or overlooked. Here one might bracket together Emily Apter on the role of Turkey in the formation of comparative literature with Susan Buck-Morss on the influence of the Haitian revolution within Hegel's thought.[20] Today we speak of global media networks, but Apter and Buck-Morss suggest that these kinds of international flows must be understood in similar ways. What was once conveniently labeled "continental thought" often reemerges as a dynamic flux embedded in global networks of unequal exchange.

In this way we want to argue that media theory is not a new link in the grand chain of critical theory, literary criticism, cultural studies, or visual culture. Rather, it exits the chain entirely, turning ninety degrees away from these disciplines. Moving orthogonally, media theory intersects art theory, screen theory, science studies, the history of technology, and many other fields. When addressing media form, a number of different questions start to swell in importance, questions about the technics, politics, and economics of certain material layers of form. Two things in particular tend to happen. First, attention tends to shift to more empirical approaches, looking at how particular media work in particular instances (the history of the book, for example). Second, in the more theoretically-tinted approaches attention tends to shift to the issue of media orthogonality itself. That is, why are media constructed *across* the heterogeneous material layers, *orthogonal* to them, rather than within a single plane (for instance the plane of the textual or the plane of the visual)? We will therefore need a theory of orthogonality itself, of layering itself.

But didn't post-structuralism with its *écriture* or semiotics with its multiplicity of signifiers already solve this problem? Has not media studies, for decades already, defined cultural production as a complex aggregate of different kinds of interrelated practices producing different kinds of interrelated artifacts? Even if this is true, we still contend that media studies today operates with a somewhat limited conception of what media are. New sorts of parochialisms have invaded the conversation, just as it was starting to get interesting. New kinds of limitations and biases have made it difficult for media scholars to take the ultimate step and consider the basic conditions of mediation. For even as post-structuralism celebrates the free play of textuality, there remains a tendency to treat the media "beneath" the text as something of a problem, as something about which one has methodological anxieties. If text (or screen, or the picture plane) is the "good" object of creative and interpretive play, media is the "bad" object of power and vulgarity. So we must fight for media theory, even as we acknowledge its capacity for stagnation and repetition.

The field of media studies today generally understands media along two interconnected axes: *devices* and *determinacy*. On the one hand, media are understood as synonymous with media devices, technological apparatuses of mediation such as the phone, the file, or the printing press. And yet such technological devices are imbued with the irresistible force of their own determinacy. Media either determine a given social, cultural, or political dimension, or media are themselves determined by the social, cultural, or political. Media makers affect media consumers and thus establish hierarchical relationships with them, or media-savvy individuals express their own desires by way of the tools and machines that extend their will. For media studies generally, media are, in short, determinative devices, and they are thus evaluated normatively as either good influencers or bad influencers.

Consider the major traditions that continue to inform media studies today. With the Frankfurt School and Adorno and Horkheimer's theses on the culture industry, one finds an emphasis on media as technologies of *domination*. The extorted reconciliation of the pop song or narrative is determined by the apparent equivalence of commodity exchange. On the other hand, Walter Benjamin stresses not so much the raw commodity form but the technical form of *reproducibility*, through which media escape property and become the perceptual apparatus adequate to the revolutionary tasks of the working class.[21]

Likewise consider the media-ecological approach of the Toronto School, which oscillates between the categories of *bias* and *synthesis*. For Harold Innis, media forms are biased either toward being space-binding or time-binding, and the relative spatial integrity or temporal longevity of a social formation is determined by its mix of media forms. For Marshall McLuhan, the questions of bias and integration operate more at the level of the individual sensorium. The bias of print toward a fragmentary rationality destroys the sacred synthesis of the senses and of logical and analogical thought.

The tradition of British and French cultural theory tries to synthesize culture, language, and ideology. Raymond Williams's subtle readings of English culture as a domain of struggle combines with Roland Barthes's extension of the linguistic turn into cultural practices, which themselves combine with Louis Althusser's notion of the ideological as a relatively autonomous "level" (which like the economic and the political levels is subject to its own specialized methods and tools). In attempting to generalize the category of the Barthesian text beyond the literary, cultural studies came to emphasize the oscillations between writing and reading, or between encoding and decoding. A theory of *polyvalent* reading thus became sufficient for explaining the transmission of ideological or creative acts.[22]

Finally, continental philosophy, and phenomenology in particular, have foregrounded the imbrication of the human in a world that both envelops it and appears (or is given) to it. Martin Heidegger's famous claim that "the essence of technology is nothing technological" not only seeks to unearth the primal processes of technological *enframing*, but also makes possible an entire analysis of technics, or what Bernard Stiegler calls "organized inorganic beings."[23] This bleak view finds again its optimistic double in Félix Guattari's mapping of the virtual domain of the *machinic*.[24]

We applaud these traditions for endeavoring to abandon the plane of the text, turning ninety degrees and pursuing a line of flight through media and technology. Yet in each of these traditions a normative approach holds sway. Each of these traditions considers media in terms of their capacity to change, alter, or intervene in the world as it exists. This often results in discussions of media determinacy, and promotes a rhetoric of danger. Likewise it often corrals the discussion back toward talk of devices and apparatuses—often rather obsolete ones—disallowing more broad discussions of modes of mediation.

Ultimately uninspired by these various options, we are tempted to join Geert Lovink in his "declaration of independence" for media studies, unlinking it from the other traditions.[25] But in the long run even this gesture might simply reproduce the same old problems stemming from the legacy of media theory: its conspiratorial sleuthing for breaks and continuities, its obsession with devices and determinacy, its bipolar enthusing and denouncing of media as form. Indeed these symptoms are already present in so-called *new media theory*. What we need is another tactic. Not so much a tactical media as a *tactical media theory*, one which poses just enough questions to get us going on a new path.

Have we not forgotten the most basic questions? Distracted by the tumult of concern around what media do or how media are built, have we not lost the central question: *what is mediation?* In other words, has the question of "what" been displaced by a concern with "how"? Have the theoretical inquiries been eclipsed by the practical ones? Is it sufficient that media be understood as simply bi-directional relationships between determining apparatuses? Is it sufficient to say that a medium is always a tool for influence at a distance?

This book directly targets such assessments of media. We target the Achilles heel of media theory, the one aspect of mediation that is so hard to accept, *the insufficiency of mediation*. Horror author Thomas Ligotti puts it thus: "In a world without a destination, we cannot even break ground on our Tower of Babel, and no amount of rush and hurry on our part will change that."[26] For there exist modes of mediation *that refuse bi-directionality, that obviate determinacy, and that dissolve devices entirely.*

Does everything that exists, exist to be presented and represented, to be mediated and remediated, to be communicated and translated? Of course, we know that the fact that one can communicate doesn't necessarily mean that there is something to say, but at the same time one cannot help notice in our media cultures the seduction of empty messages, flitting here and there like so many angelic constellations in the aether. Do we not always assume that communication is possible and even desirable—or better, do not our attitudes toward communication always presume the possibility of communication, that "there will have always been communication," even before a single word has been uttered? A common language, a common ground, an agreed-upon topic and rules of engagement . . . so much has already taken place prior to the first words being uttered or the first message being sent.

There are mediative situations in which heresy, exile, or banishment carry the day, not repetition, communion, or integration. There are certain kinds of messages that state *there will be no more messages*. Why? The reasons may vary, from the paradoxical lyricism of the ineffable ("it can't be put into words"), to the refusal to engage ("I prefer not to"), to the contentiousness of apathy ("some things aren't worth saying"), to the enigma of silence (and its impossibility).

Hence for every communication there is a correlative *excommunication*. Every communication evokes a possible excommunication that would instantly annul it. Every communication harbors the dim awareness of an excommunication that is prior to it, that conditions it and makes it all the more natural. Excommunication—before a single word has been said. Excommunication—when there is nothing more to say. We aim, therefore, to craft not so much a theory of mediation in terms of communication, for which there already exist a number of exemplars, but a theory of mediation as excommunication.

Yet even the question "what is mediation?" has been sapped and defanged of its potency, mostly because the question tends to be answered in the same old predictable ways. Perhaps this is because the question has been posed so many times, and indeed posed very early in Western philosophy. But even here we contend that excommunication was always part and parcel of any communication theory, that non-media always lurk at the threshold of media.

Plato's middle-period dialogue, the *Phaedrus*, provides an example, moving as it does across a range of topics, from erotic favors to metaphysical love, finally landing on the topic of language and the relation of speech to writing.[27] Using an argument that would eventually spark innumerable discussions among French post-structuralists and literary theorists, Socrates notes that speech is always primary vis-à-vis writing. Likewise he suggests that immediacy, which allows for a communion between souls, is always preferable to mediation, which mars such communion by unnecessarily impeding or complicating it.

The *Phaedrus* inaugurated what has proven to be the most influential philosophical approach to media and communication. The dialogue established terms of debate that have been prominent ever since: writing versus speech, absence versus presence, and mediacy versus immediacy. In this way the *Phaedrus* puts forth nothing less than *a Socratic theory of media*, in which communication is aligned with the concern for truth, meaning, and reciprocity. From this foundation, one can trace a legacy of thinking about communication, from Socrates and Plato (communication is presence), to Heidegger and the hermeneutic turn (communication is interpretation), to Habermas and discussions over the public sphere (communication is discourse).

Yet in spite of its canonization in literary and philosophical circles, the *Phaedrus* is filled with non-philosophical excursuses and adjunct exchanges typically glossed over in the secondary literature. Indeed, much of the opening is dedicated to ambling around the countryside and choosing the ideal spot to recline and chat, the ideal grounds for thinking, suggesting that an a priori locus might be necessary for thought, that the place of thought precedes thought itself.

For us, the first interesting moment happens early on in the dialogue, when Phaedrus appeals to Socrates for his opinion on the rhetoric of Lysias, the Attic orator, an opinion that Socrates tantalizingly withholds from him. Phaedrus ups the ante by making a wager, which is really an oath: he refuses to read any more texts or hear any more speeches until Socrates agrees to give his own speech and reply to Lysias's argument. In short, Phaedrus raises the threat of excommunication, promising to withdraw himself from their discussion, from his friendship with Socrates, and from discourse generally.

The *Phaedrus* also contains another interesting non-philosophical moment, that of a prayer. After having ventriloquized both Phaedrus and Lysias on the nature of love—that is, after having critiqued their speech by ventriloquizing it—Socrates, afraid he has offended the gods, makes an appeal to divine Love (Eros) for not having done justice to the concept of love. In his prayer, Socrates effectively blames Phaedrus for having misled the discussion, asking Eros to "make him cease from speeches of that kind," and to turn him toward the path of philosophy. After all, the *philia* embedded in the word philosophy is that of love and friendship. It is only after this prayer that Socrates proceeds to the main course of his views on love, writing, and speech. But here, via a prayer, Socrates excommunicates Phaedrus *from discourse itself*, on the condition that the ban not be lifted until Phaedrus's speech becomes properly "philosophical."

In the *Phaedrus*, two types of excommunication occur, one by an oath, another by a prayer. Both produce a message for the ending of messages—an excommunication that silences all

communication. Phaedrus, appealing to Socrates, "excommunicates" himself, refusing to speak or read any more unless
Socrates gives his speech, thereby communicating to Socrates
through this excommunication. And it is Socrates himself,
who, midway through his philosophical discussion with Phaedrus, makes an appeal to the gods, a prayer shot through with
irony and "divine madness" in the middle of philosophical exegesis. This strange, non-philosophical appeal is also the crux
of Plato's dialogue itself, the unquestioned and uncommuni-
cated axis on which philosophy is constructed. In this way, philosophy is made possible by prayer—but an ambiguous prayer,
to no one in particular, and very likely without a reply—except
in the form of more philosophy! In this way excommunication
seems to haunt every instance of communication.

The excommunications of Socrates and Phaedrus find their
modern incarnation in Marshall McLuhan's famous example of
electric light. For McLuhan, light is *the* medium of all media:

> The electric light is pure information. It is a medium without a
> message, as it were, unless it is used to spell out some verbal ad
> or name. . . . Whether the light is being used for brain surgery
> or night baseball is a matter of indifference . . . because it is the
> medium that shapes and controls the scale of human association
> and action.[28]

McLuhan's own associative writing often moves at light
speed, and much media theory from the last few decades has
tried to explain the various twists and turns in his famous max-
ims and arguments concerning media and material technologies. But here McLuhan's choice of light is instructive. Media are
pure presence for McLuhan, pure positivity. Yet at the same time
media such as light are never present in and of themselves. What
results therefore is a theophany of media, wherein the medium
stands in as a visible manifestation of what is ultimately a mystical or religious relation. Today such a theophany of media finds
its expression in the culture industry and its awestruck rever-

ence toward new media, digital networks, and all things compu-
tational.

In this sense, one cannot help but think of the "light theory
of media" in other contexts, quite removed from those of McLuhan. Augustine, for example, speaks of mystical experience in
terms that are at once empirical and anti-empirical, a "Light Unchangeable" that is also "not this ordinary light" of sight, optics,
and representation.[29] For Augustine, as for McLuhan, there is a
Light of all lights, a Socratic theory of media in which light, presence, immediacy, truth, and the divine become commingled in a
single revelation. The affirmative theology of thinkers like Augustine is predicated on this conjunction of the hyper-presence
of light and the transparency of mediation.

But for every affirmative theology there is also a negative
theology. For instance, Dionysius the Areopagite inverts the
Augustinian logic through a language of darkness. Dionysius's
Mystical Theology begins with a prayer, a prayer to "lead us up
beyond unknowing and light" to the point where one reaches
the simplicity of the divine, in the "brilliant darkness of the
hidden silence." Beyond the dichotomy of light/dark, Dionysius posits a paradoxical "divine darkness" amenable neither to
thought nor to the senses, one accessible only via an enigmatic
"absolute abandonment of yourself and everything."[30]

This strange darkness, at once empty and excessive, is not
without its modern (and postmodern) avatars as well. Speaking about the exigency to communication in media culture,
Jean Baudrillard notes that all communication involves a form
of going outside oneself, an *ec-stasis* that is inherent in the communicational imperative itself:

> We no longer partake of the drama of alienation, but are in the ec-
> stasy of communication. . . . It is no longer the obscenity of the
> hidden, the repressed, the obscure, but that of the visible, the all-
> too-visible, the more-visible-than-visible; it is the obscenity of
> that which no longer contains a secret, and is entirely soluble in
> information and communication.[31]

Baudrillard's postmodern apophaticism is taken to another level in François Laruelle's questioning of the hermeneutic imperative in media and communications: "Meaning, always more meaning! Information, always more information! Such is the mantra of hermeto-logical Difference, which mixes together truth and communication, the real and information." This communicational imperative reaches its highest pitch in his satirical reformulation of Hegel—"the real is communicational, the communicational is real."[32]

From philosophy we learn that excommunication is a question of language and mediation. But from theology we learn that excommunication is also a question of community, belonging, and judgment before the law. When one is excommunicated one is removed from the community of believers. Excommunication implies an original infraction, an infraction which elicits some kind of removal. The excommunicant is both the receiver of the excommunicating decree, but also the bearer of the original act or enunciation that persists during excommunication.

An act of religious excommunication removes the excommunicant from the religious community. But excommunication is different from other forms of boundary management. It is not quite banishment, which places an emphasis on the physical removal from the *topos* of community. It is also not quite exile— a term with more modern meanings—which implies the possibility of eventual return to the community or the place from which one has been exiled. The excommunicated Christian remains a Christian, but is barred from participation in Church ritual. His intermediary status is amplified by the public ritual of excommunication itself, a funerary ritual whereby the excommunicant—like the leper—is considered dead to the community, dead both in a topological sense (in the mediation between inside and outside the community), and dead in a metaphysical sense (in transcendental mediation between heaven and earth).

But excommunication is itself communicated. *Excommunication is given as a message, a message that proclaims: "there will be no more messages."* The excommunicated will no longer receive messages from the community, nor will they be able to send them. Excommunication is always "ex-," always a former communication that is no longer. As such, it is a singular communication, both unilateral and unidirectional, a communication which ultimately aims for its own negation. All that remains is the last word, the final utterance, the penultimate gesture.

At the center of excommunication is a paradoxical anti-message, a message that cannot be enunciated, a message that is anathema, heretical, and unorthodox, but for this very reason a message that has already been enunciated, asserted, and distributed. Excommunicants become this paradoxical anti-message themselves, their very material existence nothing but a residual indicator of the message. Prior to the cybernetic dichotomy of information and noise, prior to the metaphysical dichotomy of presence and absence, excommunication is the communication of "no longer communicating," the silence of "nothing more to say."

In short, excommunication is the fantasy of an absolute end to all communication. Excommunication runs counter to the Socratic theory of media and the communicational imperative. But excommunication is not an aberration of communication, despite its long and convoluted history as a political and theological form of mediation. It is, arguably, as much a part of the genealogy of communication and media as is the emphasis on Socratic presence, truth, and reciprocity. The message of "there will be no more messages" does not simply destroy communication, but evokes the *impossibility* of communication, the *insufficiency* of communication as a model. In this way, excommunication is prior to the very possibility of communication.

With this elusive topic in mind we embark as a trio, and foray into the realm of excommunication.[33] In the first of three chapters Alexander R. Galloway proposes a rudimentary theory of mediation culled from classical literature and philosophy. Rooted in the concepts of the intermediary and "the middle," this chapter begins with the most important and influential figure of mediation, Hermes, and the science of interpretation labeled hermeneutics that stems from him. Hermes is the messenger, the promiscuous one who chaperones travelers while on a journey. As the guiding god, he accompanies merchants and others venturing into foreign worlds. Hermes stands at the doorway, the threshold between the hearth and the outlands; he stands at the crossroads too, in the form of "herms" or stone pillars which serve as waypoints and boundary markers. For these many qualities Jacques Derrida famously called Hermes the "signifier god"; indeed as inventor of writing, Hermes is a key figure in any theory of mediation, producing as he does much of what we label the critical tradition.

As counterpoint to this dominant discourse, Galloway also explores the contrasting figure of Iris, the other messenger of the gods, often overlooked, who in fact best exemplifies McLuhan's notion that "light is pure information." Certain and immediate where Hermes is foggy and foreign, Iris deviates sharply from the hermeneutic tradition, launching instead the alternate tradition of illumination and iridescence. Taken together Iris and Hermes encompass the canonical media universe we have already described above: the universe of devices and determinacy, a universe in which media are either clear or complicated, either local or remote, either familiar or strange.

To venture outside of this dominant binary, Galloway proposes a third paradigm, and eventually a fourth. The third paradigm is neither the hermeneutics of Hermes or the illumination of Iris, but the infuriation of an incontinent body: the Eumenides or Furies. The Fury model is useful because it allows us to deal with complex systems like swarms, rhizomes, assemblages, and networks—the various modes of mediation that have achieved a new level of prominence today at the turn of the new millennium. Yet even as the Furies dissolve the consistency of the human body, there is another, Aphrodite, who is present at the physical communication of bodies in congress. For while Aphrodite, as her name suggests, is "born from sea foam" and hence from the spume of the wave, she is also *Aphrodite Philommēdēs* because she was born from the severed genitals (the *mēdea* in Greek) of her father. In this way the theory of the middle must communicate between, on one extreme, the exile into foreign lands, as with Hermes and the attendant textual science of hermeneutics, and on the other extreme, a "love of the middle" which returns us to a more somatic immediacy.

Eugene Thacker's chapter on "Dark Media" explores the concept of excommunication via the secret link between modern genre horror and medieval mysticism. Thacker is driven by the limit cases, those instances when one communicates or connects with the inaccessible. During these moments the traditional Kantian self-world relationship becomes untenable. The self communicates with a radically contingent real. Or further still, the real obviates the human entirely and communicates more or less autonomously within and across itself. Uncanny and strange as they are, Thacker dubs such modes of mediation "haunted" and "weird" in order to underscore the paradox of their inaccessibility. Charting a trajectory of examples from the supernatural horror of H. P. Lovecraft to the apophatic mysticism of Meister Eckhart, Thacker suggests that communication often shifts from an epistemological register (a connection between two points in a single, shared reality) to an ontological register (a disconnection between the natural and the supernatural, or the earthly and the divine). Media are thus "haunted" when they *affirmatively* span different ontological orders. Media are "weird" when they *negatively* mediate between two ontological orders. The former tends to produce artifacts, relics, and other divine objects; the latter produces very little at all, not objects but *things* receding into an obtuse and obstinate thinglyness.

In such instances, the supernatural is at once posited and yet retains a certain inaccessibility, beyond the pale of human forms of knowledge production and discursive possibility. Such a situation is conditioned by what Laruelle calls a "communicational decision"; it is made possible by the communication of something that by definition cannot be communicated. At its limit, the elements of the modern communicational apparatus (sender, receiver, channel, message) negate themselves, resulting in a paradoxical communication of the horizon of communication itself. This is neither a total lack of communication, nor is it an affirmative communication of presence and reciprocity. It is, instead, a "weird" communication in the Lovecraftian sense of the term, one that paradoxically transmits its absolute impossibility.

McKenzie Wark's chapter, "Furious Media," attends to one of the chief instances of excommunication: heresy. Restating and modifying what was proposed in the first two chapters, Wark homes in on certain infuriating aspects of excommunication. Evoking the surging poetics of the swarm, Wark proposes a political heresy, one that will deviate from both traditional media theory and the traditional left: a post-hermeneutic marxism, or "marxism of the swarm." Such a political theory would only be possible by way of recognition of the impossibility of authorized control over communication with the nonhuman.[34] Hence where Galloway deals with the Furies and Thacker with the darkness of the beyond, Wark proposes the concept of xeno-communication as a way to think through the control of mediation to and from the absolutely alien.

As in Thacker's chapter, the question of religion and heresy becomes central. Media studies in North America takes as its founding moment McLuhan's media theology, but McLuhan was a Catholic convert, and his work, however idiosyncratically, was to its author sometimes thought within the space of an orthodox faith. His dislike of print media's discontinuities, for example, is essentially a more or less veiled critique of Protestantism. But, as Wark suggests, what if heresy were necessary to communication theory? And what if communication served as a central concept for thinking about the Judeo-Christian inheritance in the West?

Here heresy—as the thought that provokes excommunication—can be usefully turned against the revival of interest in orthodox Christian texts among what are supposedly critical thinkers: Žižek, Badiou, and Agamben all reach for St. Paul; Bloch and Negri pick up Job's rage against orthodoxy, but from within the sanctioned and sanctified texts of the church. As a critical alternative, Wark turns to a series of heretical sites and figures—Simon of Samaria and Helen of Troy, the Barbelites, Epiphanes, Charles Fourier, Raoul Vaneigem, and the more contemporary figure of Laruelle—arguing that such a (non)lineage will provide a surer footing for a critical negation of media and political theory, one that might open up onto a field of "teeming life" and "the movement of the free spirit."

In sum, the book presents media as love, media as darkness, and media as fury. If the primary theme of Galloway's chapter is to tackle theories of mediation from the perspective of human experience, Thacker's chapter reverses the terms, starting not from the human but from the nonhuman, from the perspective of what Lovecraft called "cosmic outsideness." Wark continues into the great outside, exploring how alien or inhuman mediation fuses back with the human. Galloway's chapter discusses the mediations of *this* world, as either hermeneutics, the illumination of iridescence, or the complexities of the swarm; Thacker's chapter, by contrast, discusses mediations *not* of this world, when mediation arises between two different ontological orders; Wark's chapter deals with both extremes, dealing at once with orgies and swarming poetics, the sacred and the heretical, in order to arrive at something akin to a pantheist universe of passions. For Galloway it is a question of distinguishing between text, image, and system; for Thacker between the haunted and the weird, the artifact and the thing; for Wark the disintegration and reorganization of these many ingredients into a new arrangement of freedom.

Taken together all three chapters try to move beyond the canonical iterations of media and communication theory. Not simply Socrates and the separation of the medium from the self. Not simply the sender-receiver models of "naive" communication science. Not simply the break wrought by structuralism and post-structuralism, which overwhelms the sender-receiver model within an incompatible communicative alterity. Buoyed and inspired by these traditions as we are, we wish nevertheless to push media and communication theory further, out into the realm of the absolutely alien. For Galloway the absolutely alien is found in the thresholds of everyday mediation. For Thacker it is found in the opacity of "dark" media. For Wark it is found in the concept of xenocommunication, or the mediation of the alien.

The stakes for us are therefore slightly different from many of the conversations happening in media studies. In this book we pursue not so much a post-media condition but rather a non-media condition, not so much the extensions of man but the exodus of man from this world. Our task is not so much a reinvigorated *humanism*, no matter how complicated or qualified it might need to be, but rather a glimpse into the realm of the *non-human*. We seek not so much a blasphemy but a heresy, not so much miscommunication but excommunication. For only there will we find a theory of mediation adequate to our present condition.

NOTES

1. Friedrich Kittler, "What's New about the New Media?," *Mutations*, ed. Rem Koolhaas et al. (New York: Actar, 2001), 58–69.

2. Lisa Gitelman, *Always Already New: Media, History, and the Data of Culture* (Cambridge, MA: MIT Press, 2008); Jay David Bolter and Richard Grusin, *Remediation: Understanding New Media* (Cambridge, MA: MIT Press, 2000).

3. See in particular Friedrich Kittler, *Gramophone, Film, Typewriter*, trans. Geoffrey Winthrop-Young and Michael Wutz (Stanford, CA: Stanford University Press, 1999), and Friedrich Kittler, *Optical Media: Berlin Lectures 1999*, trans. Anthony Enns (Cambridge, UK: Polity, 2010).

4. Matthew Kirschenbaum, *Mechanisms: New Media and Forensic Imagination* (Cambridge, MA: MIT Press, 2012).

5. Franco Moretti, *Graphs, Maps, Trees: Abstract Models for Literary History* (London: Verso, 2007).

6. Ian Bogost, *Unit Operations* (Cambridge, MA: MIT Press, 2008).

7. Lev Manovich, "Understanding Meta-Media," *Ctheory*, http://www.ctheory.net/articles.aspx?id=493 (accessed May 24, 2012).

8. Peter Krapp, *Noise Channels: Glitch and Error in Digital Channels* (Minneapolis: University of Minnesota Press, 2011). See also Markus Krajewski, *Paper Machines: About Cards and Catalogs, 1548–1929* (Cambridge, MA: MIT Press, 2011).

9. Kenneth Goldsmith, *Uncreative Writing: Managing Language in the Digital Age* (New York: Columbia University Press, 2011).

10. Stewart Home, *Blood Rites of the Bourgeoisie* (London: Bookworks, 2010).

11. See Alister McGrath, *In the Beginning: The Story of the King James Bible* (New York: Anchor Books, 2002); Simon Winchester, *The Professor and the Madman: A Tale of Murder, Insanity, and the Making of the Oxford English Dictionary* (New York: Harper, 2005); Joseph Michael Reagle Jr., *Good Faith Collaboration: The Culture of Wikipedia* (Cambridge, MA: MIT Press, 2010).

12. Dick Higgins, *Horizons: The Poetics and Theory of the Intermedia* (Carbondale: Southern Illinois University Press, 1983).

13. Christiane Paul, *Digital Art* (London: Thames and Hudson, 2008).

14. For more on this line of reasoning see McKenzie Wark's two books *The Beach beneath the Street* (London: Verso, 2011) and *The Spectacle of Disintegration* (London: Verso, 2013).

15. Lydia Liu, *The Freudian Robot* (Chicago: University of Chicago Press, 2011); Timothy Campbell, *Wireless Writing in the Age of Marconi* (Minneapolis: University of Minnesota Press, 2006).

16. See chapter 11 of Stefan Müller-Doohm's *Adorno: A Biography* (Cambridge, UK: Polity, 2005).

17. Rita Raley, *Tactical Media* (Minneapolis: University of Minnesota Press, 2009); Kathleen Fitzpatrick, *Planned Obsolescence: Pub-*

lishing, *Technology, and the Future of the Academy* (New York: NYU Press, 2011).

18. Lisa Nakamura, *Digitizing Race: Visual Cultures of the Internet* (Minneapolis: University of Minnesota Press, 2007); B. Coleman, *Hello Avatar: Rise of the Networked Generation* (Cambridge, MA: MIT Press, 2012).

19. Brian Larkin, *Signal and Noise: Media, Infrastructure, and Urban Culture in Nigeria* (Durham, NC: Duke University Press, 2008).

20. Emily Apter, *The Translation Zone: A New Comparative Literature* (Princeton, NJ: Princeton University Press, 2005); Susan Buck-Morss, *Hegel, Haiti, and Universal History* (Pittsburgh: University of Pittsburgh Press, 2009).

21. Theodor Adorno, *The Culture Industry: Selected Essays on Mass Culture* (New York: Routledge, 2001); Walter Benjamin, *The Work of Art in the Age of Its Technological Reproducibility, and Other Writings on Media* (Cambridge, MA: Harvard University Press, 2008).

22. See Dennis Dworkin, *Cultural Marxism in Postwar Britain* (Durham, NC: Duke University Press, 1997).

23. See Martin Heidegger, *The Question Concerning Technology and Other Essays*, trans. William Lovitt (New York: Harper and Row, 1977), and Bernard Stiegler, *Technics and Time, 1: The Fault of Epimetheus*, trans. Richard Beardsworth and George Collins (Stanford, CA: Stanford University Press, 1998).

24. Félix Guattari, *Chaosmosis: An Ethico-Aesthetic Paradigm*, trans. Paul Bains and Julian Pefanis (Bloomington: Indiana University Press, 1995).

25. Geert Lovink, *Networks without a Cause* (Cambridge, UK: Polity, 2012), 76–94.

26. Thomas Ligotti, *The Conspiracy against the Human Race* (New York: Hippocampus, 2010), 127.

27. *Phaedrus* as media theory is grounded in three classic texts: Eric Havelock, *Preface to Plato* (Cambridge, MA: Harvard University Press, 1982); John Durham Peters, *Speaking into the Air: A History of the Idea of Communication* (Chicago: University of Chicago Press, 1999); and of course Jacques Derrida, *Dissemination*, trans.

Barbara Johnson (Chicago: University of Chicago Press, 1981). See also Darren Tofts, *Memory Trade: A Prehistory of Cyberculture* (New York: Craftsman's House, 1998), and McKenzie Wark, *Gamer Theory* (Cambridge, MA: Harvard University Press, 2007).

28. Marshall McLuhan, *Understanding Media* (Cambridge, MA: MIT Press, 1994), 8–9.

29. Augustine, *Confessions*, bk. 7, ch. 10, trans. E. B. Pusey (Oxford: Oxford University Press, 1853), 121.

30. Pseudo-Dionysius, *The Complete Works*, trans. Colm Luibheid (Mahwah, NJ: Paulist Press, 1987), 135.

31. Jean Baudrillard, *The Ecstasy of Communication*, trans. Bernard and Caroline Schutze (New York: Semiotext(e), 1988), 22.

32. François Laruelle, "The Truth According to Hermes," trans. Alexander R. Galloway, *Parrhesia* 9 (2010): 22.

33. We recognize that such a procedure for returning to the past to refound the critical project has many distinguished and more systematic precedents. Here we shall just mention Hans Blumenberg, *Legitimacy of the Modern Age* (Cambridge, MA: MIT Press, 1985), and Harold Bloom, *Kabbalah and Criticism* (London: Continuum, 2005).

34. In this respect, Wark's chapter reverses the procedure of Agamben's "anthro-machine," which finds the human within circuits of relays between human, animal, and machine. The procedure is rather to find the locus of the control of access to the nonhuman as a control device. See by way of a comparison the procedures of Dominic Pettman, *Human Error: Species-Being and Media Machines* (Minneapolis: University of Minnesota Press, 2011).

LOVE OF THE MIDDLE

Alexander R. Galloway

On July 7, 1688, Irish scientist William Molyneux sent a letter to his friend the philosopher John Locke in which he proposed the following hypothetical scenario. Consider a man, blind from birth, who knows the shapes of spheres, cubes, and other objects, but being blind only knows them via his sense of touch. If the blind man were suddenly given sight, would he be able to identify and distinguish between these same spheres and cubes by vision alone?

Known today as Molyneux's Problem, the thought experiment was one of the central philosophical problems of its time. Any number of thinkers proffered solutions to the problem, from G. W. Leibniz, Voltaire, and Denis Diderot, to Hermann von Helmholtz and William James. Molyneux's problem was so compelling at the time, and indeed still resonates today, because it addresses key questions in mediation, aesthetics, and the sciences of perception, and in what would become psychophysics and cognitive science.

While ostensibly a thought experiment about the cognitive relation between different modes of perception, in this case tactile and visual perception, Molyneux's Problem also speaks to

This chapter greatly benefited from research assistance by Carolyn Kane, Kavita Kulkarni, Sonaar Luthra, and Alice Marwick, and from conversations with Liv Hausken, Ben Kafka, Eivind Røssaak, Martin Scherzinger, as well as Eugene Thacker and McKenzie Wark.

greater issues within the Western tradition. Indeed Molyneux's Problem is so compelling because it is, at root, the great allegory of Greek philosophy. What role will vision play in the organization of the faculties? Can knowledge be gained simply by gaining sight? Is the path of philosophy the path that leads to enlightenment, and if so what role do light and vision play in such a revelation? In a certain sense, Molyneux's Problem is not unlike the cave of shadows and the path to light and knowledge described in Plato's *Republic*. Just as Plato's pupil must wrestle with the murkiness of false knowledge and the hope of higher cognition unified by the light, Molyneux's blind man must determine if and how his newfound sensory ability will aid the communicative interplay between self and world.

Author of the *Dioptrica Nova* (1692), Molyneux helped establish the modern science of optics, and in particular the seventeenth-century conception of visuality as translucence, as opposed to today's notion that visuality is largely a question of opaque surfaces like screens or images. Indeed the story of the blind man who learns to see, only to face the risk of being unable to assimilate his visions and thus being dazzled by that very light, shows the importance of dioptrics in particular (the division of optics concerned with light passing through materials) and of optics in general, both as a science but also as a metaphor for what enlightenment man might be.

A few years earlier, in the 1670s, Spinoza wrote his own allegorical tale of transformation. It comes near the end of the *Ethics*, and we might assign it a name, Spinoza's Poet.

> Sometimes a man undergoes such changes that I should hardly have said he was the same man. I have heard stories, for example, of a Spanish Poet who suffered an illness; though he recovered, he was left so oblivious to his past life that he did not believe the tales and tragedies he had written were his own. He could surely have been taken for a grown-up infant if he had also forgotten his native language.[1]

Himself a master craftsman in the dioptric sciences, Spinoza uses his poet to illustrate a very different kind of illumination. His is a light lost in the shadows. It points not to the *Republic* but to the *Phaedrus*, the Platonic dialogue in which Socrates notes the inferiority of writing to pure thought. Writing is an image of speech, Socrates explains, and therefore an image of the self once removed. As a mediation of speech, writing is thus something of a problem for the Platonic tradition. Following Plato, Bernard Stiegler calls this the problem of *hypomnēsis*, that is, the problem of the translation of memory into physical media supports.[2] With a "grown-up infant" who can no longer speak because he has forgotten his language, Spinoza gives a play on words. The Latin *infans* means the non-speaking, from a negation of the deponent verb *fari*, to be speaking. In this sense, media threaten to render us speechless, turning us into grown-up infants. The poet's light is a dark cloud within the self, pure opacity in a forgetting of media.

Each story deals with mediation, and each contains a metamorphosis of the communicative faculties. One is the story of reason acquired, the other of reason lost. Spinoza's Poet experiences a collapse into oblivion (*lēthē*), while Molyneux's Seer experiences a newfound revealing of the world through reason and sight (*logos*). The one is about the truth of one's own Muse, one's own memories. The other is about the journey out of chthonic knowledge (through tactile feeling) and coming to know reason. Ultimately they represent two competing assessments of seventeenth-century modernity.

The risk to Molyneux's Seer is that he will be dazzled by vision, his sense of sight uncorrelated to his sense of touch; the risk to Spinoza's Poet is that he will slip into the psychosis of amnesia, his own expressions effaced and banished from conscious memory.

If Molyneux's Problem is a modern reinterpretation of Plato's cave, which is to say an allegory about learning to recognize the world through a reorganization and cultivation of the cognitive faculties, Spinoza's Poet is an anti-cave, a story about unlearning and forgetting what one already knows. Spinoza's Poet is the story of oblivion gained (*lēthē*) instead of oblivion lost (*alētheia*). Not quite "the death of the author," nevertheless the poet in Spinoza produces works that he can no longer recognize. It is the ultimate revenge of one's own literary production, the ultimate excommunication, the ultimate betrayal by media.

***

The goal of this chapter is to tell a story about mediation, to determine a few facts as anchor points along the way, then to make an argument about a very particular transformation in the historical arrangement of media.

Many will say that mediation is of a single kind, for example the single kind of mediation evident in Spinoza's Poet. To some this single mode of mediation appears sufficient, for it captures the basic paradox of media, that the more we extend our minds into the world the more we risk being alienated from it.

Others will ratify the single kind, but complement it with a second kind: Spinoza's Poet together with Molyneux's Seer. Again, the two appear sufficient. For every danger of alienation and obfuscation there exists the counterbalance of cultivation and clarity. Even if a person loses his or her communicative faculties, there is the hope that the person will gain them again. If the world falls dark, it will soon grow light.

But there is not simply one kind of mediation. Nor is the problem solved by adding an auxiliary mode to include experiences of cultivation or enlightenment. I hope to convince you that these two are engulfed within a third middle, a third mode of mediation that is both emblematically modern and as old as the Earth.

Three modes of mediation, three middles: the first is *communication in the most workaday sense*, mediation as extension, transit, representation, reflection, mimicry, and alienation. It includes both circulation and exchange and the dangers they provoke such as disenchantment, fraud, and deception. The second is *pure and true communication*, or the kind of communication found in communion, immediacy, and immanence. The third is the *multiplicity of communication*, a complex affair in which the communicative infrastructure itself dilates and reduplicates to such a degree that it extinguishes any sort of middle whatsoever (and with it any sort of media).

Each middle has its own avatar. First is Hermes, the embodiment of communication in the most normal sense, for, as the god of the threshold, he governs the sending of messages and the journeying into foreign lands. From his name we derive the term *hermeneutics*, the art of textual interpretation understood as a kind of journeying into texts. Second is Iris, the other messenger of the gods, often overlooked and overshadowed by the more influential Hermes. As Greek goddess of the rainbow, Iris indicates how light can bridge sky and land. She presides over communication as luminous immediacy, and from her we gain the concept of *iridescent* communication. Third are the Furies, the most rhizomatic of the divine forms.[3] They stand in for complex systems like swarms, assemblages, and networks. The term *infuriation* captures well the way in which the Furies can upend a situation, thrusting it into a flux of activity and agitation.

What does this mean today? As a number of critics and theorists have observed in recent years, hermeneutics is in crisis.[4] Formerly a bedrock methodology for many disciplines across the humanities from phenomenology to literary criticism, many today consider hermeneutics to be in trouble, in decline, or otherwise inappropriate for the various intellectual pursuits of the age. Why plumb the recesses of the human mind, when the neurological sciences can determine what people really think? Why try to interpret a painting, when what really matters are the kinds of pre-interpretive affective responses it elicits—or, to be more crass, the price it demands at auction? Many have therefore spoken of a "post-hermeneutic" moment, in which stalwart interpretative techniques, holding sway since medieval scholasticism if not since antiquity itself, have slowly slipped away. But what has replaced hermeneutics? Some find inspiration in a new kind of scientism (disguised as cognitivism in many disciplines), others return to a pre-critical immanence of experience, and still others are inspired by a newfound multiplicity of "flat" experience endlessly combining and recombining through rhizomatic networks.

The task here is thus multiform. First is to define mediation as hermeneutics, by way of the figure of Hermes himself. But Hermes does not have the last word on communication *tout court*. Although he is the traveler, there are certain journeys on which even Hermes is unwilling to embark. Thus two additional journeys will be of interest: after Hermes, a second journey back to Iris and immanence, and a third out to a kind of tessellated, fractal space inhabited by the Furies.

All three modes of mediation bear witness to the paradoxes of communication. Hermes's hermeneutics acknowledges that even the clearest form of communication is beset by deception and withdrawal. Iris's iridescence brings the communicants into an ecstasy of immediacy, producing a short circuit of hypercommunication. And the Furies' infuriation destroys the primacy of sender and receiver, reduplicating communicative agents into endless multiplicity. The hermeneutic wayfarer, the ecstatic mystic, and the furious swarm are thus all excommunicants in some basic sense. They all venture beyond the human into the unknown. All three modes incorporate the logic of excommunication into themselves, since they each acknowledge the impossibility of communication, whether it be via deception, immediacy, or multiplicity.

Yet, at the same time, none of the three modes consummate excommunication entirely, for none forsake mediation altogether or attempt to communicate with the purely inaccessible. Excommunication is quite militant. Excommunication is the message that says there will be no more messages. As Thacker and Wark will demonstrate more fully in the chapters to come, excommunication refers to the impossibility of communication that appears at the very moment in which communication takes place. While my three modes of mediation make certain overtures to that effect, they forgo the ultimate step. They remain firmly rooted in this world, the human world of the here and now. So, in laying a certain terrain, I aim simply to start the conversation rather than finish it. Only by venturing out into the realm of the purely nonhuman will we be able to take stock of excommunication proper. The subjects of the chapters to come, Thacker's dark communication and Wark's alien communication, give an indication of what this realm might be, not so much an image of our world, but a message from a world in which we are absent.

HERMES AND HIS EPITHETS

The myths tell of Hermes that he was "born in the morning, by midday he was playing the lyre, and in the evening he stole the cattle of far-shooting Apollo."[5] He grows up rapidly and has no past, or so it appears. He is clever and inventive, but also cunning and deceitful. His brother Apollo calls him a "friend of dark night," and christens him "The Prince of Thieves."[6] To which Hermes, still a baby, retorts with a fart and a sneeze.

As mediator, he is perhaps best known as Hermes *diaktoros*, Hermes the messenger. A traveler from afar, he is often depicted, particularly in sculpture, in the act of binding his sandals in preparation to depart. He is that thing that is just about to leave. "Nothing in him is fixed, or stable, or permanent, or restricted, or solid," wrote Jean-Pierre Vernant. "In space and in the human world, he represents movement, passages, state changes, transitions, contacts between foreign elements. At home, his place is by the door, protecting the threshold, warding off thieves because he himself is the Thief."[7] In the Homeric Hymn to Hestia, Hermes is called *angelos*.[8] This word means messenger too, but it is also the word that gives us "angel," the divine messenger, the one who mediates and chaperones travelers while they are on a journey. Thus Hermes is the guiding god. He accompanies travelers and merchants. The Greek poet Theocritus wrote: "I go in / Awe of the terrible vengeance of Hermes the god of the wayside, / For he is greatest in anger, they say, of the heavenly powers / If anybody refuses a traveller wanting directions."[9]

Because of this he is also known as Hermes of the turning hinge (Hermes *strophaios*) and is often present at the front door of houses, that is, by the hinges of doorways. "[T]he practice [of installing Hermes at the door] might also have arisen from his power over the ghostly world; for we know that the primitive Greek was troubled by the fear of ghosts entering his house, and used spell-words . . . and other magic devices to prevent it; and a statue of Hermes at the entrance would be a natural religious prophylactic."[10] The god of the threshold is, in this way, also the god of borderlands, market places (Hermes *agoraios*), and the protector of merchants (Hermes *empolaios*). Indeed merchants are those daring souls who must travel to foreign lands in order to circulate goods, and the two terms merchant and Mercury, Hermes's Roman appellation, share a common root. "While many other deities were also *agoraioi* [among them Zeus, Athena, and Artemis], Hermes was the market-god *par excellence.*"[11] But why? "It is probable that the way-god is here again asserting his immemorial rights, acquired before the development of cities, when trade was conducted by traveling merchants, who needed the help of the deity of the road, and whose safest market was perhaps on the borderland between two communities, where a boundary-pillar of Hermes would preserve the neutrality and guard the sanctity of the spot."[12] Moving fluidly across borders, Hermes thus illustrates a high level of promiscuity. He is given, in the Homeric Hymns, the title of king of exchanges. We might therefore call him the god of circulation itself. Indeed, for this reason, Jacques Derrida called Hermes, with some brio, the "signifier-god."[13]

He is the signifier god for all of these reasons. But he is also the signifier god in a more literal sense, for Hermes is said to be the inventor of writing, the alphabet, and numbers. (That he is also the inventor of fire, before Prometheus procured it for humanity, is also rarely noted.) The Neoplatonist philosopher Plutarch recounts the following observation: "Hermes . . . was, we are told, the god who first invented writing in Egypt. Hence the Egyptians write the first of their letters with an ibis, the bird that belongs to Hermes, although in my opinion they err in giving precedence among the letters to one that is inarticulate and voiceless"—and here Spinoza's Poet again looms large.[14] The mute ibis bird, inarticulate and voiceless, stands in for the alphabet and hence writing in general as that thing both externalized and opaque. As Plato writes in the *Phaedrus*, the individual using written language must, in varying degrees, come to terms with the fact that the written text kills all forms of dialogue, for it can never speak back, only parrot over and over its own fixed contents.[15] As with Spinoza's Poet, the object of expression (the piece of writing) is that thing that is rendered foreign and unintelligible to the one person most likely to be able to commune with it, its author. The Latin writer Hyginus recounts the following on the invention of letters: "The [three Fates] Clotho, Lachesis, and Atropos invented seven Greek letters—A B H T I Y. Others say that Mercury invented them from the flight of cranes, which, when they fly, form letters."[16] The cranes in flight are not mere wildlife in this example, but a totemic incorporation of Hermes himself, the one who flies on journeys. So when the cranes take a shape, and the shape is a letter, it is at the same time Hermes who forms (invents) the letter.

The two stories that perhaps best characterize Hermes are the story of the stolen cattle and the story of the slaying of Argus. I will recount them both in turn. The myth again: "born in the morning, by midday he was playing the lyre, and in the evening he stole the cattle of far-shooting Apollo." After finding his cattle gone, Apollo, brother to Hermes, starts to investigate the crime and interviews an old man, the only witness to Hermes's cattle rustling. The old man replies to Apollo:

> My friend, it's hard to say all the things a fellow can see with his eyes. Many travelers use this road, and some come and go with very bad things in their mind, others with very good things. And it's awfully hard to know everyone. As for me, I was working all day long up until the sun set digging away in my very profitable, wine-producing vineyard. But it seems to me, my friend, I saw a child—but really, I don't know, I didn't see him clearly, I don't know who the child was that followed behind those beautifully horned cows, he was awfully young, though, a baby, and he carried a staff, and he walked along zigzag, he pushed them along backwards with their heads facing him![17]

All of Hermes's themes are here: promiscuity, travel, backwardness and trickery, circumlocution, commerce and profitability, moral ambiguity—and of course snitching. Hermes herds the cattle so they trot backward, leaving a trail of hoof prints pointing in the wrong direction. Here he is Hermes *dolios*, the deceiver, "the patron god of thieves, liars, and defrauders."[18] "Resourceful and cunning," is Hermes. "A robber, a rustler of cattle, a bringer of dreams, a night watcher, a gate-lurker."[19]

The messenger and god of borderlands is thus also a deceiver. But why should this be true? Consider those who must pass from place to place. The journeyer is also the promiscuous one, a non-native, an unknown, a potential thief or pirate. Not a benign chaperone, the wayfarer god is the one who can spout untruths in plain sight. After being apprehended for the cattle incident Zeus laughs at Hermes's lame excuses, for the lies are so transparent. Being a guide requires a certain amount of deception. But a hermetic lie is on the moral level of a white lie, for all parties involved know the truth even if they play along, propping up the lie for other reasons altogether (commerce, diplomacy, expediency, etc.). Hermes is not just a thief, he is the Prince of Thieves.

Duplicity in speech gives Hermes yet another epithet, this one explicitly linguistic and semiotic in nature: Hermes *logios*, or as one might say using current parlance the "discursive" Hermes. He governs over eloquence, persuasion, and the act of speaking. Flows of words are not unlike flows of goods and services across the borderlands, and so, as with merchants and economic commerce, Hermes too has a special connection to the dialogical and discursive economies of language that flow from the tongue of the rhetorician. And like Eros and Aphrodite, he is one of the "whisperer" or seducer gods, for he can intoxicate and seduce others either with promise of profit, or seduce simply through the sweet sounds of the lyre or the reed flute. The Hermes *logios* sculptural type depicts the god in the act of oration, for the herald is the one who, after arriving in far-off lands, must stand tall and speak clearly and convincingly. Thus travel and rhetoric—if not its more degraded form, sophistry— are connected in Hermes.[20]

From a second story Hermes derives another of his most common epithets, Hermes *argeiphontēs*, or Hermes the slayer of Argus. Siegfried Zielinski, in his book *Deep Time of the Media*, retells the story as it appears in Ovid's *Metamorphoses*:

> The mythical hero with the gaze that controls is Argus, whose name derives from the Latin *arguere* (to prove, to illuminate). He is the all-seeing one with one hundred eyes, of which only a few ever rest; the others move continually, vigilantly watching and observing. The goddess Hera set Argus to guard her beautiful priestess Io, who was one of Zeus' beloved. Supervision is the gaze that can contain envy, hate, and jealousy. Argus was killed by Hermes, son of Zeus, who made him the messenger of the gods.[21]

The epithet for Argus is crucial. He is Argus *panoptēs*, which could be roughly translated as the all-seer who illuminates— the term is of course etymologically similar to the word panopticon, made famous by Bentham and Foucault. "He had eyes in the whole of his body," wrote Appollodorus of this creature.[22]

When he slept, Argus would close his eyes only in rotation. Even if several dozen eyes were sleeping, at any given moment there were enough vigilant eyes to keep watch.

How does Hermes kill him, this ever vigilant all-seer? Forever clever, Hermes's strategy is to talk. He begins to talk and talk, and continues speaking for hours on end, telling Argus the story of how the reed pipe was invented. During Hermes's tedious monologue, all of Argus's many eyes gradually close in sleepiness, and his fate is sealed. Argus, in essence, was bored to death by the most boring thing of all, tales about technology.

So the messenger kills the panopticon in the end. Appollodorus has Hermes slaying Argus with a stone; a famous Rubens painting in Madrid's Prado museum shows a decapitation by sword. A poetic finale to the story is given by Ovid, as dozens of Argus's now lifeless eyes are plucked from his body by Hera and pasted onto the tail feathers of the peacock, where they remain to this day.[23]

Since he has so many epithets and so many aspects, it is sometimes thought that Hermes is the result of several earlier gods combined into one. Indeed it makes sense for him to be a syncretic god, for he rules over syncretic behavior among men, that is, the amalgamation and exchange of foreign cultures and economies. In the end Hermes does not die out with the old Greek cults, but instead merges again with the Egyptian god Thoth into Hermes Trismegistus, the author of the *Hermetica*, a supposed bridge to Christianity, and thus the patron saint of alchemists, Gnostics, and mystics of the Middle Ages.

THE CRITICAL MIDDLE

Why does the word hermeneutics come from Hermes? The answer is that Hermes has a special relationship to discourse, exchange, and rhetoric. In hermeneutic mediation there is never simply a direct relationship to truth, there is always a *confrontation* with truth. In the hermeneutic tradition, texts are not self-evident, they do not reveal truth in a clear and direct way. The hermeneutic interpreter of texts must coax meaning out of sometimes obfuscatory and contradictory signs existing in the material, whether it be biblical scripture, or the semiotic performances of human affect. The confrontation with truth is led by and released through various economies of meaning, be they social, political, or commercial. Always *about* the real, the hermeneutic tradition is also in some basic sense *against* the real.

The confrontation with truth may be mapped out more explicitly within the critical tradition. It consists of three steps:

❶ exegesis → ❷ hermeneutics → ❸ symptomatics

Note the hierarchy of reading that lingers in the critical tradition. First comes *exegesis*, or the realm of practical explanation. This is *logos* in its most workaday sense: speakers exchange across and within discourse with the goal of elucidating and analyzing the subject at hand. Exegetical readings typically run "with the grain" of the work, they unfold in a stance that is considered sympathetic to the author's intent, and indeed sympathetic to the existence of any author whatsoever. An exegetical claim comes in the form: "This is how artifact *a* works . . . ," or "This is what text *b* says . . ." To some the exegetical read is illuminating, to others it is evidence of mere complicity with latent meaning, with the status quo.

Second is hermeneutics proper, what is often simply called critique. The origins of hermeneutics are in textual and scriptural interpretation. Hermeneutics tries to, as it were, unmask the status quo, focusing on a development or reform of the work. As in Hermes's voyages abroad, hermeneutics assumes that the work is itself a foreign land that must be visited. Thus any hermeneutic reading will tend to run "against the grain" of literal or latent truth visible in the work. Stuart Hall's essay "Encoding/decoding" is an excellent source to consult on this point, as he shows how readings do not necessarily follow the literal fact of the text.[24] Finding value in the counterintuitive fact, hermeneutical critique accepts that the exegetical framework exists, but nevertheless insists that it is somehow wrongly crafted or that it is covering up some deeper more significant truth. Thus, critique will tend to contextualize or historicize the work, but likewise it will also collide the work with new arguments and counterarguments. The discovery of flaws or gaps in the work only helps in the process of hermeneutic interpretation, for, like Hermes *dolios* (the deceiver), the work itself is considered to be, at a certain manifest level, obviously false. Alternate levels of meaning are opened up, be they hidden or repressed or erased.

For this reason Marx and Freud are important entries in the history of hermeneutic methodology. Marx's reading of the commodity is textbook hermeneutics in that it discounts the latent read, the deceptive form-of-appearance, in subordination to a more daring voyage across the borderlands and into the very heart of the matter (how value is created). Freud's model of the psyche follows a similar logic, as the unconscious resides in a latent reality behind the manifest layer of the conscious mind. For this reason both Marxism and Freudianism are sometimes called "depth" models of interpretation because they obey Hermes's basic principles: mediation involves obscurity and deception; mediation requires a "deep" voyage to or from some faraway land.

Thus, instead of asking "How does artifact *a* work?," critical hermeneutics asks "Do artifacts have politics?" (as Langdon Winner once put it).[25] The artifact may be read on its own terms, but the truth of the artifact is exposed *using external rubrics*—i.e., a critique of a novel using the external rubric of historical materialism. Paul Ricœur has famously called this a "hermeneutics of suspicion," a libidinal-political suspicion rooted in Marx and Freud, to be sure, but also in Nietzsche and his suspicion toward classical models of aesthetic judgment.

The third moment of the critical narrative is the moment of the symptom. If the previous phase can be associated with structuralism, this phase is associated with post-structuralism in general and deconstruction in particular. Unlike the hermeneutic phase, the symptomatic reading does not accept the exegetical framework at all. It suggests that the framework is in some sense a decoy, an expedient explanation that must be effaced entirely, not in an attempt to probe the depth of the work, but in a topological parsing of signs on the surface of the work. If hermeneutics proper runs orthogonal to the text, the symptomatic reading runs back and forth across the face of it, skeptical toward any attempt to return to the origin of the work, or to appeal to some essential truth lying within it. Instead stress is given to the reading of "clues" (symptoms) in the work to reveal structured absences, contradictions, misunderstandings, the work's "epistemological other," or what is "not said" in it.

An example of the symptomatic mode is given elegantly in the epigraph to Donna Haraway's book *How Like a Leaf.* "Both chimpanzees and artifacts have politics, so why shouldn't we?"[26] What is Haraway saying here? Recall that the hermeneutic position would try to argue something different, that artifacts have politics. Haraway's claim however is "symptomatic" because it throws out the exegetical and hermeneutic frameworks entirely, accepting the counterintuitive claim not as provocation but as fact (that chimpanzees and artifacts have politics), and then nominates a new claim (that "we" should have politics). The new claim is in a certain sense beyond provocation because it is almost tautologically true—since the Greeks, mankind has been defined as the political animal. So to dare to assert the claim as something worth arguing about is to insinuate that the whole framework of knowledge must be, at some basic level, obsolete.

These three modes—exegetical, hermeneutic, and symptomatic—have thus far been described as a "narrative" or a "hierarchy" because in the critical tradition these three modes tend to be arranged, if not strictly chronologically, then in terms of a normative sequence with a beginning, middle, and end: mere exegesis is that stuffy old technique that must be denuded, in the hermeneutic tradition, as so much ideological cant; while later the hermeneutic tradition itself is undercut by its own eventual blindness toward the unconscious of the text, an absence that can only be approached by the newfound techniques of the symptomatic reading. Thus, (1) exegesis is solved by (2) hermeneutics, which is solved again by (3) symptomatics. Or to narrate it using some terms and names commonly heard, the (1) ghosts of bourgeois social theory are *denaturalized* by (2) Marx, who himself is *complicated* by (3) Fredric Jameson or Jacques Derrida. The first explains, the second denaturalizes, and the third complicates. These three moments are all contained within the many aspects of Hermes.

The tale of Spinoza's Poet retold at the outset is important because it describes the basic dilemma of the critical tradition. The relationship to oblivion—the fate of the poet—is precisely the same relationship that people have with media. Cast off from the self, media are forever those things foreign to us. They must be picked apart, tamed, but still kept at bay, so that the process of signification can take place. Again, always *about* the real, critique is also forever *against* it.

Many accounts of the critical tradition would end here. And to the informed reader the story thus far will have been quite familiar territory. Beyond exegesis, hermeneutics, or symptomatics, what else does critique have to offer? Have we said all that needs to be said about the essential modes of mediation? Not hardly, for in order to understand theories of mediation in any broad sense, the journey has only begun. Other things await us: a secondary world parallel to that of the critical tradition, and a third waiting to annihilate it. (A fourth will be conserved for the end as a kind of synthesizing postscript, before handing the reins over to Thacker and Wark.)

MEDIATION AS IRIDESCENCE

Ants bring their eggs above ground, the crane takes to flight, the heifer snorts, and the great bow drinks (*bibit ingens arcus*). In Virgil's great pastoral *Georgics* all these things happen when a storm comes; by sure indicators (*certis signis*) we know of its arrival.[27] The great bow, when it drinks, is one of the unfailing signs.[28] The bow appears in the clouds, opposite the sun, creating a perfect arc of color that connects the heavens to the earth. The sign imparts meaning immediately. It is no omen, no mysterious sign that must be deciphered. It says what it is. The great bow is as certain as it is sudden. The sign and what it conveys are one and the same: a storm is nearby.

The great bow, Iris, provides an alternative mode of mediation, incompatible with Hermes and hermeneutics. Iris's characteristics include an *immediacy* in time and space, a physical *immanence* with itself, and absolute *certainty* as regards what is to be known.

Iris has no story of her own, no mythology. She is the rainbow and, with Hermes, one of the two messengers of the gods.[29] While Hermes has a long list of epithets, Iris has only a short list. Indeed there are fewer iterations of her, fewer diverging aspects that must be reconciled into a single form. Unlike Hermes who withdraws and deceives, Iris is fully present at all times.

She is Hera's maiden. With ears alert and head slanted, Iris is like a totemic animal, the eager companion and assistant to the queen of the gods:

> And by [Hera's] golden throne [Iris] sat like Artemis's
> hound, who when the day's hunting is done,
> crouches beside the Huntress's feet, her ears cocked,
> always ready to welcome the Goddess's shout;
> in the same way, the daughter of Thaumas crouches
> by the throne, her head slanting a little,
> she sleeps. She never ungirds her robe
> or swift boots, lest her mistress speak some
> sudden word.[30]

In Homer, Iris is "humanized, but not earthy; thoroughly practical, but most ethereal," to borrow a description from William Gladstone.[31] The epithets given in Homer will paint a fitting picture of the goddess of mediation. At various times she is called (A) *angelos*, the messenger; *metangelos*, the intermessenger; (B) *chrysopteros*, golden-winged, saffron-winged; (C) *kraipnōs memauia*, keenly eager; (D) *okea*, swift, or *podas okea*, the swift of foot; *tacheia*, nimble; and (E) *aellopos*, the storm-footed, or *podēnemos*, the wind-footed.[32] These epithets have all been culled from Gladstone's analysis, but I shall add two additional ones: (F) *thaumantos*, daughter of Wonder (Thaumas); and (G) *dea clara*, the bright goddess.

Like Hermes, Iris is a messenger. She is a middle. She operates in the zone of intermediate action between two individuals. She moves quickly. Her movement is spatial and decisive; she is neither a straight line, nor a tortuously complicated one, but an arc, a bow. Her duties are to Zeus and Hera, and whereas Hermes is often a chaperone for a person or a conduit for something, Iris is a pure relay, carrying and repeating messages that she carries within her own physicality.

The textual record on Iris often contains a two-part echo structure: first she receives a message from someone (often Hera), and second she travels to the receiver and verbalizes the original message. Her retelling is often slightly different from the original message, as would be expected when something is repeated from memory. Her commands are usually unidirectional, for example from god to man—a feedback loop is not necessary in the iridescent mode of mediation. Sometimes the original message is told to Iris, but the repetition of the message is only indicated in passing, giving us an example of mimetic repetition *without* difference. Consider for example the following, in which Hera gives a multipart command to Iris which she relays to three separate receivers, Thetis, Hephaistos, and Aiolos:

So [Hera] spoke, and Iris promptly launched herself from
    Olympos,
light wings outspread, knifed through the air, and plunged
into Aigaian waters, where Nereus has his domain.

First she visited Thetis, and passed on the whole message
that Hera had given her, commanding Thetis's presence;
next she sought out Hephaistos, made him silence his iron
hammers that instant, choke off the breath from the smoky
fire blasts. Then, thirdly, Iris called upon
Aiolos, far-famed son of Hippótas.[33]

Sometimes the reverse is true, that the original message is
merely referred to, then verbalized in the retelling. In either
case the logic is one of doubling or rote repetition. Hermes is
the interpreter, *erméneus*, but Iris gains her name from the word
eirein meaning to tell.[34]

Can there be a tele-telling, a telling at a distance? Hermes's
hermeneutic mediation will always answer in the affirmative,
claiming that all telling happens at a distance, from the closest conversation, to the most far-flung mediations of space and
time. Iris's iridescent mediation will always answer in the negative, claiming that no telling happens at a distance. One cannot
yell from the mountains. The past does not speak to us. Or rather
in the yelling and in the speaking both space and time are instantly transcended. To tell is to touch, no matter how far away,
and thus for Iris any mediation is mediation in the here and now.

With all this in mind, it is possible to expand what it means
for a mode of mediation to follow the model of iridescent immanence by way of a series of qualities.

(1) *Nearness.* The critical narrative, with hermeneutics as its
central gesture, claims that meaning is found in remote loca-
tions. But Iris claims something else, that meaning is found in
what is close at hand. Or to be more precise Iris claims that *the
nearby has an experience*—a claim that Hermes could never hope
to utter. To be sure, whether or not the nearby has a *meaning* is of
marginal importance; handwringing over meaning is a neuro-
sis of the hermeneutic variant alone. For Iris whatever appears
appears as near, never far or foreign. Thus the trick of the rainbow's pot of gold is not simply that it never gets nearer, but that,

in the chase, it never gets further away either! This is why Iris is a model of immanence. The immanent communion of two things produces a mediative relation of nearness in which both parties remain within themselves such as they are.

With its attention to nearness, the Iris mode is profoundly uninterested in questions of circulation and exchange, and hence could never be affiliated with the production of value or meaning through such systems of exchange (as is the prevailing view of many decades' worth of freudian-marxian theory). Iris exists at the person-to-person level. She is neither systemic, nor structural. If hermeneutics is a tortuous epistemology, iridescence is merely a bowed or curvilinear one.

(2) *Ecstatic surpluses.* In the most technical sense, meaning as such does not exist in iridescence, for meaning is the domain of hermeneutics. Instead iridescence overflows with an immense surplus of expression. This is what we might call the baroque quality of iridescence, or following Erwin Panofsky, the "lordly racket" of it all. Granted, "surplus" is a term borrowed from the hermeneutic mode. So some imagination will be required here: the "surplus" of the iridescent mode comes in the form of unmotivated—which is to say meaningless and sourceless—aesthetic output. For example, the rainbow in the sky emits an immense surfeit of expression in order to say something that is already quite obvious, that *it rained.* Or consider the examples of the iris of the eye or the iris flower. With their pure unmotivated beauty, both say "too much" in order to say very little, that *there is splendor in the world.*

If hermeneutics is cognitive and verbal, iridescence is affective and thus profoundly dumb—although in a non-pejorative sense of the word, as in the expression "I was dumbstruck." After all, Iris is called *thaumantos*, the "daughter of Wonder." (And in this sense the ultimate villain for immediacy is pornography, for it forever reveals too much, and in doing so commits violence toward that thing that is most intimate to it, the real, while the ultimate villain for hermeneutics is fetishism, for it forever sets up two absolutely unconnected things, turning the first into a hidden source and the second into an obscure device for veiling and unveiling the first.) So even though Iris gains her name etymologically from *eirein*, to tell, she is also the one who, as Roland Barthes writes, "has nothing to say." She is contentless. She tells, but does nothing more. It is simply a question of being present at hand to tell. Once relayed, the telling is already consummated.

(3) *Certainty*. Certainty goes hand in hand with the two previous points, that the iridescent mode is experienced in nearness and that it is felt through unmotivated aesthetic abundance. Consider certainty in both a quotidian and technical sense. First, Iris's rejection of deception (leaving deception to the kingdom of Hermes) means that inconstancy and caprice fade away and one is left with a world in which things happen rightly, clearly, and in a known manner. All the de Manian rhetoric about blindness versus insight must be thrown out in the iridescent mode. That drama finds no inroads here. If Iris appears in the sky, one does not have to wonder if the sun is out and whether there are water droplets in the air. One can claim this with certainty.

But there is also a more technical aspect to certainty. This refers to the ability for the rainbow to be turned into something of a technical science. Take this in the most prosaic way: there is a bona fide "hard science" of iridescence, the science found in the analytical geometry of Descartes's or Spinoza's writings on refraction and reflection within water droplets, or in François d'Aguilon's color arc or Newton's color wheel, or in any number of scientific approaches to dioptric and iridescent phenomena. This is not unimportant, for it is not possible to say the same thing about hermeneutics, bracketing of course the lofty scientific aspirations of structuralism or semiotics.

In other words, the hermeneutic mode can never truly be articulated as a strict matheme or logic. Whereas it is quite normal for the iridescent mode to be articulated in this way. Iris *can and will be mathematized*. Yet at the same time, since immanent iridescence, as a mode of mediation, is also closely associated with a kind of pathos or romantico-poetic affect vis-à-vis one's existence, the following might be a slightly more appropriate formulation: Iris is "objectively" a matheme, but "subjectively" a patheme (i.e., an expression of pathos, a poem).

At this point in the discussion it is possible to synthesize what has been said so far about Hermes and Iris and extrapolate a bit from it. I have been referring to these two avatars as modes of mediation, but it is also possible to assign specific media formats to each. In the most general sense, the privileged format for the critical middle is *text*, and the privileged format for the iridescent middle is *image*. (In a moment, for the Furies, it will be *system*.) Given the convoluted twists and turns of Hermes's travels, the text is best understood as a *problem*. Likewise, given the aesthetic gravity of immediate presence in Iris's bow, the image is best understood as a *poem*. Thus, whereas hermeneutics engages with the problem of texts, iridescence engages with the poetry of images be they visual or otherwise. Hermeneutics views media (of whatever kind, be it text, image, sound, etc.) as if they were textual problems needing to be solved. Yet iridescence views these same media as if they were poetic images waiting to be experienced.

By assigning these modes their own privileged formats I do not wish to indicate that a specific mode of mediation will operate exclusively within a single media format, but rather that there exists a hegemonic relationship, which is to say a relationship of negotiated dominance, between a certain modality of aesthetic mediation and a certain format. In fact, in many actually existing media artifacts, textual, visual, and systemic elements will operate in concert. Certain elements may very well require other elements and, further, may actively seek to break down the distinctions made among them.

In shifting between modes, the challenge is to replace the primary format and the primary method. In other words, to shift from Hermes to Iris one must swap text for image and criticism for illumination. Then, once we have described the Furies in greater detail, the final challenge will be to swap image for system and illumination for infuriation.

AGAINST HERMES

Recall the great mantra of phenomenology, *to the things them-selves!* Over the years many philosophers and critics have tried to understand what this might mean. Does the mantra proclaim an allegiance to Hermes or to Iris? Does the stress fall on the *to,* highlighting the journey that must be taken, the distance that must be traveled to transit from perceiver to thing? Or does the stress fall on the *themselves,* hinting that this kingdom of things might be easily reachable after all, because, in a certain sense, the perceiver is already in residence there?

Such is the great divide straddled by Martin Heidegger and the special kind of phenomenology espoused by him. From one perspective Heidegger is devoted to the cult of Hermes. Truth is an ambling *Weg* that must be followed. Nothing is immediate about being; it appears only in a relationship to those who seek it. Yet from another perspective Heidegger is devoted to the cult of Iris, for his version of phenomenology does not entirely ac-cept the perpetual deferral of exchange and circulation associ-ated with Hermes. Being is mysterious in Heidegger. But it is also illuminated. It is far away, like Hermes, but it is also clear, transparent, and immediate like Iris. "Being is farther than all beings and is yet nearer to man than every being, be it a rock, a beast, a work of art, a machine, be it an angel or God. Being is the nearest. Yet the near remains farthest from man."[35]

Those lines were written by Heidegger shortly after World War II. Several years later, in 1964, a young Susan Sontag penned one of the great indictments levied against Hermes and his style of mediation. "Transparence is the highest, most liberat-ing value in art—and in criticism—today," she wrote. "Trans-parence means experiencing the luminousness of the thing in itself, of things being what they are."[36] "Against Interpretation" was the title of her manifesto, but the identical titles "Against Hermes" or "Against Hermeneutics" would have served just as well.

Experience things as what they are, she cried. *To the things themselves!* These things are transparent; they illuminate and are luminous. They share little with Hermes's mode of mediation, but instead evoke Iris's iridescence, an illumination borne from immediacy, even the intimacy of the erotic. Recall the most famous line of the essay: "Instead of a hermeneutics we need an erotics of art."[37]

Sontag found such luminousness in Alain Robbe-Grillet and the *nouveau roman*. She found it in Pop Art, Symbolist poetry, and certain kinds of abstraction. The key was to throw out all systems of art founded on the age-old hermeneutic tropes and techniques—hiding and showing, repressing and revealing, nativizing and othering—and likewise any intellectual endeavor that must chaperone the reader or viewer away from danger, be it allegory over utterance, or criticism over craft. In the postwar intellectual climate, Sontag's suggestions represented a fearless and fresh wind blowing through the dusty old hermeneutic disciplines. Yet they were not uncontroversial, for they required new blood sacrifices, including a renunciation of Freud, an abandonment of cultural marxism, and a skepticism toward other methods rooted in interpretation.

Today Sontag's fight against Hermes has been taken up by many others. Opportunists leverage the fight as a way to shoot holes in what they see as the many Potemkin villages fabricated by the likes of Derrida, Lacan, or other undesirables. Hermes has essentially become synonymous with "theory" as a whole, and thus to rail against the shortcomings of theory requires a certain antipathy toward Hermes.

Yet others, even those who remain friendly to theory, while not wishing to scuttle the critical project entirely, admit that something has gotten off track. Hence in recent years there has been a profusion of writings that reflect inwardly on the status of theory (particularly theory understood as criticism or hermeneutics) and its relevance for the future, from Bruno Latour's more skeptical reassessment of how knowledge is produced

("Why Has Critique Run Out of Steam?"), to D. N. Rodowick's and Hans Ulrich Gumbrecht's eulogies to Hermes ("An Elegy for Theory" and "A Farewell to Interpretation," respectively), to the more recuperative and reinvigorating tone of Michael Hardt ("The Militancy of Theory").[38] Gumbrecht in particular has been keen to pursue the argument all the way to the end. In the book *Production of Presence: What Meaning Cannot Convey*, he argues that humanities disciplines should not be understood primarily as disciplines devoted to the quest for meaning, as they have been known for generations. Rather, Gumbrecht proposes that intellectual work oscillate between the kingdoms of both Hermes and Iris, which is to say, between both the old "meaning effects" of hermeneutic mediation, and the alternate, parallel "presence effects" of iridescent mediation.[39]

Gumbrecht, Sontag, and others in the post-hermeneutic turn gesture toward one possible exit from interpretation, but there are still others that should be identified. One is the new cognitivism that is infecting a number of branches of the humanities including cinema studies and literary analysis.[40] But another is the so-called speculative realist school (inspired in various ways by an unlikely polyglot of Gilles Deleuze, Bruno Latour, François Laruelle, and Alain Badiou), which has leveled a stinging indictment against what it terms "correlationism," a cousin of the hermeneutic position. This new turn is exciting in that it represents the first real development in continental philosophy in quite some time. Yet the result is, at least in Quentin Meillassoux's book *After Finitude*, only partially appetizing. Meillassoux seems to paint himself into a new corner immediately after breaking out of the old trap of correlationism, by setting up a sort of gnostic, mystical absolute that goes by the name "Chaos," the most elemental of the Greek divine aspects.[41] Laruelle's approach is more appealing, as Thacker and Wark will explain in their chapters, for it shows more definitively what kind of mediation might possibly exist once the constraints of this world are removed.

The question is not so much if Hermes and Iris should be superseded, but how. For it should be reiterated, if it is not already clear, that the post-hermeneutic turn is fueled in no small measure by something of a nostalgic if not altogether reactionary political bent. In tossing out correlationism—which encompasses disciplines like post-structuralism (rooted firmly in the hermeneutic tradition, no matter how much it complicates that tradition) and phenomenology (fueled by its unique fusion of hermeneutics and iridescence)—one is thus obligated, just as Sontag said several years ago, to discard Marx and Freud and all the others. This may be fine, a spring cleaning before the invention of something new. But are we not at risk of discarding the good with the bad? Is the post-hermeneutic turn a positive development, or a regression back to some kind of "pre social" or "pre political" moment?

So where are we now? And where should we go? At the risk of cultivating a host of new enemies, I will revisit two sources of inspiration from the recent past and two from the present. From the recent past we would be wise to return to Heidegger and Deleuze. For, in a general sense, one of Badiou's recent observations holds, that Heidegger is the last universally recognized philosopher. Methodologically speaking, Heidegger became central in the post-structuralism of the late 1960s to the extent that he provided a way to locate a foundational instability within the ontological apparatus itself. Indeed phenomenology exists as one of the great anti-Enlightenment philosophical movements born out of the nineteenth century. Yet Heidegger is at the same time an extension of the grand German tradition of romanticism, and it is for this reason that he cleaves so closely to the poetic-iridescent arc. Yet perhaps Heidegger did not go far enough. Perhaps it is not so much a question of the end of metaphysics, but the end of ontology. Or to put it in more detailed terms: perhaps it is a question of the end of a hermeneutic ontology, an ontology centered around having an interpretive relationship to the world. Heidegger wished to do away with a certain breed of ontological thought, and in phenomenology he achieved his wish. But the real challenge may be to do away with ontological thought altogether, or at least to do away with its claims to primacy.

Deleuze represents the first real movement out of the shadow of Heidegger. What this means is that Deleuze is the first to elaborate an alternate philosophical project that can not be reduced in some capacity to the various schools existing at the time, such as semiotics, structuralism, dialectics, phenomenology, psychoanalysis, or positivism. Instead Deleuze choose to reinvent a tradition of materialist philosophy drawing on Spinoza and others. Like hermeneutics, dialectical thinking, with its cycle of negation and ascetic self-denial, was retrograde if not outright fascistic in Deleuze's view. Yes Deleuze was Marxist in an intimate, fully internalized sense. He confessed as much in a late interview. But while Marx appears often in *Anti-Oedipus* and again in some other works, and while he was apparently writing a book on Marx before his death in 1995, Deleuze gave much less attention to Marx than his peers. Likewise Deleuze's desire to bury Freudian psychoanalysis, or at least the repressive models of subjectivity that Freud came to represent, was formidable, and it is considered a key pillar of his overall project.

After Heidegger and Deleuze, the third figure is Badiou, whom I call "present" simply because in the Anglo-American context he was only addressed in any substantive way after the turn of the millennium, despite being only a few years younger than Deleuze. Why Badiou? Because after Heidegger and Deleuze, Badiou's intervention represents the third significant philosophical project of the twentieth century.[42] Badiou is engaged in the core pursuit of philosophy, which since the Greeks—or some might say since Heidegger's reading of the Greeks—has been engaged with the problem of ontology. Deleuze and Badiou are so close in political spirit it is often a surprise to learn how entirely incompatible they are philosophically. Badiou is part of a trend today that Deleuze would intractably oppose, a metaphysical, even idealist, revival that has no qualms about evoking the name of someone like Hegel, Deleuze's nemesis. Badiou, Slavoj Žižek, and even figures like Derrida and Jean Baudrillard, all contribute to this revival. That Badiou is also a self-described Platonist is a sign of the times. Marx or no Marx, it is acceptable to be an idealist again. Further, Badiou's ability to express his project using concepts that are readily adaptable to other areas—the generic, fidelity, infinity, militancy, the universal, truth, subtraction—makes his ontological project particularly amenable to methodological coöptation and migration. So while Badiou indicts Deleuze's project, as he did before with Heidegger, by labeling it a "poetic" ontology, Badiou ends up being touched by the muse himself, if not in form—shocking the reader by confirming in no uncertain terms that the void is the proper name of being—then certainly in pep and spirit, for what could be more poetic than an ontology that obligates us to meditate on love, fidelity, and truth?

The fourth figure is Laruelle, ultimately the most important author today for any theory of excommunication. If I do not say much about Laruelle here, it is not for lack of interest. (On the contrary, because he deserves so much attention only a future monograph will suffice.) Indeed Laruelle's theory of mediation, if it can be called that, is so absolutely incompatible with the things being discussed in this chapter as to be practically unrecognizable. In short, Laruelle defines the world directly in terms of the mediative relation. There can be no world that is not already a world of mediation. As he writes, the real is what is communicated and the communicated is what is real. Thus to dwell on excommunication as the impossibility of communication will require the wholesale elimination of the world as we know it. In other words, Laruelle's theory of mediation requires a non-world. It requires what he calls a non-standard reality in which there is no reciprocity, no correlation, and no mediation in the normal sense. My task here is to deal with the excommunicative thresholds of this world, the standard world. For the world beyond, I cede to Thacker and Wark who both devote some attention to Laruelle in their respective chapters.

AN ORGANIZATION OF MEDIATION, OR WHY *ALĒTHEIA* PRECEDES *LOGOS*

Even after their passage from ancient Greek religion to modern Western secularism, both the Iris and Hermes modes of mediation remain profoundly theological. In the most literal sense hermeneutics is theological because it derives from the deciphering of scripture. But the issue is more complicated than that. To explore the text, *one must first know*. With hermeneutics one knows only too well what the text says beneath the skin, or at least what it should say. It is simply a matter of lining up the signifiers in such a way as to unlock the pattern. In scriptural exegesis, for example, the textual question is never, say, whether or not God is love—this is known to be true definitively in advance—the question is simply how one can read a particular passage in such a way as to bring it in accord with the divine fact. One knows what the *Bible* says; the real work of hermeneutics is allowing the text to say the same thing. Thus the proper method of hermeneutics is a mystico-theological method: to explicate, one must first know. And yet the miracle remains, that once meaning is revealed, the truth of the text hits the reader like a lightning bolt, like some sort of mystical revelation.

But iridescence is a theological mode too. Here the spiritual aspect is less a question of untangling a terrestrial work in response to some divine commandment ("always historicize!" "denaturalize ideology!"), but is instead a unified experience of balance, self-identity, and the communion of essences. If iridescence has a divine law it would be "to see things as they really are." Consciousness acts spontaneously; there are no human-bound commandments, only the physical incontestability of fate. Iris's is not a theology based on discipline and faith, but one based on a destiny or "way" of the world. The world shines, but the truth of the world is found in the human heart.

History is not simply that thing that converts the Hermes type into the hermeneutic narrative and the Iris type into the iridescent arc, it is also, as Marcel Detienne tells us, the imposition of a structured relation between the two mediators, between iridescence and hermeneutics. In this way history may be understood as the *organization of mediation*. But it is an organization of mediation that, at the same time, invents mediation. "*Alētheia* precedes *logos*" is one way of rendering the relation. The overall result of this organizing of mediation is twofold: the hermeneutic mode is placed chronologically after the iridescent mode and hence gains something of a trump card when it comes to matters of thinking and reflecting, yet in being placed at the origin the iridescent mode gains primacy in all matters of being, for with Iris there is nothing more pure, nothing more rarified, nothing more holy. Hermeneutics is privileged epistemologically; iridescence is privileged metaphysically. Presence comes first and reflection second.

Paul de Man has written on the great themes of blindness and insight in literature and literary theory. It is true that in de Man the Hermes and Iris arcs are somewhat collapsed into one history, where literary immanence is the notion that a text exists in and for itself and literary interpretation is a kind of mediation that, like literature itself, contains a necessary blindness. Yet it is also possible to separate the two in such a way that Hermes stands in for blindness and Iris for insight. On the one hand, the hermeneutic tradition suggests that meaning is ultimately not native to representation. The trick is not that meaning is somehow special, or parasitic, or beyond expression, but that *representation is not native to itself*. Thus, since representation is always alienated from itself, meaning is too by virtue of association. For de Man, criticism is a kind of literature, just as literature itself contains a kind of criticism within it. And hence blindness is something at the very heart of how hermeneutic interpretation works. On the other hand, the iridescent tradition suggests that meaning is indeed native to representation. Presence itself means something regardless of interpretation. Being in the world is an undivided act within which the self and the lifeworld are produced hand in hand. Thus insight is the natural state of the iridescent mode, for the world always already reveals itself.

In this way, blindness and opacity are Hermes's keywords, while illumination and insight belong to Iris. The shining of Iris becomes, in Hermes, the loss of the self into shadow. What is expression and radiance in Iris becomes accumulation and circulation in Hermes. The iridescent mode aspires to something like a scientific law in the world, as things transpire with a beautiful sheen of natural necessity. The rainbow is a phenomenon of the optical sciences, after all. Iridescence says that the world shines; one must simply let it reveal itself. Hermeneutics, by contrast, comes in the form of a commandment, not a material law: "always historicize!" or "denaturalize ideology!" The hermeneutic commandment is a response to blindness; while the iridescent law is a mere recognition of insight. The first happens in the domain of naming and discourse, the second in the domain of presence, experience, or feeling. The culminating moment of hermeneutics is always a type of mystical revelation, a lightning strike. Yet the culminating moment of iridescence is an aurora, a blooming, the glow of a sacred presence. And finally, to return to the opening themes, the Hermes type is found in the eerie disorientation of Spinoza's Poet, while the Iris type is found in the illumination of Molyneux's Seer.

There is an assumption, in de Man and elsewhere, that, in the twentieth century and certainly by the 1960s, hermeneutics is brought back as a way to work through the problems of hitherto existing crises in reading. "Well-established rules and conventions that governed the discipline of criticism have been so badly tampered with that the entire edifice threatens to collapse," wrote de Man in 1967. "One is tempted to speak of recent developments in Continental criticism in terms of *crisis*."[43] Twentieth-century critical theory tended to say that insight was itself naive, and that any sort of iridescence, coming in the form of an immediate insight into the object at hand, was a fool's errand. But of course the final step of the critical tradition (labeled "symptomatics" above, but deconstruction would have worked just as well) was really just a new hermeneutics in disguise. There is nothing in the symptomatic reading that was not already there in the hermeneutic reading. The very fact that the symptomatic reading requires that the text be something of a "crisis" or a "trick" means that it is still firmly in the land of Hermes *dolios*. So if de Man predicted the crisis, he did not predict what would happen next.

FURY AND INFURIATION

Figures like Gumbrecht and Sontag were responding to an event, and, I would argue, responding in a misguided way by trotting out the familiar humanist comforts of nostalgia, transcendence, or gauzy metaphysics, as with Gumbrecht's zen-like spin on the old phenomenological themes. What is this event? The event is the event of the modern, to be sure, but it is more specific than that. Daniel Bell called the event the end of ideology. Francis Fukuyama rather smugly called it the end of history. Economists call it postfordism, while those in industry refer to the rise of information technologies. In 1964 Paul Baran described the event in terms of "distributed" communications. In 1980 Deleuze and Guattari described the same event via the propagatory structure of the rhizome.

After Hermes and Iris, instead of a return to hermeneutics (the critical narrative) or a return to phenomenology (the iridescent arc), there is a third mode that combines and annihilates the other two. For after Hermes and Iris there is another divine form of pure mediation, the distributed network, which finds incarnation in the incontinent body of what the Greeks called first the Erinyes and later the Eumenides, and the Romans called the Furies. So instead of a problem or a poem, today we must confront a system. A third divinity must join the group: not a man, not a woman, but a pack of animals.

"Effaced. With faces sagging. Ruined. Decomposed. Collapsed. Shredded. Bit by bit. Pulverized. Particle by particle. *Par-*

tes extra partes. Dispersed. Split. Deconstructed. Fragmented. Disseminated. Scattered. Emulsified. Blunted. Unfolded. Folded up. Incomplete. Becalmed. Calmly. Carefully. Continuously. Obstinately."[44] The Furies signal noncompliance with both immanence and hermeneutics, an abdication of both presence and difference. They signal the triumph of multiplicity, heterogeneity, parallelity, rhizomatics, horizontal topology, complexity, and nonlinear systems. But what exactly are we dealing with?

The Furies are prehistoric. They move through contagion. They are called a "bloody ravening pack" by Aeschylus, and often described as animals or swarms. The Furies are essentially indeterminate in number; in the literary record their numbers change depending on the source. If Hermes is the god of the signifier, and Iris is the goddess of immanence, the Furies are the gods of the incontinence of form. As Vernant wrote, the Furies are a kind of evil spirit representing the unindividuated self,

> a sinister *numen* that manifests itself in many guises. . . . It is a power of misfortune that encompasses not only the criminal but the crime itself, its most distant antecedents, its psychological motivations, its consequences, the defilement it brings in its wake and the punishment that it lays in store for the guilty one and all his descendents. In Greek there is a word for this type of divine power. . . . It is *daimōn* . . . an evil spirit.[45]

"The Erinyes are the huntresses but they are huntresses that are purely animal," notes Pierre Vidal-Naquet, referring to the raw animality of the Furies. "They are serpents and they are also bitches. Their purely animal nature is very strongly emphasized, by Apollo . . . : 'You should make your dwelling in the cave of some blood-gorged lion instead of coming to defile others by inflicting your foulness in this temple of prophecy.'"[46]

If Hermes always responds with "maybe," and Iris with "yes, of course," the Furies are forever "never." They bring punishment, but not the kind of retribution wrought by the "modern" juridical power of Athena. They bring only the punishment of the ages.

Their weapon is a strand, a link, a rope. If Hermes is a self, and Iris is a life, the Furies are an ecosystem, a swarm, a cloud.[47]

Deleuze is something of a patron saint for the Fury mode. In one of Deleuze's summaries of some of the main characters in Nietzsche's work, he inserts an entry for "spider" that reveals much about the nature of the Furies:

> *Spider (or Tarantula):* It is the spirit of revenge or resentment. Its power of contagion is its venom. Its will is a will to punish and to judge. Its weapon is the thread, the thread of morality. It preaches equality (that everyone become like it!).[48]

Yet the difficulty with assimilating Deleuze fully into the present schema is that he was interested in both immanence and multiplicity. (Whereas he resolutely hated Hermes in all his many guises.) Thus Deleuze has a special relationship to both iridescence and infuriation. For every reference to assemblages and rhizomes in Deleuze, he also expresses a commitment to pure immanence. This is why Deleuze can mix the two terms, as he did in a text on Hume and the "real empiricist world." Such a world is "a harlequin world of multicolored patterns and non-totalizable fragments where communication takes place through external relations."[49] The radiance of iridescence and the fragmentation of infuriation thus coexist in Deleuze. The reason for this is that Deleuze was primarily interested in overturning the hermeneutic tradition—what he viewed as the same claptrap of depth and division, of dialectical subterfuge coming to a head in the great mistakes of Descartes, Kant, or Hegel, the progenitors of the modern subject. Pure multiplicity undoes all that tat, but so does pure immanence. Hence both options were philosophically appetizing to Deleuze. Thus pure multiplicity and pure immanence coexist in Deleuze with equal measure: the univocity of being consists of pure multiplicity.[50]

In the classical account, the Furies were born from the bloody testicles of Ouranos. The part of the severed members that fell on the land as drops of blood became the Furies and the Giants, while the part that fell on the sea washed out into the ocean and flowed back to shore again atop the sea foam, giving life to Aphrodite. Aphrodite is the goddess of the sexual media, that is the genitals (in Greek, the *mēdea* [μήδεα]), yet we may ascribe a very different kind of role to the Furies who, in stalking the gap between individuals and their fate, seem bent on tearing up any sort of media whatsoever. In short, if Aphrodite or Hermes or Iris are media, the Furies are quite literally anti-media.

So the bilateral model of mediation discussed thus far—whether as Spinoza's Poet and Molyneux's Seer, or Hermes and Iris, or hermeneutics and iridescence—must be amended with a third term that is quite resistive of the model itself. If the Hermes middle is a narrative and the Iris middle is an arc, it is only possible to say, in very limited terms, that the Furies middle is a *system*. The reason for this is that, while iridescent immanence is also elemental and prehistoric, the Fury middle neuters any attempt to establish a grand arc of history. The Furies run next to the real, but they are never *about* it. They reflect nothing, they reveal nothing, and they most certainly do not let something "shine forth in what it is" as Iris's phenomenology teaches us. They demonstrate that truth is not inside or even outside the real, but simply alongside it, nipping at its heels. (For this reason the Furies follow Laruelle's logic, that non-philosophy is "alongside" philosophy but never "of" or "about" it.[51]) The Furies can put the world in flight but, beyond that, they can neither interpret it nor immanently "remain within" it.

To project these ideas across the many centuries, one might say provisionally that the ancient world, the hermeneutic world, is cryptographic, as in the famous saying *physis kryptesthai philei*. The modern baroque or iridescent world is prismatic, separating the white light of the sky into its component rainbow spectrum. But by the middle twentieth century the world became systematic, synthesizing all diverse colors into a global machine. If Hermes is dark metaphysics, and Iris is light metaphysics, then the Furies are nothing at all related, merely a microphysics of links and vectors.

THE HERESY OF THE SWARM

If both Hermes and Iris remain profoundly theological, the Furies type allows us to conceive of a truly secular, and hence nihilistic, mode of mediation. As a being, the Furies do not exist in any durable sense, like a material object. Instead they exist in a general state of agitation and sensuous energy. As they hound their prey, the Furies exhibit an energy of antagonism, an agitation *against* some target of persecution. Because of this the most useful branches of philosophy are not ontology or aesthetics, neither Iris's immanent being nor Hermes's interpretive journeys. In order to understand the third type of mediation, we must turn to *politics*, that branch of philosophy that deals most directly with force and physical transformation.

Military and social theory have long examined the pure energy of antagonism known as the asymmetrical threat. Its names are many: insurgent, partisan, irregular, riot, crowd, popular rebellion, or guerrilla—these are some of the many synonyms for the Furies and their mode of mediation. The asymmetrical threat carries great force. It encounters the power center not as an equal, but as an unholy monster, seemingly formless and ungovernable.

There are many great thinkers who have explored this mode, from Sun Tzu and Carl von Clausewitz's writing on military theory, to the extension of these ideas in the writings on guerrilla warfare by V. I. Lenin and Mao Tse-tung. Yet I will not catalog and interpret these many writings, nor will I try to commune with them. There will be no dark hermeneutics or luminous ecstasy in the case of the swarm. In deference to the third mode of mediation, I will merely constitute a kind of assemblage and cite a few passages from the very crucial late-modern phase, crucial because of the special relationship that has arisen historically between the Fury mode and the middle to late twentieth century:[52]

- *Robert Taber*—Author of *War of the Flea* on guerrilla insurgencies and their relationship to state power. "The guerrilla fights the war of the flea, and his military enemy suffers the dog's disadvantages: too much to defend; too small, ubiquitous, and agile an enemy to come to grips with. If the war continues long enough—this is the theory—the dog succumbs to exhaustion and anemia without ever having found anything on which to close his jaws or to rake with his claws."[53]

- *Elias Canetti*—The celebrated novelist who wrote on the animalistic qualities of the infuriated pack (the "crowd"). "The first thing which strikes one about the pack is its unswerving direction; equality is expressed in the fact that all are obsessed by the same goal, the sight of an animal perhaps, which they want to kill."[54]
- *Guy Brossollet*—The French soldier and military theorist who described a system of "non-battle" arising from within the logic of Cold War nuclear deterrence. A fighting force made up of "pinpricks," not "fists," deployed across a "mesh" of "presence modules" and supported by communication networks that can produce a "series of minor but statistically consistent actions."[55] The new flexible, network-centric warfare is, in his estimation, "[m]ultiform, maneuverable, [and] omnipresent."[56]

Any number of additional books and articles exist today that try to describe contemporary media as infuriated, contagious, or antagonistic.[57] Like the web itself, they constitute nodes in a network. Without the methodologies of deep reading or aesthetic appreciation borrowed from hermeneutics and iridescence, we may simply enumerate, scan, or possibly reorganize them. Following Franco Moretti's method of distant reading, the infuriated media become a vast database, and the scholar becomes a counter of entities, a diagrammer of data, or a visualizer of information.[58]

These writings help explain what the Fury mode of mediation looks like today, whether it be rhizomatics, distributed networks, swarming clouds, or impersonal agents. Yet they also help support a much more important claim. Not simply a description of the Furies, such writing demonstrates that, at this moment in history, we are living through a new hegemony in which one of the three forms has achieved a new negotiated dominance over the other two. The network form has eclipsed all others as the new master signifier. Today it explains all manner of things, from social networks, to neural nets, to network-centric warfare. Indeed it is no coincidence that Deleuze's growing popularity at the end of the twentieth century paralleled the ascension of the new postfordist and networked epistemes such as game theory, cybernetics, ecology, graph theory, etc. These are some of the many fields that have contributed to the dominance of furious media.

Thus for media theory, the following normative claim begins to emerge: hermeneutic interpretation and immanent iridescence are, at the turn of the millennium, gradually withering away; ascending in their place is the infuriation of distributed systems. In other words, and in more concrete terms, we can expect a tendential fall in the efficiency of both images and texts, in both poems and problems, and a marked increase in the efficiency of an entirely different mode of mediation, the system, the machine, the network.

*
* *

The conversation on media and modes of mediation has only barely gotten underway. It is not exhausted by the three middles discussed thus far, not nearly. All three of the avatars discussed here deal with the complexities of excommunication. Hermeneutics deals with the first and most fundamental paradox of communication, for it addresses the way in which media always betray us when they pass beyond our grasp. Like the problem described by Spinoza's Poet, media objects are excommunicated from our own consciousness, and in so doing carry the human mind into foreign and otherwise unknown lands. In the next chapter Thacker will describe this process in terms of a darkness or blind spot that always exists in any instance of communication. Iris's iridescent media deal with a different aspect of excommunication. The problem with Iris is not so much the alien or the outside, but the immanent relation to the self. As Wark will say later, the problem with Iris is a kind of ecstasy of hyper-communication in which communication becomes impossible precisely at the moment of its own self-consummation. Finally, the Furies interface directly with the paradox of excommuni-cation, for they embody the nonhuman form most completely. Swarms and systems threaten the sanctity of the human more than animals or things or ghosts. They violently reduce mind to matter, disseminating consciousness and causality into a frenzy of discrete, autonomous agents, each with their own micro func-tions. Where Iris achieves a kind of immanence of the self, the Furies achieve what Deleuze called the material univocity of im-manence, that is, a purely material immanence that "speaks in one voice" across the many different multiplicities of being.

Yet even as these three modes of mediation, these three middles, gesture toward the paradoxes of excommunication, none of them reside entirely within the great beyond. If I have opened the door it will be for Thacker and Wark to walk through. Thacker will venture first into the realm of the unseen, recast-ing media in terms of their own horrible absence. With his dark media, Thacker addresses anti-humanism proper and tries to describe what it would mean to communicate directly with the inaccessable. This will take him to the most remote corners of the communicative utterance, to the haunted, the weird, the horrible, the fantastical, and the mystical. Wark begins and ends his chapter with the swarm. If I have only gestured here at the fundamentally heretical nature of the infuriated swarm, Wark describes a pantheist universe of passions in which her-esy emerges as the key constituting force. The excommunicant is not banished in Wark but celebrated as the very antihero of a new kind of society.

But before passing the baton, I will outline one final kind of mediation that has not been adequately addressed thus far. Son-tag used the heading "erotics" to label her media of transparency and luminousness. And, as she knew, erotics means love or intimacy, not sexual desire per se, as is typically assumed in puritan society.[59] So consider one last, salutatory mode, one that borrows a little bit from all the others.

Aphrodite, whose name means "rising up out of the foam," is a mixture of desire, lust, and sex. Aphrodite spans two different poles, two different aspects, often typified by Aphrodite *ourania* and Aphrodite *pandēmos*, the one sprung from her father Ouranos and the other disseminated into the pandemonium of the common people:

> In the fourth century we find Aphrodite separated into two aspects: higher, celestial love, Aphrodite *Ourania*, and the love of the whole people, Aphrodite *Pandemos*, who is responsible for lower sexual life and in particular for prostitution. Both names of Aphrodite are old and widespread cult epithets, but the original meanings are quite different. The Heavenly One is the Phoenician Queen of Heaven, and *Pandemos* is literally the one who embraces the whole people as the common bond and fellow-feeling necessary for the existence of any state.[60]

Desire: from Hermes she gains the mediatory promiscuity of mixing, inseminating and cross-fertilizing; from Iris she gains a somatic immediacy, appearing as surging waves and surging bodies; from the Furies she gains a generic commonality, resulting in non-reproductive sexual desires, a non or pure desire. Aphrodite might be best understood, then, as a kind of pure mediation. She is the mediation of the middle as such—never lost in foreign lands like Hermes, or so ethereal and light like Iris, or horrifyingly chthonic and nonhuman like the Furies. Aphrodite is in the middle of the middle, the governor of the middle.

Perhaps this is why Lucretius evoked *alma Venus* the *Aeneadum genetrix* as his muse to launch *De Rerum Natura*. She is one of the governors of things, and through her "things make their primordial entrance."[61] She is thus a mediator, as in the Greek *medō* [μέδω], meaning to take care of, protect, rule over, or guard.

"[T]he root *med-* is very important," recounts Pierre Chantraine, for the root and its derivatives "express the notion of a thought that rules, commands, moderates . . . 'he who utters the law.'"[62] This is why, in the two homeric hymns devoted to him, Hermes is called Κυλλήνης μεδέοντα, meaning the "lord" or "ruler" of Kyllene, his birthplace. And why the gorgon bears the name Medusa, for she is the protectress or guardian. And why "medicine" comes to mean the-one-who-rules, in this case who rules over disease. The rulers are the mediators. They arbitrate and exercise dominion in the middle of a kingdom of relations. The mediator is the one who takes care, who directs or leads with attention to the entities at play.

But Lucretius's poem is about the atoms of things, the *primordia*, the seeds, the semen of things (*semina rerum*). Is there not, then, some still more primordial linkage between *medō* and *mēdea*? Both Boisacq and Chantraine list two entries for *mēdea*: they are the genitals, but they also refer to one's thoughts, concerns, and designs.[63] The seeds are the governors and progenitors of the world, but they also engender cares and desires. Here, then, Aphrodite unites both lust and seed, as someone who is solicitous and seductive, who froths up the foam of the waters in successive surges of birth and rebirth. "The foamy surface is birth itself, it is the goddess who is born and who is divine only in being born in this way, on the crest and rim of each wave, and in each of the hollows into which the foam spills and spreads," writes Jean-Luc Nancy. Aphrodite stands for "the pitching, rolling, and swelling of the waves, movement upon movement, the incessant backwash, the lapping, the wake. . . . Aphrodite is not born: she *is* birth, emergence into the world, existence."[64] But why choose between these sources? Desire is both mediator, ruler, and sex. The body and mind, when under the seductive lusts of Aphrodite, are oriented, preoccupied, infatuated, and impassioned.

Part of the Aphrodite story includes an oscillation between the determination and indetermination of sexual mediation.

The masculine and the feminine are born when she, born-from-sea-foam, "rises up" from the waves (Aphrodite *anadyomenē*), inaugurating the bilateral synthesis of sexual reproduction. "It is only after the castration of Ouranos by Kronos and the distance that this creates between the masculine and the feminine, that the sexual act assumed a new character and became truly fertile in producing, from two beings, a third, different from its progenitors."[65] But "how could Aphrodite divide the sexes?" asks Nancy in his encomium to Aphrodite. "She is merely their apportioning, between one and the other. Aphrodite is one in two, not two in one. Not 'bisexual' but one in two sexes, and in such a way that there cannot be one without two (ultimately, there cannot be one at all). No sex is one, unique. Nor is Aphrodite one."[66] And just as Aphrodite *pandēmos* represents a kind of sexuality common to all—a generic, disseminating sexuality associated across "all people" (*pandēmos*), but also the promiscuities of prostitution and the brothels—she will also eventually recombine and procreate with that other promiscuous mediator, Hermes, into the indeterminate intersex of Hermaphroditus.[67]

Aphrodite is often called *genial*. She is the amiable goddess, good-natured and convivial. But why this word, why *genial*? To be genial is to smile, and Aphrodite is the gay one, the one who likes to smile. But the word genial, like genius and genitals, comes from the root meaning to beget or procreate, to spring from an origin, a sexual origin.[68] So, in being *genial*, is Aphrodite "the smiling one," or "the one who springs from the sex"?

There is some discussion around a certain passage in Hesiod in which the poet describes Aphrodite as *philommeidea*.

> White foam surrounded the immortal flesh [of Ouranos],
> And in it grew a girl. . . .
> Her name is Aphrodite among men
> And gods, because she grew up in the foam [*aphros*],
> . . .
> [And she is called] Philommeidea from
> The genitals, by which she was conceived.

. . .

From the beginning, both among gods and men,
She had this honour and received this power:
Fond murmuring of girls, and smiles, and tricks,
And sweet delight, and friendliness, and charm.[69]

Hesiod appears to be playing with words here, as Aphrodite's common epithet, *philommeidēs* (lover of smiles, or more colloquially the smiling one), is defined as if it ended with *mēdea* (genitals). Chantraine and others chalk this up to a play on words by Hesiod. However he admits too that there is disagreement over the interpretation of the epithet, and cites, among others, a "bold hypothesis" by A. Heubeck, that "φιλομηδής [*philomēdēs*] was an older form, which in Homer was secondarily altered to be φιλομμειδής [*philommeidēs*]."[70] And therefore the pun in Hesiod may be due to the similarity, and fungibility, between these two meanings, old and new. (In Homer, Aphrodite is not borne from Ouranos's members, but is the offspring of Zeus and Dione; thus for him there is no need to wordsmith *mēdea* into the poem.)

The two words are often collapsed into one by later authors. The epithets are translated differently depending on one's proclivities, from she-who-loves-genitalia (Hesiodic, anatomically explicit), to she-who-loves-smiles (Homeric, useful for more polite company), to she-who-loves-laughter (euphemistic, etymologically imprecise).

But perhaps the two words are neither pun nor bowdlerization. Perhaps they represent a simple equation. For the smile and the sex are, in Aphrodite, very often the same thing. A lover's smile brings arousal, just as lovemaking invokes smiles of pleasure. Somatic bonds join the smile and the sex into a singular, body-wide organ. The smile of sexual desire links back to sexual arousal in the body. So Aphrodite is indeed a kind of genial mediation. Such an observation would not have surprised Plato who structured the *Phaedrus* around a twin theme: not just love and the soul but writing and mediation too, not just Eros but the *hypomnēmata* too.

Neither mouth nor groin reside at the top of the psyche. Nor at the bottom. They reside in the *middle*. The faculty of vision is certainly sidelined during lovemaking (discounting the spectacular or fetishistic variants), as is that of one's active, quotidian consciousness; instead there are skin, mouth, torso, breast, vagina, hand, penis, anus. All these reside in the body, *in the middle* of the body. Perhaps this is the ultimate answer to why the smile and the sex are unified in Aphrodite. As a mediator she is the "lover of smiles" just as she is the "lover of the sex." Indeed it would be difficult to have one without the other. To combine these two—the genitals and the affability of the smile—one might say, simply, the *genial* Aphrodite, or the genial middle. So sex is a middle too, irreducible to the endless elusive promiscuities of Hermes, or the translucent immanence of Iris, or even the propagatory tessellations of the Furies. And in this sense, Aphrodite is, like us, *philomēdēs*, fond of smiles, fondler of media, and lover of the middle.

NOTES

1. Baruch Spinoza, *Ethics*, scholium to part 4, proposition 39, in *The Collected Works of Spinoza*, vol. 1, trans. Edwin Curley (Princeton, NJ: Princeton University Press, 1985), 569. Curley notes that the poet was probably Luis de Góngora.

2. "*Hypomnémata* include all artificial memory supports: from prehistoric engraved bone or the Australian *churinga*, to Personal Digital Assistants (PDAs) and MP3 players, by way of biblical writing, the dialogues of Plato, the printing press, photography, etc." Bernard Stiegler and Ars Industrialis, *Réenchanter le monde: La valeur esprit contre le populisme industriel* (Paris: Flammarion, 2006), 37n3.

3. The canonical Greek names are either the Erinyes or the Eumenides. But given the appeal of the Roman name Furies, I have chosen to mix the Roman and Greek nomenclature.

4. See for example Bruno Latour, "Why Has Critique Run Out

of Steam? From Matters of Fact to Matters of Concern," *Critical Inquiry* 30, no. 2 (Winter 2004): 225–48.

5. "To Hermes" (lines 17–18), *Homeric Hymns*, trans. Martin West (London: Harvard University Press, 2003), 115. One of the more delightful refrains from Hermes is a phrase he repeats: I was born yesterday, I was born yesterday . . .

6. "To Hermes" (lines 290–91), *Homeric Hymns*, trans. West, 137.

7. Jean-Pierre Vernant, *Mythe et pensée chez les Grecs*, vol. 1 (Paris: François Maspero, 1982), 126.

8. "To Hestia" (line 8), *Homeric Hymns*, trans. West, 212.

9. Theocritus, *Idylls and Epigrams*, trans. Daryl Hine (New York: Atheneum, 1982), 88.

10. Lewis Farnell, *The Cults of the Greek States*, vol. 5 (Oxford: Clarendon, 1909), 19–20.

11. Ibid., 26.

12. Ibid.

13. Stiegler gives a similar description: "Hermes and Mercury arrive at the point when . . . mnemotechnics allow the writing of the superego. They are the two messengers of interpretation, writing, and telecommunications, that is to say, of telecracy." Bernard Stiegler, *La télécratie contre la démocratie* (Paris: Flammarion, 2006), 185.

14. Plutarch, *Table-Talk*, IX, question 3, trans. Edwin Minar et al. (Cambridge, MA: Harvard University Press, 1961), 235.

15. Plato, *Phaedrus* (line 275d), trans. R. Hackforth, in *The Collected Dialogues of Plato*, ed. Edith Hamilton and Huntington Cairns (Princeton, NJ: Princeton University Press, 1961), 521.

16. Hyginus, "Fabulae 277: First Inventors," *The Myths of Hyginus*, trans. Mary Grant (Lawrence: University of Kansas, 1960), 178. For related interest see also Plato, *Phaedrus* (line 274d), 520, and Derrida on Thoth and Hermes in Jacques Derrida, *Dissemination*, trans. Barbara Johnson (Chicago: Chicago University Press, 1981), 84–94.

17. *The Homeric Hymns*, trans. Charles Boer (Dallas, TX: Spring Publications, 1970), 32.

18. Lewis Farnell, *The Cults of the Greek States*, vol. 5 (Oxford: Clarendon, 1909), 23.

19. "To Hermes" (lines 14–15), *Homeric Hymns*, trans. West, 115.

20. One additional epithet is worth mentioning in this context: *hēgemonios* (the leader, the supreme, the imperial), particularly when paired with the aforementioned *empolaios* (the merchant-protector). Empire, public opinion, and commerce share a special relation, for the mobilization of empire across borders, through diplomacy or commerce, typically relies on a skillful orchestration of public opinion. The three are joined in Hermes. Yet Hermes bears many epithets, and there are still others, including *psychopompos*, the conveyor of souls, and *enagōnios*, the patron of the gymnastic games.

21. Siegfried Zielinski, *Deep Time of the Media*, trans. Gloria Custance (Cambridge, MA: MIT Press, 2006), 38.

22. Appollodorus, *The Library*, vol. 1 (book 2, i, 2), trans. James George Frazer (New York: G. P. Putnam's Sons, 1921), 131.

23. "Juno took the eyes and set them in the feathers / Of her own bird, filling the tail of the peacock / With starlike jewels": Ovid, *Metamorphoses* (book 1, lines 775–77), trans. Stanley Lombardo (New York: Hackett, 2010), 27. The Prado's "Mercury and Argus" (Peter Paul Rubens, c. 1636–1638) is the most exciting, the most baroque, of Rubens's several depictions of Argus's slaying and its aftermath. But more sophisticated and enigmatic is Rubens's "Juno and Argus" (c. 1609–1611) hanging at the Wallraf-Richartz Museum in Cologne. Here the perpetrator of the crime, Hermes, is not depicted, or at least not directly. Instead Iris appears, with her signature bows and billows in color and cloth. I have tried to make some sense of these two paintings, along with a few others relating to Hermes and Iris, in the essay "The Painted Peacock," in *And They Were Two in One and One in Two*, ed. Nicola Masciandaro and Eugene Thacker (New York: MagCloud print on demand, 2011), 36–44.

24. Stuart Hall, "Encoding/decoding" in *Culture, Media, Language: Working Papers in Cultural Studies, 1972–79*, ed. Stuart Hall et al. (New York: Routledge, 1992), 128–38.

25. See Langdon Winner, *The Whale and the Reactor* (Chicago: University of Chicago Press, 1986).

26. Donna Haraway and Thyrza Nichols Goodeve, *How Like a Leaf: An Interview with Donna Haraway* (New York: Routledge, 1999).

27. See Virgil, *Georgics* (book 1, lines 380–81), trans. H. Rushton Fairclough (Cambridge, MA: Harvard University Press, 1999), 124.

28. In Genesis, chapter 9, the great arc is a sign of a similar but slightly different sort, for it is the *signum foederis*, the contractual sign, that is, the sign of the covenant between God and Noah, the inaugural covenant signaling the beginning of the second age.

29. It is also important to reference Morpheus, one of the *oneiroi*, who is also strictly speaking a messenger of sorts. He is associated with divination and the bringing of messages through dreams. Morpheus shares a relationship with Iris, and is connected to her in Ovid.

30. Callimachus, "Hymn IV: To Delos" (lines 251–62), *Hymns*, trans. Stanley Lombardo and Diane Rayor (Baltimore: Johns Hopkins University Press, 1988), 28.

31. William Gladstone, "The Iris of Homer: And Her Relation to Genesis IX.11–17," *Contemporary Review* 32 (1878):140–52, p. 140.

32. Adapted from Gladstone, "The Iris of Homer," 141–42. Gladstone points out that with the Homeric Iris there is a general absence of color epithets, and thus that Iris should be understood is a messenger first and an optical phenomenon second. But this argument is unconvincing given the color-rich way she is described in other texts, and given the fact that the Greek mind did not consider divine forms to be personifications as we like to think of them today—neatly cleaving corporeal body to divine concept—but rather unified, singular presences.

33. Apollonios Rhodios, *The Argonautika* (book 4, lines 770–78), trans. Peter Green (Berkeley: University of California Press, 1997), 171.

34. See Plato, *Cratylus* (line 408b), trans. B. Jowett, in *The Collected Dialogues of Plato*, 444.

35. Martin Heidegger, "Letter on Humanism," in *Basic Writings*, trans. Frank Capuzzi (New York: Harper Collins, 1977), 234.

36. Susan Sontag, *Against Interpretation, and Other Essays* (New York: Picador, 1966), 13.

37. Ibid., 14.

38. See Bruno Latour, "Why Has Critique Run Out of Steam?";
D. N. Rodowick, "An Elegy for Theory," *October* 122 (Fall 2007): 91–109; Hans Ulrich Gumbrecht, "A Farewell to Interpretation," in *Materialities of Communication*, ed. Hans Ulrich Gumbrecht and K. Ludwig Pfeiffer (Stanford, CA: Stanford University Press, 1994): 389–402; and Michael Hardt, "The Militancy of Theory," *South Atlantic Quarterly* 110, no. 1 (Winter 2011): 19–35.

39. Hans Ulrich Gumbrecht, *Production of Presence: What Meaning Cannot Convey* (Stanford, CA: Stanford University Press, 2004), 2.

40. John Rajchman, evoking the late Deleuze, clarifies this cognitivist trap: "Written in a strange interval before his own death, 'Immanence . . . a life' has been regarded as a kind of testament. What is clear is that Deleuze took its 'last message' to occur at a time of renewed difficulty and possibility for philosophy. As with Bergson, one needed to again introduce movement into thought rather than trying to find universals of information or communication—in particular into the very image of the brain and contemporary neuroscience. In the place of artificial intelligence, one needed to construct a new picture of the brain as a 'relatively undifferentiated matter' into which thinking and art might introduce new connections that don't preexist them—as it were, the brain as materiality of 'a life' yet to be invented, prior and irreducible to consciousness as well as machines." John Rajchman, "Introduction," in Gilles Deleuze, *Pure Immanence: Essays on a Life*, trans. Anne Boyman (New York: Zone, 2001), 20.

41. "Our absolute, in effect, is nothing other than an extreme form of chaos, a *hyper-Chaos*, for which nothing is or would seem to be impossible, not even the unthinkable," writes Meillassoux. "We have succeeded in identifying a primary absolute (Chaos), but contrary to the veracious God, the former would seem to be incapable of guaranteeing the absoluteness of scientific discourse, since, far from guaranteeing order, it guarantees only the possible destruction of every order." Quentin Meillassoux, *After Finitude: An Essay on the Necessity of Contingency*, trans. Ray Brassier (New York: Continuum, 2008), 64.

42. In the opening to *Being and Event*, Badiou himself maps the current methodological landscape slightly differently. He includes another tradition as significant, the logical positivism of the Vienna circle, while omitting Deleuze (in *Being and Event* at least). In addition to positivism, Badiou cites the other two key traditions as first phenomenology, for which Heidegger is the stand-in, and second what Badiou calls a post-Cartesian theory of the subject, essentially a catchall for Marx, Lenin, Freud, Lacan, and all of what is known today as critical theory and post-structuralism. See Alain Badiou, *Being and Event*, trans. Oliver Feltham (London: Continuum, 2005), 1.

43. Paul de Man, *Blindness and Insight: Essays in the Rhetoric of Contemporary Criticism* (Minneapolis: University of Minnesota Press, 1983), 3.

44. Jean-Luc Nancy, "Les Iris" (trans. Leslie Hill), in *Multiple Arts: The Muses II* (Stanford, CA: Stanford University Press, 2006), 65–66.

45. Jean-Pierre Vernant, "Tensions and Ambiguities in Greek Tragedy," in Jean-Pierre Vernant and Pierre Vidal-Naquet, *Myth and Tragedy in Ancient Greece*, trans. Janet Lloyd (New York: Zone, 1988), 35–36.

46. Pierre Vidal-Naquet, "Hunting and Sacrifice in Aeschylus' Oresteia," in Vernant and Vidal-Naquet, *Myth and Tragedy in Ancient Greece*, 157.

47. For more on what might be called the "web of ruin" see my chapter titled "Networks," in *Critical Terms for Media Studies*, ed. W. J. T. Mitchell and Mark Hansen (Chicago: University of Chicago Press, 2010).

48. Gilles Deleuze, *Pure Immanence: Essays on A Life*, trans. Anne Boyman (New York: Zone, 2001), 94.

49. Ibid., 38.

50. For more on the concept of univocity in Deleuze, see in particular Gilles Deleuze, *Difference and Repetition*, trans. Paul Patton (New York: Athlone, 1994), 39–41, and Gilles Deleuze, *The Logic of Sense*, trans. Mark Lester (New York: Columbia University Press, 1990), 179–80. Alain Badiou's book *Deleuze: The Clamor of Being*, trans. Louise Burchill (Minneapolis: University of Minnesota Press,

2000), is also an instructive overview and critique of Deleuze's theory of univocity.

51. Laruelle spends a lot of time parsing prepositions like these, determining which words help the non-philosophical project and which inhibit it. See, inter alia, François Laruelle, *Principes de la non-philosophie* (Paris: PUF, 1996).

52. For a deeper exploration of the special relationship between networks and the late-twentieth century, see my own *Protocol: How Control Exists after Decentralization* (Cambridge, MA: The MIT Press, 2004), and the book co-written by Thacker and me, *The Exploit: A Theory of Networks* (Minneapolis: University of Minnesota Press, 2007).

53. Robert Taber, *War of the Flea* (Washington, DC: Potomac Books, 2002), 20.

54. Elias Canetti, *Crowds and Power*, trans. Carol Stewart (New York: Farrar, Straus and Giroux, 1962), 93.

55. Guy Brossollet, *Essai sur la non-bataille* (Paris: Belin, 1975), 67–78, emphasis removed from original.

56. Ibid., 15.

57. See for example Jussi Parikka, *Digital Contagions: A Media Archaeology of Computer Viruses* (New York: Peter Lang, 2007); Tony D. Sampson, *Virality: Contagion Theory in the Age of Networks* (Minneapolis: University of Minnesota Press, 2012); and Michel Serres, *The Parasite*, trans. Lawrence R. Schehr (Minneapolis: University of Minnesota Press, 2007).

58. See Franco Moretti, *Graphs, Maps, Trees: Abstract Models for Literary History* (London: Verso, 2007).

59. Nietzsche has quite pointedly attacked what he viewed as the dubious Christian moral presuppositions maligning all things desirous or erotic. "Christianity has succeeded in transforming Eros and Aphrodite—great powers capable of idealisation—into diabolical kobolds and phantoms by means of the torments it introduces into the consciences of believers whenever they are excited sexually. . . . Must everything that one has to combat, that one has to keep within bounds or on occasion banish totally from one's

mind, always have to be called *evil*! Is it not the way of *common* souls always to think an *enemy* must be *evil*! And ought one to call Eros an enemy? The sexual sensations have this in common with the sensations of sympathy and worship, that one person, by doing what pleases him, gives pleasure to another person—such benevolent arrangements are not to be found so very often in nature! And to calumniate such an arrangement and to ruin it through associating it with a bad conscience!" Friedrich Nietzsche, *Daybreak: Thoughts on the Prejudices of Morality*, trans. R. J. Hollingdale (Cambridge: Cambridge University Press, 1997), 45.

60. Walter Burkert, *Greek Religion*, trans. John Raffan (Cambridge, MA: Harvard University Press, 1985), 155.

61. Jean-Luc Nancy, "Paean for Aphrodite" (trans. Jonathan Derbyshire), in *Multiple Arts*, 54.

62. Pierre Chantraine, *Dictionnaire étymologique de la langue grecque* (Paris: Éditions Klincksieck, 1974), s.v. μέδω, 675.

63. See Émile Boisacq, *Dictionnaire étymologique de la langue grecque* (Paris: Librairie C. Klincksieck, 1938), and Chantraine, *Dictionnaire étymologique de la langue grecque*.

64. Nancy, "Paean for Aphrodite," 52, 53, 59.

65. Jean-Pierre Vernant, "Preface," in Jean Rudhardt, *Le Rôle d'Éros et d'Aphrodite dans les cosmogonies grecques* (Paris: PUF, 1986), 6. Later in the book, Rudhardt explains in greater detail: "The mutilation of Ouranos most certainly limited the spontaneity and permanence of desire, but the myth tells us also that it did not weaken the powers of love: what desire lost finds itself again in another form, in the goddess that came out of the mutilated genitals. . . . The castration of Ouranos does not abolish sexuality, it defines the conditions of how it is exercised" (17).

66. Nancy, "Paean for Aphrodite," 54. Nancy's language here echos Irigaray's mediations on a sex *qui n'en est pas un*. See Luce Irigaray, *This Sex Which Is Not One*, trans. Catherine Porter (Ithaca, NY: Cornell University Press, 1985).

67. Deleuze, in his "Three Women of Masoch," describes Aphrodite as a courtesan who dissolves into pansexuality: "Her life, in her

own words, is dedicated to love or beauty; she lives for the moment. She is sensual; she loves whoever attracts her and gives herself accordingly. She believes in the independence of woman and in the fleeting nature of love; for her the sexes are equal: she is hermaphrodite." Gilles Deleuze and Leopold von Sacher-Masoch, *Masochism: Coldness and Cruelty & Venus in Furs*, trans. Jean McNeil (New York: Zone, 1989), 48.

68. Genial may refer to the chin or jawline, from the Greek *genus*, the part of the face animated by the smile (if not also the animation of a physiognomic "kind"), but it also refers to the nuptial bed and hence to fertility and marriage. Derrida has written on what he calls "the line of words belonging to the same family in *g*," words like generation, genitalia, genesis, genealogy, genre, gender, genial, or genius. For a particular emphasis on genre theory in literature including a discussion of Maurice Blanchot, see Jacques Derrida, "The Law of Genre," trans. Avital Ronell, *Critical Inquiry* 7, no. 1 (Autumn, 1980): 55–81. For the question of genius (on the occasion of Hélène Cixous's archive being acquired by the Bibliothèque Nationale de France), see Jacques Derrida, *Geneses, Genealogies, Genres, and Genius: The Secrets of the Archive*, trans. Beverley Bie Brahic (New York: Columbia University Press, 2006). See also the chapter on "Genius" in Giorgio Agamben, *Profanations*, trans. Jeff Fort (New York: Zone, 2007). For a rather different perspective see Michel Serres's discussion of multiplicity in *Genesis*, trans. Genevieve James and James Nielson (Ann Arbor: University of Michigan Press, 1997).

69. Hesiod, *Theogony* (lines 197–206), trans. Dorothea Wender (New York: Penguin, 1973), 29, translation altered.

70. Chantraine, *Dictionnaire étymologique de la langue grecque*, s.v. μειδιάω, 677.

DARK MEDIA

Eugene Thacker

ALONE AT LAST

It is said that the shortest horror story ever written is Frederic Brown's story "Knock," published in the December 1948 issue of *Thrilling Wonder Stories*. The story, in its entirety, is as follows:

> The last man on Earth sat alone in a room. There was a knock on the door . . .

A variation on the story appeared few years later, in the July 1957 issue of the *Magazine of Fantasy and Science Fiction*. There Ron Smith published "The Horror Story Shorter by One Letter Than the Shortest Horror Story Ever Written":

> The last man on Earth sat alone in a room. There was a lock on the door . . .

While they differ only by a single letter, each story encapsulates within itself a very different kind of horror—the horror of an

This chapter has grown out of my "Dark Media" seminar, given at The New School. My thanks to those who have participated in it over the years. Portions of this chapter have previously appeared in other publications, including Alexander Galloway et al., *French Theory Today* (The Public School/Erudio Editions, 2010), *Die technologische Bedingung*, ed. Erich Hörl (Surkhamp Verlag, 2011), and *Conveyor Magazine* (issue no. 4, 2012).

unknown mediation that is about to happen, and the horror of the absence of mediation that has already happened. Who—or what—is it that could be knocking at the door? Who—or what—has put the lock on the door? How should one answer a knock from beyond, and where is the key to a lock that at once shuts one in and shuts some other entity out? Which is the greater horror, the something that wants to come in, or the impossibility of ever going out, that something unknown that is locked out, or that something all-too-familiar that is locked in?

However, what both stories have in common is that they present to us situations in which communication is impossible. This is one sense of the term excommunication—the impossibility of communication, that is nevertheless presented or "communicated" as such. In these stories, communication is impossible because we are dealing with the last man on Earth, one of those imaginary end-of-the-world scenarios so popular in the genres of horror and science fiction. When there is only one, communication serves no purpose; at best one speaks to imaginary others or, what amounts to the same thing, one speaks to a redoubled self. Only delusion, glossolalia, and madness can result. Just another day, this same room, the same chair, the same daylight or darkness, and the enigmatic door, suspended in ambiguity. Sooner or later, some sort of communication must take place—the knock must be answered, the lock must be removed. In fact, a life without communication seems unthinkable, if not unlivable. It is as if there is a communicational imperative that haunts every possibility of solitude, refusal, and silence; it is as if communication must have its say, even if it necessitates the dissolution of the subject it is meant to reaffirm and bolster.[1]

It is for this reason that these two little stories are of interest. They encapsulate an impossibility of communication that is at the heart of the communication concept itself. But notice that this initial impossibility of communication—being the last man on Earth—immediately fails. In the first story, it turns out that either one is mistaken (one is not the last man on Earth, another is knocking at the door) or that one is correct (one is the last man on Earth, yes, but there are other beings that await, perhaps impatiently, just outside the door).

Something similar takes place in the second story, except here the ambivalent promise of solitude is interrupted by a different sort of gesture. It is not the affirmative gesture of a knock that interrupts, but the more negative gesture of a lock that prevents passage. Here, as in the first story, either one has put the lock there themselves (but what is there to fear, since there is no one else outside?), or someone or something else has put the lock there, and without first asking permission.

The end result of both stories is the same. In both, the solitude implied by being the last man on Earth is immediately interrupted by the communicational imperative. But this is a communication that can never really take place, for how can one communicate with someone—or something—that is presumably beyond the pale of all human notions of communication? And how can communication take place when the only gesture of communication—a lock on the door—forbids it? In both instances the form of communication remains intact, though its content either exceeds it or withdraws from it. A communicational imperative is expressed, but one either confronts an otherness beyond all possible communication, or communication's possibility is enigmatically foreclosed and withdrawn.

In the preceding chapter, we saw how Alexander Galloway invoked excommunication across three different modes of mediation. Each mode shows how communication encounters its own impossibility. Tied as Hermes is to the idea of hermeneutics, excommunication comes to be understood as an always contentious and often confrontational testing of the limits of communication. Hermes is the messenger who is a deceiver, the wayward guide, the trusted courier whose own words involve entanglement. At the same time, the luminous communication of Iris presents a different window onto excommunication. Rather than the threat of excommunication into foreign lands,

Iris represents the reverse threat, that communication will cease entirely as the communicational structure collapses into itself, resulting in pure immediacy. Finally, there is a third mode, the swarming exemplified by the Furies. The Furies are a flat assemblage, and as such lapse into the absolute vacuity of a kind of non-communication.

By contrast, in the chapter following this one, McKenzie Wark proposes another approach to the excommunication concept. Rather than taking excommunication as the always-negotiating, always-critical in-between (where both signal and noise uneasily co-exist), Wark suggests that excommunication be thought of in relation to massively distributed forms of communication that exceed normative—and human—forms of communication. Either the nonhuman punctures normative human communication in an excommunicational rupture, or communication itself is so radically transformed and alien that to speak of communication at all makes little sense.

Proceeding from this, we can add another dimension to the notion of excommunication, and that is the way in which excommunication collapses the two extreme poles of mediation— that of pure immediacy and that of total opacity. It seems that there is always the communicational imperative, even if it is to respond by saying no, refusing, or ignoring the imperative. This is a more melancholic form of mediation, a mediation that seems to have already failed before the drama has even begun. In this sense, communication cannot be thought of apart from its own annulment, even though, in this possibility of annulment, one always seems to return to the knock or the lock on the door. We can thus propose another definition: *excommunication is a double movement in which the communicational imperative is expressed, and expressed as the impossibility of communication.* In excommunication, the very possibility of communication is annulled. Excommunication employs a logic of negation, a logic that dreams of an absolute negation, though the truth is that this negation is always shadowed by an engimatic residue—the message that says "there will be no more messages."

THE REALISM OF THE UNSEEN

In the sections that follow, this double movement of excommunication will be traced through cultural examples drawn mostly from the genre of supernatural horror, examples that are expressed through a variety of media, including literature, film, television, and the graphic novel. These examples will eventually take us into the shadowy corners of medieval mysticism, particularly that branch known as apophatic mysticism (from *apophanai*, "saying away," or speaking by negations). The aim is to undertake a sort of experiment—to think about communication, media, and mediation less in terms of technical artifacts or technical processes, and more in terms of the capacity of media to at once mediate between two points, while at the same time negating this very same form of mediation. This means understanding media as not simply defined by on/off states or the obligation to stay connected, and not simply as technical conductors for a vitalistic, communicational flux and flow, but understanding media as embodying a basic paradox: mediation as those moments when one communicates with or connects to that which is, by definition, inaccessible. I will be calling this enigma—the mediation of that which cannot be mediated—*dark media*. Dark media are, in a way, the consequence or the effect of excommunication. And, if excommunication precedes or conditions every communication, we might likewise say that dark media precede or condition every mediation.

One example of dark media is given at the birth of cinema—which also coincides with the birth of the horror film. Georges Méliès, known to many for his innovative use of special effects in early cinema (and generally credited with the first horror film), gives us three interesting examples of mediation that combine a fascination with new technologies while also evoking a sense of the supernatural.

In the film *Long Distance Wireless Photography* (*Photographie électrique à distance*, 1908), a young bohemian inventor demonstrates to his benefactors his unique invention—a machine that captures the living, animated image of a person on a screen. The invention itself is a hodge-podge of steampunk-like devices, including a mirror-like "camera," a large cinematic screen, and an assembly of gears and turbine engines driving it all. At first, the machine faithfully captures still images, which then take on a life of their own on the screen. But something goes awry, as the benefactor and his wife sit to have their images "animated" on screen. The benefactor's wife has her rather pudgy face magnified into contorted, grotesque expressions, while the benefactor himself is transformed on screen into a monstrous, clown-like monkey. A minor riot ensues, culminating in the overheating and destruction of the machine itself.

Another Méliès film, *The Mysterious Retort* (*L'Alchimiste Parafaragamus ou La cornue infernale*, 1906), depicts an aged alchemist who attempts to use magic from a grimoire to call up angels, demons, and other unnamed creatures. The lab itself features a large glass container set atop a brick alchemist's stove. The glass container itself is centrally displayed like a screen, within which we see a sequence of figures (a mythical female figure bearing gold, a monstrous spider with a human head, and finally the Devil himself).

Finally, in the film *The Black Imp* (*Le diable noir*, 1905), a bourgeois lodger at a hotel is perplexed when furniture in his room suddenly disappears. Chairs vanish just as he is about to sit down; tables and wardrobes suddenly move as he is about to unpack. When he tries to put everything back in place, the furniture magically multiplies out of control. Eventually a demon-like figure becomes visible as the trickster behind it all; a chase ensues and eventually the entire room is destroyed, leaving only the laughing demon behind.

Like many of Méliès's films, these films can be read as allegories of the "new" medium of cinema, a medium as magical as it is technological. Taken in sequence, these three films give us three views of media and mediation. In *Long Distance Wireless Photography*, mediation takes place via media, in the sense that we understand "media" to be commensurate with technological devices and the machine apparatus. While Méliès has fun with the baroque complexity of the machine in the film, it also serves a kind of pedagogical function as to the inner workings of cinema itself, as we witness first the proper mediation from the thing itself to its (animate, living) representation, and then the accidental or unexpected mediation of the benefactor and his wife into grotesque monsters. But between the thing itself (the living body in a space) and the mediated image (animate on the screen), there is the medium of the machine, the apparatus, the device. In a sense *Long Distance Wireless Photography* is the encapsulation of media in the era of industrial capitalism, at once transparently mediating between the thing and its representation, while also providing some value added, either in terms of enhancement or synthesis.

But the next two films, while they still take up the issue of mediation, do something different. *The Mysterious Retort*, borrowing as it does from Renaissance alchemy and the Faust myth, analogizes modern industrial technology in terms of another "technology," that of magic, alchemy, and the occult. Instead of cameras, turbine engines, and cinematic screens, we see a grimoire, magical potions, and an alchemical glass. Again, both the expected and unexpected happen—the alchemist does get his gold, but he also gets more than he bargained for, as the alchemical lab—like the technological lab in *Long Distance Wireless Photography*—is eventually consumed in smoke and fire. Importantly, the alchemist—like the inventor in *Long Distance Wireless Photography*—is rarely in control of the medium or of the process of mediation. In *The Mysterious Retort*, the Devil seems to be coordinating everything we see in the alchemical glass, while in *Long Distance Wireless Photography* it seems to be the machine itself that generates the surprising images of its own accord.

The third film, *The Black Imp*, effaces mediation altogether, at least in the traditional sense. There is no machine or device, no book of spells or alchemical lab—simply a devious and unseen demon arbitrarily causing things to appear and disappear, to magically move or suddenly multiply. There is also no screen or glass upon which or within which the products of mediation appear, separating their "virtual" reality from that of the real characters themselves. The demon and the vanishing/appearing furniture are just as much a part of a shared reality as is the unsuspecting hotel lodger. Indeed, in *The Black Imp*, Méliès only shows the demon to us the viewers at the beginning and the end of the film. Otherwise the demon is invisible to both the character and viewers—we as viewers do have the added advantage of knowing that the demon is invisibly present in the room, but we also are left to fill in the relations of causality that we subsequently witness, in effect speculatively inserting the demon—as a mediator—into the supernatural events of the vanishing table or multiplying chairs.

These, like many of Méliès's films, appropriate the vernacular of supernatural horror (monsters, ghosts, spirits, demons, magic, and the occult), but they do so not without a good deal of humor. The apparatus always breaks down and consumes itself, the inventors or magicians always lose control, and in the end it is the demon that has the last laugh. Méliès's films chart the enigma of media and mediation, an enigma at once technological and theological: how to make something present that is absent, how to make something alive that is dead, how to create something out of nothing. In spite of Méliès's overt humor, there is always something that recedes into a shadowy, unspoken region: the machine that shows us more truth than we are prepared to see, the magic that calls up forces beyond human comprehension, or the everyday apprehension of an invisible nexus of causality, behind the veil of what can be seen and heard and felt. Méliès's "horror" films are not only pedagogical moments of mediation, but they also point to the shadowy absence at the core of all mediation. In any given moment of mediation, there is always a minimal separation, a differential, a gap, lacuna, or fissure . . . a blind spot. This is both what conditions and what undermines mediation, but it is also the reason why the media that fully succeed are also the media that fail. The most perfect mediation comes in *The Black Imp*, in the form of demonic possession; but for us as viewers to realize this, it must be remediated as a special-effects film, and we must be shown the demon, so that we can go back to viewing the scene "as if" the demon isn't there. The fantastical element of Méliès's films is to be able to see what media and mediation usually don't make visible— this is why Méliès's films are about film, and more broadly, about technological mediation. But it is, of course, only through the medium and its "special effects" that one can gain a glimpse of what is not mediated.

Perhaps this can serve as a description for the types of media and mediation we will be calling "dark media." Dark media have, as their aim, the mediation of that which is unavailable or inaccessible to the senses, and thus that of which we are normally "in the dark" about. But beyond this, dark media have, as another aim, the investigation into the ways in which all mediation harbors within itself this blind spot, the minimal distance that persists in any instance of mediation, however successful or complete it may be. Dark media inhabit this twofold movement—seeing something in nothing (e.g., the animate images appearing on the screen or the alchemical glass), and finding nothing in each something (the paradoxical absence or presence of the "demon" behind each thing).

As a concept, dark media takes up concerns at once technological and theological. But this is not to say that dark media is simply "about" religion. Dark media is not to be found in the representation of religion in the media, where media act as a purely formal container for a separate religious content (be it faithfully rendered or not). In such instances, media serve as the image of religion. Dark media is also not to be found in the use of media by religious communities or within religious rituals, in spite of the ubiquity of multi-media in churches and the long-standing use of media to further religious ideology. Here media are the tools of religion. Lastly, dark media is not the latest avatar of religion-as-media, in which one would retrospectively interpret premodern religion in terms of modern concepts of discourse, rhetoric, or mass communication. Dark media is neither the image, the tool, or the discourse of religion. Although it invites us to consider a premodern genealogy of media, one that would stretch back to medieval mysticism and beyond, dark media is not reducible to religion.

Instead, we can ask how dark media is "religious," from *religo* "I bind"—a binding between the human and the divine, between the subject and God, between members of a religious community, a binding to the institutions and values of a religion, and ultimately the binding or un-binding within one's self. All these bindings are ways of relating and mediating, not just in the secular domain (between one person and another, between believers and nonbelievers), but also in an exceptional type of binding— that between the human and the divine (even in those instances in which the human is divine, the divine "in" the human). Perhaps we can even understand this in a post-secular context, in which there is a *religo* specific to dark media: the relation between the human and the nonhuman, but a nonhuman that is not necessarily outside the human or separate from it. With dark media there is an "anti-humanism" at work, a form of mediation that ultimately does away with the terms of mediation itself.

These instances of dark media invite us to think about media and mediation as religious problems.[2] In his lectures on religion and mysticism, William James notes the strange status of "objects of belief" in mystical accounts, neither fully adhering to the Kantian framework of coherent intuitions given over to the understanding and reason, nor simply arbitrary statements of unreason. James suggests that this intuition—of something present and non-empirical—is not just of the order of mystical experience, but of everyday experience as well. James calls this "the reality of the unseen":

It is as if there were in the human consciousness a *sense of reality, a feeling of objective presence, a perception* of what we may call "something there," more deep and more general than any of the special and particular "senses" by which the current psychology supposes existent realities to be originally revealed.[3]

In language that also serves as an apt description of media and mediation, James suggests that the Kantian framework holds in both directions—not only is our reason only as good as our sensory apparatus, but our sensory apparatus also sees what it is prepared to believe. "The truth is that in the metaphysical and religious sphere, articulate reasons are cogent for us only when our inarticulate feelings of reality have already been impressed in favor of the same conclusion."[4]

The question is what role media and mediation play in this charged space between scientific reason and religious belief. This is the reason why the supernatural horror tradition is of interest, presenting us with extraordinary phenomena, to which we may respond with philosophical skepticism or religious acceptance. Méliès's films present media as having this dual nature of skepticism and belief, ghosts and the machine, the engineer's ratiocination and the mystic's laughter.

COMMUNICATIONS HORROR

Historically speaking, our modern ideas of media are largely influenced by postwar cybernetics and information theory. In the well-known communications model put forth by Claude Shannon and Warren Weaver in the 1940s, a sender and receiver are connected by a channel, which serves as the conduit for an informational message.[5] The channel is a medium, and as such it both connects and separates two points that are physically or geographically remote from each other. The channel presumes the distinction between sender and receiver, as well as providing a means for connecting them, just as the message presumes a relative autonomy with respect to the sender and the receiver. Even though there may be "noise" along the communications channel, the aim of the mediation is to provide as seamless and as transparent a connection as possible, "as if" sender and receiver were physically co-present.

Shannon and Weaver were adamant that this was ostensibly an engineering concept; they even stress that the informational message has to be viewed as purely quantitative, a certain amount of data sent at point A and received at point B. Their research would go on to influence the modern concept of the information network as well. In the 1960s, communications engineer Paul Baran would expand the "Shannon diagram" to encompass multiple point-to-point communications.[6] Most notably, Baran provided a way of understanding how the Shannon diagram could be scaled up to form a fully distributed network of computers, each sending and receiving messages within a system based on this basic relationship of sender-channel-receiver. Very quickly the idea was taken up by different groups for different applications, from Cold War era "first strike" scenarios to idealistic proclamations concerning the freedom of information sharing and virtual communities. Our twenty-first-century lingo of social networks, WiFi, and trans-media are in many ways extensions of these same concepts.

The technical detail of such research has not prevented the Shannon diagram from entering the broader cultural discourse surrounding information and communications technology, especially as computers ceased to be Moloch-like, military mainframes and entered the workplace and gradually the home. Shannon's diagram has become part of the standard way in which we view media today—it is the common vernacular of media literacy, intuitive interfaces, and the constant urge to become early-adopters of the newest of media. It puts into a formal language what we take for granted—that a medium is some device X that connects two separate points A and B. It is modular, scalable, and applicable across a wide spectrum of everyday examples, from the most personal of computers to the most social of networks. Within the Shannon diagram, the media industries themselves discover a message as powerful as it is direct—everything everywhere is always available and connected. What was previously inaccessible—due to the contingencies of space or time or corporeality—is rendered accessible via media and the process of mediation. This is the promissory rhetoric of new media, in whatever capacity it is used, and for whatever purposes it is deployed.

From a philosophical perspective, the Shannon diagram is important because it implies that *media* and *mediation* are the primary ways through which one lives in modern, technologized cultures. At the same time, however, these concepts of media and mediation have an extensive philosophical genealogy. Media and mediation are central to the Western philosophical tradition, whether it be in terms of the relation between self and world (the metaphysical monism found in presocratic thinkers like Parmenides, Anaxagoras, or Heraclitus), the relation of self to others (the ethical, human-centric turn of Socrates and his followers), or the relation of thought to an intelligible reality, whether or not that reality be apparent to the senses (the emphasis on language and rhetoric in Plato, the emphasis on logic in Aristotle).

The pioneers of modern cybernetics and information theory were engineers and not philosophers, but even so, their concepts also presume some minimum ground of mediation as the basis for any possible communication. In the Shannon diagram, a starting presupposition is the interplay of identity and difference—I am who I am in part because I am not you, my body does not occupy the same space as your body, and I am at point A while you are at point B. The individuation of "point A" is dependent on its separation from a "point B" with which it is communicating, and in fact the possibility of connecting points A and B relies on this notion of a prior separation—the conditions of connection relying on a prior state of disconnection. We might even say that the very possibility of communication lies in the presupposition of a prior discommunication. Connection is a way of formally articulating a prior (and perhaps, primordial) state of disconnection.

While the Shannon diagram ostensibly has, as its goal, the connection of points A and B, it is what happens between those two points that is of special interest. Thus, we can ask: What happens when media cease to mediate—at least in the conventional sense of the Shannon diagram? With media and mediation, everything happens in the middle; it is the locus where things go smoothly or fail to connect at all, the place where one not only finds information, but noise as well. Likewise, are there also instances in which media work "too well," that is, instances in which media and mediation seem to operate beyond the pale of human capacity or comprehension. Another question presents itself: Might there be instances in which the former are also the latter, instances in which the "failure" of media are also an indication of the limits of our ideas of media and mediation?

We know that in nineteenth-century Europe there were many instances of "new" media devices being used in unorthodox ways, from the popularity of spirit photography, to phantasmagoria shows such as those found in the Parisian *Cabaret du Néant*, to the use of modern media in early examples of "ghost hunting" carried out by groups such as the Society for Psychical Research and the British Ghost Club. While this moment is unique, it also looks forward to similar uses of video and digital media today, just as it reaches back to a premodern understanding of mysticism, magic, and occultism. Given this, what should we make of the many contemporary examples of handheld cameras used to prove the existence of ghosts, or the use of digital audio to record the voices of the dead, or the use of photography and Photoshop to capture spirits or the aura of an individual? In our skepticism, we often dismiss such fringe uses of media as mere gimmicks; we are more likely to attribute to media the ability to produce novel aesthetic effects, generating a momentary "as if" experience that is, nevertheless, always framed by our secular, scientific understanding of such effects as effects. Arguably, we no longer believe that media can trick us, if this was ever the case (indeed, accounts of nineteenth-century spirit photography and phantasmagoria suggest that we've always known, and always played along, "as if").

At the same time, we seem to take pleasure in imagining media behaving in unorthodox ways. We often sublimate such media trickery into entertainment, perhaps allowing ourselves a nostalgic, ironic longing for a belief in the supernatural that could, at the same time, be verified via the technicity of new media. Nowhere is this combined skepticism and fascination more apparent than in popular culture, and in particular the horror genre. From TV programs such as *Twilight Zone* and *Fringe*, to films such as *Poltergeist* and *Paranormal Activity*, we see representations of a range of media that attempt to make contact with the supernatural. In contemporary horror film, video tapes, digital cameras, mobile phones, and webcams are used in such ways that they provide a link to what American author H. P. Lovecraft once referred to as "cosmic outsideness."

Indeed, a cursory glance at the horror genre today reveals a number of examples in which everyday objects—and in particular, media objects—become infused in some way with the supernatural or the paranormal. In these stories the innocuous and even banal ubiquity of media objects, from cell phones to webcams, enters a liminal space, where such objects suddenly reveal the ambivalent boundary separating the natural from the supernatural, the uncanny from the marvelous, the earthly from the divine. Furthermore, in our contemporary trans-media culture, the representations of such supernatural media themselves take place via one or more media forms—novels, films, TV, comics, video games, and so on. Thus what we are witnessing is not a single, master medium that represents all possible cases of the supernatural, but a variety of media that mediate or remediate other media: a novel about a cursed videotape, a film about haunted webcams, a videogame that uses a paranormal camera.

Consider the case of contemporary Japanese horror (also referred to as "J-horror"). Some stories portray media as normative technologies that behave in abnormal ways, serving to mediate between the living and the dead, or between the natural and the supernatural. The best-selling novel *Ring* and the film based on the book use the videotape and the video image as the point of mediation between the natural and the supernatural. In the *Ring* film, there are scenes in which the object of the videotape is itself imbued with vitalistic and supernatural properties, contagiously passing from one person to another. But there is also a key scene in the film where a mysterious figure in the video crosses the threshold of the screen, actually emerging from the TV into the room in which the TV is being watched by a horrified viewer/character. In such moments, it is less the media object that is the source of horror, and more the fact of mediation itself that is horrific, a mediation that strangely seems to work all too well. Kiyoshi Kurosawa's atmospheric film *Pulse* takes this idea a step further, showing us webcams and chat rooms that are portals to the dead. The media themselves are quite quotidian, and even, by today's standards, out of date. A simple laptop anywhere will do. But it is the form of mediation itself—this time via webcams—that makes the mysterious contact with the supernatural possible.[7] These motifs are also apparent in the video game franchise *Fatal Frame*, in which the player, moving about a haunted landscape searching for clues, must "kill" the menacing creatures there—by taking a photo of them with a special camera. The near opposite of *Pulse*, in which media passively mediate ghosts and the dead, the *Fatal Frame* games re-imagine media in terms of active "capture"—in which capturing and killing become identical. In these and other examples we see readily familiar media objects—videotapes, TVs, computers, cameras—which continue to function as media technologies, albeit at another level.

But not all horror films characterize media in this way. In many ways the first lesson of the horror genre is that the body itself—as living, dead, or possessed—is the medium of all media. Other examples of J-horror move beyond the use of technological devices, and show us the ways that the human body can serve as a medium. This not only points back to the earlier, nineteenth-century sense of a spiritual "medium," but it also dips back deeper into the cultural history of funeral rites and the preparation of the corpse. For instance, author Koji Suzuki's sequel to *Ring*, entitled *Spiral*, shows us the corpse as a medium, with DNA and informational code eerily emerging from the organs of the body. Another of Kurosawa's films—*Séance*—more directly plays with the double sense of medium, and the manga series *Kurosagi Corpse Delivery Service* combines the detective genre and gallows humor to tell the story of a group of college students at a Buddhist seminary, who make money on the side by performing exorcisms and capturing ghosts with a range of strategies, both high-tech and low-tech.

Yet another iteration in the J-horror story is one that understands space itself as a point of mediation. The "old dark house" motif is perhaps the most familiar motif of the horror genre, emerging as it does out of the gothic novel tradition, and forming a staple within horror film to this day. But what happens when the mediation of the supernatural occurs not via media devices, and not even via the body—but in and through physical space? Space and place themselves serve as points of mediation, and such haunting is also scalable, from the suffocating confines of a coffin, to the domestic space of houses or apartment buildings, to the dark cavernous spaces of the city's underground. The film *The Grudge* (*Ju-on*) is a well-known example, borrowing as it does both from the gothic novel, as well as from Hokusai's *manga* and the *yokai* folklore tradition. The tight spaces of a bedroom, a shower, even one's own bed, all become occasions for a sudden dilation of physical space, revealing impossible beings suddenly present in incongruous spaces. The reverse also takes place, in which large spaces suddenly constrict and focus on particular spaces—an elevator, a corridor, a corner on the stairwell. The scope is expanded to an entire apartment building in *Dark Water*, and to an entire haunted city in the film *Marebito*.

J-horror is interesting because it pushes the idea of media and mediation outward, from everyday media devices, to the body, to space and place. A last iteration occurs in which it is thought itself that is haunted, thought itself that is the point of mediation between the natural and supernatural. Junji Ito's metaphysical horror manga *Uzumaki* offers what is perhaps the strangest theory of media. A small seaside town becomes obsessed with the abstract geometrical shape of the spiral. Soon spirals are cropping up everywhere in eerie ways, from the strangely shaped grass on the hillside, to the noodles in a bowl of udon soup, to the patterns on traditional kimonos, and so on. The spiral craze causes one character—a potter—to begin to make grotesque pottery, with contorted spiral-like limbs. After another character commits suicide (by attempting to cut out the spiral-shaped cochlea in her head), her burned ashes at the funeral ascend into the sky, forming a gigantic black spiral of smoke. An abstract horror, a kind of black matheme, seems to arbitrarily haunt the town and its inhabitants—in a spectacular perversion of Plato, their ultimate obsession is to become spirals, which one character attempts by impossibly contorting his body, with all the studied discipline of an ascetic.

One can detect a final stage beyond even this, in which it is, finally, being itself that mediates the supernatural, and being itself that is also the source of horror. The low-budget film *Long Dream* follows this motif, but on the level of temporal rather than spatial transformation. Based on a manga story by Junji Ito, the main character, Tetsuro Murkoda, can't stop dreaming—he is an example of an inverted insomniac. As he looses all sense of (waking) time, his body begins to change and adapt in grotesque ways. He soon loses his eyelids, the his eyes themselves become hypersensitized, able only to see an unnamable "beyond" that bears no relation to what can normally be seen. The gradual disintegration of body and mind is elaborated in the manga version of the story. Murkoda's skin becomes scaly and crystalline, he loses his hair and his head elongates, his senses withdraw, his nose, ears, and even eyes gradually receding into his unhuman body. Attended by physicians in a hospital, Murkoda's dreams get longer and longer, though the actual time he sleeps is the same. His "long dreams" eventually span years, decades, centuries, and beyond, into an unhuman, timeless time. Near the end of the story, a grotesque, alien-looking Murkoda mumbles, "What happens to the man who wakes from an endless dream?" In the final scenes, Murkoda's body disintegrates completely, leaving behind only strange, crumbling, unidentifiable crystals lying in his hospital bed. Paradoxically, mediation reaches its endpoint once it becomes absolute, once there is no longer anything to mediate except the pure form of mediation itself.

In all these examples, we see the communications diagram at work, though in anomalous ways. Media shift from the connection of two points in a single reality, to an enigmatic and ambivalent connection with an unnamed "beyond." We begin with "media" in the colloquial sense of technological devices, and we end with the mediation as equivalent to thought and being itself. J-horror takes up the communcations diagram and stretches it to its extreme point, provoking us to wonder where mediation ends and something outside mediation begins.

ON WHAT CANNOT BE SAID

If examples such as these are any barometer for our post-secular culture, it appears that the supernatural has returned—not in the guise of answered prayers or divinely sanctioned holy wars, but via the panoply of media objects that satellite us and that are embedded into the very material fabric of our bodies, cities, and lives. No longer is there a great beyond, be it in the topographies of the afterlife or the mythical journey of reincarnation. Instead, the supernatural is embedded in the world here and now, manifest via a paradoxical immediacy that constantly withdraws and cloaks itself. The supernatural seems to be as immanent as our media are—distributed, ubiquitous, in the "cloud" and enveloping us in its invisible, ethereal bath of information and noise.

The function of media is no longer to render the inaccessible accessible, or to connect what is separated. Instead, media reveal inaccessibility in and of itself—they make accessible the inaccessible—in its inaccessibility. To reveal the manifestation of that which does not exist—this is not simply a matter of data visualization or the construction of augmented realities. *This is a religious impulse.*

John Durham Peters, writing about the role of language and communication in the work of Augustine, puts it succinctly:

> For Augustine, the appearance of God to humans is essentially a media problem. For how could God, he asks, "appear" to the patriarchs and prophets when God has no appearance or physical form? If God appeared to appear, he was resorting to deception, donning a disguise to meet the crudity of human sense organs. Theophany is either deception (of humans) or debasement (of God).[8]

This dilemma is laid out in Augustine's *Confessions*, where the possibility of communication with the divine is characterized through an analogy between communication and "light":

> Into myself I went, and with the eyes of my soul (such as it was) I discovered over the same eye of my soul, over my mind, the unchangeable light (*lucem incommutabilem*) of the Lord: not this vulgar light, which all flesh may look upon, nor yet another greater of the same kind; as if this should shine much and much more clearly, and with its greatness take up all the room.[9]

Augustine analogizes a light that is superlative to all empirical or optical light, in order to describe a type of communication beyond all human or earthly communication. The pinnacle of communication surpasses the senses, language, and even the human activity of meaning-making; in effect, Augustine evokes a kind of mediation that, in its very description, is always surpassing itself into the ever-higher realms of divine communion and union.

But this is also a problem, for the divine by definition cannot appear, cannot be mediated, and cannot communicate. Even when the usual forms of theological mediation are employed—the notion of Christ, the God-man, as mediator; the role of various "spiritual creatures," including angels, to deliver divine messages—even in these instances there is still the duplicitous combination of something mediated that itself cannot be mediated. While Augustine arbitrates this problem by parsing God's mediation into two forms (the divine and its mediation are two different things), the problem of the mediation of the supernatural persists.

At the heart of this is the problem of presence, lyrically evoked by Augustine in a well-known passage in which he asks, "Whom do I love when I love God?"[10] Augustine's first reply is to separate the love of God with the love of earthly or worldly things: "What now do I love, whenas I love thee? Not the beauty of any corporeal thing . . . not the brightness of the light which we do behold . . . not the pleasant melodies of songs of all kinds . . ." But just as he separates them, Augustine acknowledges that the divine and earthly cannot be separated in this way, noting "and yet I love a certain kind of light, and a kind of voice, and a kind of fragrance, and a kind of meat, and a kind of embracement, whenas I love my God; who is both the light and the voice, and the sweet smell, and the meat . . ." In a remarkable rhetorical turn, Augustine seems to imply that the divine is not separate from the earthly, because the divine is "in" the earthly—the divine seems to be both that which is fundamentally separate from the earthly, but which is also identical with it.

This is where the duplicity that Peters points to appears. When Augustine asks "Whom do I love when I love God?," the problem is the opacity of the divine and the necessity of discovering some form of mediation.[11] In this latter view, where the divine seems to be identical with the world, mediation is rendered unnecessary, since God "is" the world and vice versa. But Augustine is in no way asserting a position of pantheism, for it is clear that the transcendence—the absolute separation and opacity—of the divine is never under question. Augustine arbitrates this through theological forms of mediation between the divine and earthly, supernatural and natural (the creation of the creatures by a Creator; the manifestation of the divine via earthly signs and symbols; the miraculous intervention of the supernatural into the natural). As he notes, divine mediation is the moment when "that light shineth into my soul, which no place can receive; that voice soundeth, which time deprives me not of; and that fragrancy smelleth, which no wind scatters; and that meat tasteth, which eating devours not . . ." Such mediation is unidirectional, a one-way communication that only becomes a two-way communication in the theologically exceptional moments of miracle, mercy, or grace.

Augustine's own reflections on divine mediation map out a problem central to the mediation concept itself—how to connect without also separating, insofar as connection implies a separation (and, in the case of divine mediation, an absolute separation). The link between a premodern and modern concept of mediation is summarized by Peters: "Augustine's account of divine communication with mortals foreshadows modern communications and the problem of how to conjure the credible presence of an absent body for an audience remote in time, space, or degree."[12]

In the horror genre, the mediation of the supernatural is always problematic, either because what is being mediated (e.g., ghosts, demons, and disembodied spirits) is not accessible by the senses, or because it is, in its very existence, a contradiction (e.g., living corpses, words made flesh, hybrids and monsters). In the J-horror examples above, something appears that has no appearance, or something appears that shouldn't appear. Something defies the litmus test of the empirical, or something defies natural law and the production of knowledge. In each case, something is given that is also withdrawn, a presence asserting itself only through absence, a *disbelief* that has two sides to it—I can't see what I believe, or I can't believe what I'm seeing.

It is this push-pull of mediation that Augustine identifies in the citations above. While Augustine attempts an affirmative reply (the divine can be mediated, though the divine itself is not mediation), the early-sixth-century mystic Dionysius the Areopagite opts for another approach, distinct from, yet in conversation with, that of Augustine. For Dionysius, the communication with, or mediation of, the divine can only take place through a practice of negation. If the human capacity of the senses, language, and ultimately thought are limited, and if the human is attempting this communication with that which is, by definition, beyond the human, then it would seem that any such communication or mediation would have to confront, or even embrace, the paradox of mediation—mediating that which cannot be mediated. No superlative analogies will do, nor will any attempts to cloak the divine by inserting intermediaries such as angels, demons, or theophanies. The problem remains the same—how to mediate that which cannot be mediated—but the approach is different. In contrast to Augustine's analogy of light, Dionysius offers the analogy of darkness; in contrast to Augustine's affirmationism of divine mediation, Dionysius explores a negative form of mediation. The contrast is brought out in Dionysius's influential text *The Mystical Theology*:

> The fact is that the more we take flight upward, the more our words are confined to the ideas we are capable of forming; so that now as we plunge into that darkness which is beyond intellect, we shall find ourselves not simply running short of words but actually speechless and unknowing.[13]

It is this negative method of stripping away and emptying that characterizes Dionysius's text and the negative theology tradition it inaugurates. Whereas with Augustine the self and God are mediated via an attenuated union of creatures and Creator (God as absolutely apart from the world, and yet identical with it), with Dionysius the mediation of self and God are mediated via a process of abandonment and self-abnegation. In a complex phrase, the author repeatedly asks how we can know the "ray of divine darkness": "By an undivided and absolute abandonment of yourself and everything, shedding all and freed from all, you will be uplifted to the ray of the divine darkness (Θειου σκοτους ακτινα) which is above everything that is."[14] In this enigmatic evocation of divine darkness, Dionysius is elaborating a logic of negation that is neither simply privative nor oppositional, but instead a kind of superlative negation, a "negation beyond every assertion." In this use of the analogy of darkness, Dionysius attempts to mediate that which cannot be mediated, while also preserving the opacity of the divine, an opacity that is characterized in negative terms ("dark," "shadow," "abyss").

As with Augustine, for Dionysius the task of mediating that which cannot be mediated requires a method. In the *Mystical Theology*, Dionysius outlines two paths of mystical knowledge: an affirmative path, or the *via affirmativa*, and a negative path, or the *via negativa*. In the former, one arrives at knowledge of the divine through successive affirmations, as when one describes individual human acts as "good" but the divine as "the Good" or "Goodness" in itself. The latter approach arrives at the divine through successive negations, as when one describes the divine as that which is not created or not existing in time. The *via affirmativa* implies what can be positively said of the divine, or a "kataphatic" approach (*kata-phanai*, literally to "come down" or "descend" in order to speak), while the *via negativa* implies what can be negatively said of the divine, or an "apophatic" approach (*apo-phanai*, "to say no," or to speak by not speaking). For Dionysius it is this second path, the *via negativa*, that yields the most profound results, based on the author's metaphysical commitment to a concept of the divine that is fundamentally inaccessible. As he notes, "[s]ince the Divine is the Cause of all beings, we should posit and ascribe to it all the affirmations we make in regard to beings, and, more appropriately, we should negate all these affirmations, since it surpasses all being."[15]

But even this approach must necessarily fail (and Dionysius seems readily aware of this), for the logical extension of the *via negativa*'s language is the failure of language and logic itself. While Dionysius—like Augustine—never doubts the transcendence of the divine and its super-essential character, there is a sense in which the *via negativa* is ultimately a kind of performative failure, a failure which ends up serving as this mediation of that which cannot be mediated. Denys Turner puts it in the following way:

> It is of the greatest consequence to see that negative language about God is no more apophatic in itself than is affirmative language. The apophatic is the linguistic strategy of somehow showing by means of language that which lies beyond language. It is not done, and cannot be done, by means of negative utterances alone which are no less bits of ordinarily intelligible human discourse than are affirmations. Our negations, therefore, fail of God as much as do our affirmations.[16]

Turner recaps his points within the terminology of analytical philosophy: "there is a very great difference between the strategy of *negative propositions* and the strategy of *negating the propositional*," the latter of which describes the ultimate point toward which Dionysian mysticism tends.[17] Through a successive stripping away of attributes, through the negation of affirmation, Dionysius puts forth a concept of darkness that is, first, an anti-empirical one (in that one moves away from what is seen and sensed), and then an anti-idealist one (in that one moves away from what can be thought and put into language), before arriving at a stage the author can only describe as "unknowing." For Dionysius, the divine can only be discussed through a language pushed to its limit—the divine as a "brilliant shadow," the "divine darkness" or the "darkness beyond every light."

Dionysius is, of course, talking about the way in which the divine is enigmatically inaccessible to us as human beings. But he is also talking about mediation, and its possibility or impossibility. This emphasis on the impossibility of mediation, or the negation of mediation itself, brings us back to the tradition of supernatural horror. We can suggest the following distinction: in the everyday context, mediation is epistemological, while in supernatural horror, mediation is ontological. In the former case, one assumes a certain practical knowledge of how media work and how they can be used. The questions one asks are questions of knowledge that presume a basic ontological framework: What's your number? Who's calling me? Can you hear me now? And so on. By contrast, in supernatural horror one still assumes a certain working knowledge of media, but something goes wrong—fundamentally wrong. Ironically, the problem is not that the media in question are broken; if anything, the problem is that media are working *too well*—we get more than we bargained for, as specters turn up in our photos, the dead appear on our computer screens, and that videotape, well, you probably shouldn't watch that. Here one cannot presume a common ontological ground, as the mediation is really a mediation between different realities, or between different ontological domains—the natural and the supernatural, the normal and the paranormal, life and the afterlife.

While we may use media today in an everyday context, it seems that we also like to imagine media having the exceptional ability to mediate between a world here-and-now and a world that remains mysteriously inaccessible to us without the use of media. In the horror genre, what we witness is an evocative concept of the supernatural as itself mediated, often through objects that are at once overly familiar and highly technical, objects that are everyday and opaque at the same time. In the broadest sense, the mediation of the supernatural prompts us to wonder whether the supernatural is by definition always mediated.

CINEMA AND DEMONOLOGY

In this triangulation of media, horror, and religion we see a concept of the supernatural deployed that is at once opaque and transparent—the supernatural appears to inhabit the domain of pure affective experience beyond the reach of words or images, and yet, in the examples we've pointed to, the supernatural is only ever apparent via some form of mediation. This presents us with a dilemma: If the supernatural exists, to what extent can it be experienced? Given that the supernatural is, in itself, beyond the senses, what then would be an "experience" of the supernatural? If the supernatural cannot be experienced, how are we to distinguish it from mere subjectivism—an illusion, a dream, a drug, a bit of visual trickery . . . ? The dual specters of realism and idealism haunt media and mediation—either "it's all in your head," or everything is reducible to the engineered and technical manipulation of sensory and cognitive affordance.

The literary theorist Tzvetan Todorov has a name for this dilemma, and he calls it the "fantastic." Drawing on the literature of supernatural horror, he provides a definition of the term: "The fantastic is that hesitation experienced by a person who knows only the laws of nature, confronting an apparently supernatural event."[18] Todorov goes on to elaborate on the logic of the fantastic:

> In a world which is indeed our world . . . there occurs an event which cannot be explained by the laws of this same familiar world. The person who experiences the event must opt for one of two possible solutions: either he is the victim of an illusion of the senses, a product of the imagination—and the laws of the world then remain what they are; or else the event has indeed taken place, it is an integral part of reality—but then this reality is controlled by laws unknown to us. . . . The fantastic occupies the duration of this uncertainty."[19]

Instances of the fantastic abound in the "weird fiction" tradition, most often associated with authors such as H. P. Lovecraft, and pulp magazines such as *Weird Tales*. But the fantastic inhabits not just a single moment, but a certain duration, in which it is carefully parceled out in failed attempts at description, in confessional language, or in quasi-scientific arguments between characters. In Lovecraft's 1936 novel *At the Mountains of Madness*, an expedition to the Antarctic reveals the massive, black ruins of a "cyclopean city," whose very existence questions all human knowledge. In the bowels of these ruins, the characters discover weird creatures that defy category and even description—the "Shoggoths." At once formless and geometric, oozing with malefic intent and swarming with temporary eyes, these creatures confront the explorers with their radically unhuman character, rendering them catatonic: "The shock of recognizing that monstrous slime and headlessness had frozen us into mute, motionless statues. . . . It seemed aeons that we stood there, but actually it could not have been more than ten or fifteen seconds."[20]

In this frozen moment, the testimony of the characters' senses are absurd, language falters, and thought becomes equal to silence: "I might as well be frank—even if I cannot bear to be quite direct—in stating what we saw. . . . The words reaching the reader can never even suggest the awfulness of the sight itself."[21] In a last, desperate attempt to comprehend their situation, Lovecraft's characters resort to what is essentially a negative language, the language of negative theology:

> We had expected, upon looking back, to see a terrible and incredibly moving entity if the mists were thin enough; but of that entity we had formed a clear idea. What we did see—for the mists were indeed all too malignly thinned—was something altogether different, and immeasurably more hideous and detestable. It was the utter, objective embodiment of the fantastic novelist's "thing that should not be."[22]

This is the moment of the fantastic, a moment that tenuously tips to one side (it must be accepted and yet it cannot not be accepted), and tenuously tips to the other (there must be some explanation, scientific or otherwise). In this apophatic silence of language and thought, what results is an all-pervasive stillness of everything except the furtive, lurking revelation of a limit. Lovecraft's stories are replete with such revelations, expressed through the kind of purple prose that has become a hallmark of the weird tale. At the same time, these revelations point to a limit that Lovecraft's characters can only negatively articulate: the beyond, the unnamable, the nameless thing, and so on.

For Todorov, the fantastic presents a fork in the road—either one accepts what appears to be exceptional, but then everything must be rethought (what Todorov calls "the marvelous"), or one discovers a rational explanation for what only seemed exceptional, and both natural law and social norm remain intact ("the uncanny").[23] However, Todorov says very little about what role media have in this fork in the road, and he says nothing about the ways that media themselves may serve as the conduit to either the marvelous or the uncanny.[24] In short, the *how* of the fantastic is left an open question. That the supernatural is mediated, and that it is by definition mediated—this is taken for granted in Todorov's analysis. At the same time, in our examples thus far, a character experiencing the fantastic nearly always comes up against a loss of words—in short, *the fantastic in supernatural horror has the structure of apophatic mysticism.* The characters in the stories of authors like Lovecraft, Algernon Blackwood, or Izumi Kyoka experience the fantastic in terms of the *via negativa*; like Dionysius the Areopagite, they can only resort to either negative terms or to passages filled with aporia and self-annulling contradictions. All that remains is this bare activity of mediation, a mediation that almost immediately negates itself.

This turning of mediation upon itself is not only voiced by early mystical thinkers such as Dionysius, but it is further expanded in later mystics working in the apophatic tradition. The sermons of Meister Eckhart provide an example. Eckhart frequently uses the Middle High German term *niht* and its cognates to describe the "nothing" or "nothingness" of both finite creatures and infinite divinity. In one sermon, Eckhart derives two basic senses of the term *niht* from a passage in Acts 9:8 ("Paul rose from the ground and with open eyes saw nothing").[25] The first is the "nothing" of finite creatures (creatures are "nothing" in the sense that they are created in time and in the world as flux and flow, as coming-to-be and passing-away; but also, creatures are "nothing" in that they are founded on a primordial, pre-existent, non-being). This nothing is, as we've noted, the moral-theological notion; nothing in this sense is both privative and subtractive. A second sense has to do with the *niht* specific to the divine (the "nothing" of God as that which is outside of time, space, and modality; God is "nothing" in so far as God is not a being among other beings). But Eckhart expands even this second sense of the term *niht* beyond "God" to what he terms the "Godhead" (*Gottheit*), in which the divine is purely apophatic, the divine to which no attributes, properties, or even names can be given (what Eckhart enigmatically calls "the One"). The Godhead bears no relation to the categories of Being or Non-Being. In one sermon Eckhart asserts, "God is all, and is one." Elsewhere he notes that the Godhead is "a non-God, a non-spirit, a non-person, a non-image; rather, He is a sheer pure limpid One, detached from all duality."[26] Nothing in this second sense is at once superlative and nullifying.

On the one hand, there is the nothing of creaturely life, the non-substantiality of what is ephemeral and temporary, the nothing of the all-too-human in its creaturely finitude. On the other hand, there is the nothing of the Godhead, the nothing that superlatively encompasses everything, including the very dichotomy of something and nothing, being and non-being.[27] The problem of divine mediation leads to a dilemma, a fork in the road between two types of mediation: either that there is no relation to the divine, or that there is a pure relation to the divine . . . as "nothing." For Eckhart this is ultimately a false dilemma, in that his aim is often to show that the *niht* of the divine is inseparable from the mystical subject, the divine immanently "in" the subject—but one must abrogate some of the most basic principles of philosophical and theological thinking to reach this point. For Eckhart, divine mediation has little to do with a negative that must be overcome by a positive; instead, divine mediation is the collapse of negative and positive, privative and superlative, into the strange negative immanence, an immanence of "nothing" that Eckhart terms the Godhead.[28]

Eckhart does point out that divine mediation is different from the everyday mediation of human beings with other human beings or with their surroundings; but he also borrows the *form* of this human mediation to describe divine mediation. Eckhart at once implies the necessity of mediation, at the same time that mediation is ultimately that which is negated, as the fulfillment of the mediation of the divine—a fulfillment that leads to "the desert of the Godhead." Caught between the necessity of mediation and its impossibility, the divine appears as that which is immanent to all that exists, but which is also in itself "nothing" or not-existent.[29] In short, Eckhart outlines the two forms of mediation central to dark media, understood as the mediation of that which cannot be mediated:

- A mediation of a relation to the divine, but the divine understood negatively, as "nothing." Here mediation itself is positive, but that which is mediated is negative; positive relation and negative divinity. This generally describes a type of mediation we can call *immediation* (also immediacy, immediate).
- A mediation of no relation to the divine at all (except in the positing of this opacity). Here what is mediated is positive, but mediation itself is negative; negative relation, positive divinity. This generally describes a type of mediation we can call *antimediation* (also antimediacy, antimediate).

While "immediation" and "antimediation" have a premodern genealogy in early modern mystical discourse (Dionysius, Eckhart), they reach a certain pitch in the nineteenth and twentieth centuries, as the introduction of "new media" such as photography and film co-exist uneasily with a range of spiritual practices, from Spiritualist séances to black magic and the Black Mass. Often, one finds that the two overlap in complex ways, from spirit photography of séances, to belief in the animistic, magical properties of early cinema. What is more, the ambivalent religious impulses behind such instances of dark media are often brought into the foreground in the space between religion and horror, and the horror genre provides one key site in which we can witness an early theorization of media and mediation as inseparable from the concerns of negative theology, apophaticism, and "dark mysticism," a trend that has been extended into our own cultural moment.

A case in point is the "breaking-through" motif in horror film. While many horror films point outside themselves to the real world of the audience, some films allegorize this through a scene in which some menacing, unknown force crosses the media threshold of the screen *in* the film, only to suggest a similar transgression of the screen *of* the very film the viewer is watching.

The 1982 classic *Poltergeist* (directed by Tobe Hooper, co-written and co-produced by Steven Spielberg) features a newly built suburban home that has been constructed on top of a cemetery. Hauntings abound throughout the house, and finally the family must call in a high-tech team of ghost hunters to investigate the problem. Armed with video cameras, microphones, and CCTV monitors, the team stakes out the house, waiting for the first evidence of the supernatural. The key scene occurs late at night, as a glowing, ethereal specter floats down the staircase in the living room. Importantly, the first witness to this event is not the human characters, but the camera itself, which turns of its own accord toward the staircase.[30] The camera rolls and the audio begins recording. Eventually the characters in the film do witness the ghost (evidenced by the facial expressions of the characters, in what is by now the trademark effect of the Spielbergian sublime), but just as quickly the ghosts pass by. Immediately, without a word to each other, the ghost hunters and the family go to the video deck to play back the scene they have just recorded. We again see their faces, this time crowded around the glow of video monitors, as they re-watch the scene they have just experienced, with the same expression of awe and wonder.

Poltergeist is here performing the same pedagogy that we found in the films of Méliès—this is how it works, this is how one watches, and this is how one reacts. It also serves as a comment on supernatural horror (e.g., this is how one reacts to the experience of supernatural horror, and more importantly, to the viewing of supernatural horror). The media devices (camera, audio, an EEG-type readout) serve as the eyes, ears, and nervous system of the human characters in the house. In one instance, the scene even goes so far as to simultaneously show us the actual ghost descending the staircase, and the correlating image on the video monitor (all of which is, of course, viewed by us on a movie screen, on a TV, or, nowadays, on a computer).[31] Media here serve both to verify and to reify the supernatural, whether or not it has been actually experienced. The panoply of devices ready to capture suggests an immediation, and, while the capture is successful, the ghosts appear to lie in a realm so far beyond human comprehension that this immediation can only be an antimediation. Even after recording, viewing, and re-viewing, one has learned nothing.

Something different happens in a film such as *Demons*, the 1985 project of Lamberto Bava and Dario Argento. The premise of the film is simple. The entire film takes place inside a movie theater, where there is a screening of a new horror film. The film-within-the-film appears to be a supernatural slasher, featuring a group of students who come across an old book, which contains a spell to call up demons. While this film-within-the-film is running, we are introduced to the various characters in the movie theater who are watching the film. Eventually we as viewers realize that the curse in the film-within-the-film has spilled over into the audience in the theater. The key scene comes

when the death of a character in the film-within-the-film perfectly coincides with the death of a character in the theater. A
study in self-reflexivity, both scenes involve a breaking-through
(or slashing-through)—in the film-within-the-film, a demon at-
tacks a girl camping in a tent, slashing through the canvas of the
tent; while in the theater itself, another girl, grotesque and possessed, has wandered to the back of the theater screen, where,
choking and rabid, she claws her way through the canvas screen
of the movie theater itself, at the very same time the canvas of
the tent is slashed.[32]

Demons looks forward to the breaking-through motif in films
such as Ring, but it also looks back to the reflexivity of genre horror in films such as Madhouse (1974) and Targets (1968; which features Boris Karloff as an aging horror actor, attending a drive-in
screening of his actual 1963 film The Terror, while a deranged
sniper shoots at viewers in their cars). While Poltergeist contains
mediation within media devices themselves (which serve the
perfunctory role of capture and playback), in Demons the very
function of media is to hyper-mediate, to mediate in a way that
constantly spills over and crosses boundaries. In Demons, mediation is so immediate that it is always transgressive, jarringly
passing with contagious ease between human, machine, and
demon. This transgression also applies to the way that the film
comments on film itself: in Demons, the entire movie theater is
at once a haunted house, a medium for the passage of demons,
and a film set for the film Demons. Viewers and characters exchange places, as media-as-representation becomes media-as-
transmission, infection, or possession. And yet, the source of
the transmission/possession remains a mystery, receding into
an antimediacy, as the strange non-being of the demonic curse
passes with ease between one person and the next.

The next step is the film that deals with immediation/anti-
mediation at the level of form itself, a move that necessitates
a shift from narrative to non-narrative film. While the horror
genre is notoriously conventional when it comes to film narrative, the tradition of avant-garde horror film takes mediation

to this formal level.[33] These "art horror" films combine the formal experiments of the avant-garde with the tropes and motifs of genre horror, often resulting in films that themselves either become threateningly life-like, or take on a menacing life of their own.[34] A case in point is the short film *Outer Space* (1999), by the Austrian filmmaker Peter Tscherkassky, known for his meticulous deconstruction and reconstruction of appropriated film footage. *Outer Space* uses film technologies old and new to imagine a kind of cinematic demonology. Tscherkassky uses footage from *The Entity*, a 1982 film featuring Barbara Hershey about a purportedly real case of demonic possession in the modern world. One need not have seen *The Entity* to appreciate *Outer Space*; it extracts, but also abstracts the concrete narrative into its minimalist basics. But more than this, *Outer Space* also displays a cinematic tension between the demonic possession in the film and the possession of the film itself. Ultimately, the film itself becomes "possessed," until both image and sound overload the medium so completely that all we are left with is the actual, physical, material film itself (the frame of the film is evident, as it clips and slows down, the audio waveform made visible, the screen flickering into black and white). *Outer Space* borrows from the avant-garde tradition of Stan Brakhage and Michael Snow, but it couches its formal experiments in relation to the horror genre and the motif of demonic possession. The film becomes so immediate that it overtakes and consumes the material and formal aspects of film itself, dovetailing into an antimediacy that ceases to visually or acoustically communicate at all. The logical extension of the narrative ("in" the film) is that it crosses over into an excessive, material, non-narrative domain ("of" the film).

Perhaps the final stage in the "breaking-through" motif of horror film is when the mediation in the film and the mediation of film itself collapses, the point at which immediacy is also antimediacy. This is one way of understanding Kenneth Anger's oft-cited provocation that "cinema is magic." In films such as *Invocation of My Demon Brother* (1969), Anger carries out this idea of film as "casting a spell." While other films of his *Magick Lantern* cycle portray rituals of magick within the film, *Invocation of My Demon Brother* is itself structured like a ritual. Montage and sound serve as its primary techniques, the media-equivalent of magic circles, divination spells, and grimoires. One does not so much watch *Invocation of My Demon Brother* as one, by watching, participates in it. Iconographic images of Satanism and the occult are juxtaposed to strobing effects, experiments in color, and a trance-like electronic soundtrack (performed by Mick Jagger). Anger's film represents what is perhaps the furthest limit of the breaking-through motif—the desire to dissolve all remnants of representation in film, using the motifs of the horror genre to do so.

This is, of course, the idea (or ideal). We are well aware that, for instance, films like *Invocation of My Demon Brother* are most often seen in the context of film and film history, not in the context of actual ritual or practical magick. All the same, however, these variations on "breaking-through" point to an ambivalent form of transgression, one that displays a will to annul all semblance of mediation, in effect dissolving the boundary between the screen in film and the screen of film. But such films also display an equal desire to activate a special kind of mediation that would allow one to witness the gulf or the abyss of there being "nothing" to mediate. Georges Bataille notes this ambiguity when he notes that "[t]here exists no prohibition that cannot be transgressed. Often the transgression is permitted, often it is even prescribed." Furthermore, the effect it brings about is also an ambivalent combination of a brilliant emptiness, a saturated negation: "More than any other state of mind consciousness of the void about us throws us into exaltation. This does not mean that we feel an emptiness in ourselves, far from it; but we pass beyond that into an awareness of the act of transgression."[35]

This dual desire is analogous to the attempt in mystical texts to "get at" the divine through a language of negation, contradiction, and apophatic terms. In this sense horror film takes up the lessons of mysticism and the *via negativa*. Language negating itself in its articulation, film consuming itself in its being shown, a body distending itself because it is possessed by another life—in these instances, it appears that the endpoint of mediation is the negation of mediation itself.

In fact, we can note a subtext that runs throughout our investigations thus far: that *the modern horror genre takes up a set of concerns that were previously the provenance of apophatic mysticism and negative theology.* Furthermore, supernatural horror does this in a way that highlights the dual meaning of media and mediation—as a modern fascination with new technologies, and as a premodern concern with the limits of media and mediation.

DARK MEDIA, DARKER OBJECTS

Though it is possible to regard supernatural horror as taking up the earlier concerns of mysticism, there is one element that makes modern horror unique, and that is the function of different objects in any tale of haunting and the supernatural. In other words, what is at stake in these stories is not just the experience of a subject, but the mediation of and through an object. The concept of the supernatural is here not simply oriented toward a subject, as a locus of unmediated and authentic experience. It is also oriented toward the many objects that themselves embody or mediate the supernatural, objects that elusively slide between the everyday and the exceptional, between their artifactual transparency and their strange aura of opacity. The question, then, is whether it would make sense to think about the supernatural less in terms of a subject-oriented approach, and more in terms of an object-oriented approach—and what such an object-oriented approach might mean for us, as subjects.

There are, of course, many precedents both ancient and modern for doing this. In a modern context, there is the example of the later Heidegger, who meditates at great length on "the thing" (*das Ding*) as an ontological category, resulting in his tongue-twisting phrase, "the thingness of the thing."[36] What Heidegger calls "the thing" is defined by such characteristics as "self-supporting," "standing-forth," and above all the dynamic, active process of "gathering." Less a tool or object of knowledge, the thing is for Heidegger that intersection or congealment of materials, production processes, and ideologies that is encapsulated in his phrase "the thing things, and thinging gathers."

More recently, the work of Bruno Latour has investigated the interface between humans and objects, particularly in the history of scientific experiment, where a whole panoply of gadgets, gizmos, and dooleywhigs form a complex apparatus for the production of knowledge. Objects act on us, and condition our own actions, just as much as we act on them. Searching for a middle term between subjects and objects, Latour uses the phrase "nonhuman actants" to describe the intermediary agency of objects on us as subjects. As he notes, "[e]ach object gathers around itself a different assembly of relevant parties. Each object triggers new occasions to passionately differ and dispute." For Latour, objects are not simply passive and inert entities waiting to be acted upon. Rather, "objects—taken as so many issues—bind all of us in ways that map a public space profoundly different from what is usually recognized under the label of 'the political.'" Latour suggests a renewed engagement with the Heideggerian concept of "the thing," focusing on the political aspects of assembling and gathering: "If the *Ding* designates both those who assemble because they are concerned as well as what causes their concerns and divisions, it should become the center of our attention: *Back to Things!* Is this not a more engaging political slogan?"[37]

These aspects of objects abound in contemporary philosophy.[38] A recent attempt to think about objects is the so-called object oriented ontology (OOO) school, which directly takes up Latour's slogan. As OOO argues, Western philosophy, in its almost exclusive focus on the relation between subject and object, has elided the equally important "perspective" of objects in relation to each other. Thus, in place of the relation between subjects and objects, Graham Harman suggests we think about object-object relations, and their separateness from the cognitive and aesthetic framework of human subjects. As Harman notes, "object-oriented philosophy has a single basic tenet: the withdrawal of objects from all perceptual and casual relations."[39]

But this is an agenda that must grapple with its own problems, though they may be different from those of subject-object relations. As Harman notes, this approach "immediately implies a single basic problem: how do relations occur?" He continues: "[g]iven that an object always remains aloof from its dealings with the world, causality can only be *indirect*, can only occur through some medium other than the things themselves, since these forever elude any sort of relation."[40] While it suggests an evocative image of objects as constantly withdrawn and elusive, OOO also sidesteps the central problem of objects—that of mediation and its paradoxes, the dual necessity and opacity of all mediation, not just that of objects in relation to each other. Hence the central blind spot of OOO, which Harman himself encapsulates: "It will need to be shown concretely how two objects can be absolutely hidden from each other *and* capable of affecting one another."[41]

Whether or not a comprehensive philosophy of objects is possible, without simply being recuperated into the double-bind of the object-for-us (Latour) and the thing-in-itself (Heidegger), we must always be brought back to the persistence of that most peculiar of objects—the subject. For our purposes here, what is important to note is how objects exist in this contradictory movement of givenness and withdrawal. Even in their most intimate, phenomenal interaction with us as subjects, objects still maintain some reservoir of inaccessibility—in short, for every object there is an inaccessible more-than-object. Indeed, it seems that this almost perfectly describes the objects that populate the supernatural horror genre.

To get at this in more detail, let us step back a bit into the history of philosophy. Philosophically speaking, objects are different from things, and it is important to note that not all media are objects or things. To clarify our terms, let us return to Kant's distinction between objects and things, since Kant provides a number of key points that undergird the various strands of post-Kantian philosophy today.

In Kant's critical philosophy objects are never simply objects. In fact, Kant tends to use a number of different terms for what we would, in English, term objects. These include: the term *Objekt*, which denotes objects of experience that are made into objects for knowledge through the unity of apperception; the term *Gegenstand*, which denotes objects of experience that conform to the structures of intuition and/or the categories of understanding; and the term *Ding* (also translated as "thing"), which denotes the object in itself apart from any given experience or knowledge of it. With this last term *Ding* we arrive at an entity that serves an important philosophical function for Kant: the logical necessity of there being something "out there" rather than nothing, but a something that can never be known in itself. It is a something that provides the ground for *Gegenstand*, and allows it in turn to become *Objekt* for a subject. The more we probe into it, the ground for our relation to the world as subjects to an object becomes rather shaky and uncertain. Kant encapsulates this enigma:

> That there is something real outside us which not only corresponds but must correspond to our external perceptions can likewise be proved to be, not a connection of things in themselves, but for the sake of experience . . . for we have nothing to do with other objects than those which belong to possible experience, because objects which cannot be given to us in any experience are nothing for us.[42]

While all these terms Kant employs may be translated as "object," this last term—*Ding*—is also referred to by Kant as *Ding an sich* or the "thing-in-itself." The "thing-in-itself," or simply "the thing," is for Kant a limit concept. It serves a transcendental function, in that it provides the guarantee that there is an actual, independently existing world out there that we as subjects relate to, even though we can never know it in itself, in its independent existence.[43]

Let us abbreviate this a bit by suggesting that for Kant there is a basic distinction between "objects" and "things," a distinction that corresponds neatly to Kant's overall critical framework. While objects can be sensed and intuited, and while we can produce knowledge of objects based on such intuitions, things remain forever beyond the pale of human experience and comprehension. Yet, in spite of these distinctions, Kant is forced to note a basic contradiction, which is that things—being inaccessible and unknowable—are still posited by us as thinking subjects (even if they are posited as a limit concept). Thus they can only ever be negative concepts. The most we can do, according to Kant, is to simply note the logical necessity of the thing-in-itself. Beyond that there is only silence . . .

Or is there? For Kant, what both the object and thing have in common, strangely enough, is that they both bear some minimal relation to a subject. The difference is that in the former that relation is positive, while in the latter it is negative. And, while contemporary philosophers want to shift our thinking from subject-object to object-object relations, there is another type of object-oriented thinking implicit in Kant's critical philosophy. That is *the relation between objects and things*, between that which exists for us as subjects, and that which remains indifferent to subject-object relations altogether—that is, between the domain of phenomena and the domain that Kant calls noumena.[44]

Schopenhauer, admittedly a pessimistic reader of Kant, often refers to this strange opacity of objects as occult qualities (*qualitates occultae*). Though the effectiveness of philosophy may lie in its explanatory power, there is always some prior assumption that enables such explanations to be carried out in the first place. In the Western philosophical tradition, Schopenhauer cites one such assumption, commonly known as the principle of sufficient reason—everything that exists has a reason for existing.[45]

For Schopenhauer, there is no *reason* to assume that something exists, much less that it exists for a reason (which, for Schopenahuer, almost always amounts to a reason for us as self-interested human subjects). Even the sciences must assume this prior principle, else the work of scientific experiment and hypothesis cannot carry on. As Schopenhauer notes:

> Thus we see mechanical, physical, and chemical effects, as well as those of stimuli, ensue every time on their respective causes without on that account ever thoroughly understanding the process. On the contrary, the essential element of this remains a mystery, and we then attribute it to qualities of bodies, to natural forces, and even to vital force, all of which, however, are nothing but *qualitates occultae*.[46]

It should be noted that this is not simply an anti-science position; Schopenhauer's target here is as much philosophy and logic as it is the sciences. The occult qualities are those qualities that, by definition, can never be elucidated; they inscribe the radical contingency of the human sensorium and cognitive apparatus, and they outline the contour of no object for us as subjects. What Schopenhauer terms the *qualitas occulta* is the form of dark media; it describes a paradoxical, empty aesthetic form in which the thing-in-itself is at once mediated and not mediated. For Schopenhauer this applies equally to the mediation of philosophy as it does to science and technology: "[e]very natural scientific explanation must ultimately end up in an occult quality, and hence in something completely obscure."[47] Things are hidden, but in an absolute way, an occulted relation in which there is no content to be revealed, no knowledge to be gained, and no philosophical system to be constructed.

Thus, while one can trace a genealogy of philosophical thinking about objects, one is always confronted with the stark and simple realization that one is always thinking about objects, arbitrating a form of mediation in increasingly esoteric ways. By way of summary, we can list these different relationships as follows:

- Relation of subject-object (Kantianism, phenomenology)
- Relation of object-object (actor network theory, object oriented ontology)
- Relation of object-thing (occult qualities, dark media)

In this last relation—that between objects and things—we are not considering traditional subject-object relations, nor are we interested in the uncanny object-object relations. Instead, we are considering the possible passages between objects and things, between that which is readily accessible to us as human subjects, and that which enigmatically withdraws into a region that we can only describe as the "thing-in-itself." Note that, strictly speaking, there can be no relation between object and thing. This is the "relation" of object-thing. While objects are always objects as they appear to us as subjects, things occupy a dark, nebulous zone outside of subject-object relations altogether (including object-object relations). If objects are always objects for a subject, then things are like impossible objects, occult objects, or better, apophatic objects—objects absolutely withdrawn, leaving only a strange, fecund emptiness, an inaccessibility that knows no limits.

MYSTICISM AND NON-MYSTICISM

This enigmatic emptiness of the Kantian "thing" is, however, still relative to a conceptual apparatus that thinks it as such. As Jean-Luc Marion notes, this remains so even in the contentious case of mystical experience, where the object of experience is qualified precisely by its receding into a shadowy background of the ineffable and the unintelligible. For every subject, an object (even if an object replaces the subject, in a series of object-object relations), and for every subject-object relation, there is an a priori framework that grounds every possible intuition and conditions all possible knowledge. Such knowledge is, for Marion, marked by "the primacy of the knowing mind over what it knows," and what it is preconditioned to know:

By "object" here, according to the received idea of what a science should be, we shall mean the result of a synthesis (or of the constitution) of a sensible given of a delimited concept, or the result of the synthesis (or of the constitution) of a sensible given by a determined concept in such a way that this product would be able to be delimited, produced, undone, and reproduced at will (or almost at will) by the mind that takes and maintains the initiative.[48]

Marion's somewhat technical recapitulation of Kant describes the blind spot of mystical experience with respect to philosophy—not that mysticism somehow transcends philosophy, but that, in its evocation of the limits of experience, language, and thought, mysticism evokes the limits or the arbitrariness of the a priori conditions of experience, language, and thought.[49] The passage also reads as a summary of the basic preconditions for any media theory, tethered as media often are to the human body and sensorium, and to the desire to codify, capture, and redesign that sensorium. In fact, we can suggest that it is precisely in the rift between these two understandings of the Kantian framework—the mystical and the medial—that what we've been calling "dark media" come into play.

Borrowing from the phenomenological tradition and from the philosophy of religion, Marion's approach is to suggest that the domain Kant called "noumena" or the "thing-in-itself" is not so much a closed-off, forbidden, and inaccessible zone beyond which philosophy stops and faith begins. Instead, the thing-in-itself is actually the site of phenomena that fail to adhere to the Kantian framework, "phenomena that cannot appear according to the a priori conditions that a finite mind imposes on experience."[50] This is either because there is no pre-existing category within which such phenomena can be adequately understood, or because their inconsistency and variability prevents them from adhering to the sensible form of intuition. By definition, such phenomena cannot be prepared for in advance, and in this failure of experience, the cognizing mind recognizes its own finitude and its own conditions. Thus, almost any attempt to create new categories for knowledge must do so as a conciliatory gesture—as the product of a failure or finitude built into cognition itself. "Within these phenomena, intuition is not limited to filling or fulfilling the finite measure of the concept and/or the signification but spills over to the point of saturating it."[51] Marion calls these "saturated phenomena," and they range from the aesthetic experience of listening to music, to the ethical confrontation with a stranger, to the ongoing public contestation over the meaning of political events.[52] While saturated phenomena do dovetail with the more common notion of experiences that are ineffable or sublime, Marion is careful to note that saturated phenomena have less to do with the shutting down of experience or cognition, than with a rift or sudden shift that ends up producing thought and language. Elsewhere Marion provides more analytical descriptions of a saturated phenomenon: "The saturated phenomenon will be described as invisable [from *viser*, that which cannot be aimed at] according to quantity, unbearable according to quality, absolute according to relation, irregardable according to modality."[53] Borrowing from the Kantian framework, Marion argues in each case that saturated phenomena are related to the "categories" via their excess, by their "passing beyond the concept."

Kant left the thing-in-itself to itself; it was the boundary at which philosophy stops, and something else non-philosophical begins. But Marion's suggestion is that the confrontation with this horizon of thought is itself an intuition, though of a special type. For Marion, the genealogy of the saturated phenomenon can be traced back to early Christian mystical literature, in which the divine is frequently characterized in negative terms:

> Portrayed in theological words, this issue may be summed up, according to the Greek fathers, in the fact that God is invisible, unspeakable, uncircumscribable, and incomprehensible. Yet the experience of not being able to comprehend, see, or think God can

be taken seriously as a positive experience. We can be confronted with something completely outside our reach and nevertheless present as such, as absent.[54]

It is tempting to read this passage as a synthesis of Kant and the mystics—God is a thing, or, what amounts to the same thing, God is nothing. But what Marion outlines here and in other works is a more nuanced version of the Dionysian *via negativa*. At its core lies something that is absolutely inaccessible, and thus can only be speculative—what for Kant is a secularized thing or noumenon, for the mystical tradition is God or the divine (or in Eckhart's terms, the "Godhead"). Beyond this, we find the contradictory language of the *via negativa*, in which language is stretched beyond its self-inscribed limits to describe the indescribability of the thing-in-itself or of the divine—hence Dionysius's contradictory notions of "brilliant darkness" or the "ray of divine darkness." And beyond this, the use of the more familiar mechanisms of figurative language to produce inexact analogies (e.g., the ocean, the desert, the sun as figures of the divine). In what appears to be a broadly Neoplatonic approach to the inaccessible and unintelligible, Marion suggests that the Kantian impasse of the thing-in-itself be understood as an intuition—though one that can only be obliquely stated, either through negative definitions ("not finite," "not temporal") or through superlatives ("beyond space and time").

Yet Marion's approach intentionally characterizes the saturated phenomenon in terms of generosity and fecundity; there is an implication that saturated phenomena are always "more" than what we intuit and know, and more than what we can ever possibly intuit and know. In a way, for Marion *all* phenomena are saturated phenomena, both because they were at one point (and have since entered the narrower, legitimate halls of Kantian conceptualization), and because saturated phenomena are this very horizon of possible intuition and knowledge. In short, Marion not only characterizes the Kantian domain of the thing-in-itself as an intuition, but he does so though what we might term a *metaphysics of generosity*:

> To the limited possibility of phenomenality, shouldn't we . . . oppose a finally unconditionally possible phenomenality, whose scope would not be the result of the finitude of the conditions of experience? To the phenomenon characterized most often by lack or poverty of intuition (a deception of the intentional aim), indeed, exceptionally, by the mere equality of intuition and intention, why wouldn't there correspond the possibility of a phenomenon where intuition would give *more, indeed immeasurably more*, than the intention would ever have aimed at or foreseen?[55]

In this metaphysics of generosity, there is always something more, something beyond, something larger within which we as cognizing subjects are always-already interpolated. In a sense, calling this something-more the "thing-in-itself," "the Absolute," or "God" matters little. The structure it articulates remains that of philosophy's primordial encounter between Thought and World, and it is qualified by the phenomenological priority of the givenness of World to Thought. Thus, what appears to be a negative theology turns out to be an affirmative theology; what in effect begins on the path of the *via negativa* discovers that it was on the path of the *via affirmativa* all along. Human finitude is revealed less in terms of its poverty and more in terms of its richness: "Finitude is disclosed more in the encounter with the saturated phenomenon than with the poor phenomenon."[56]

One can easily characterize approaches such as those of Marion in terms of affirmative theology and the *via affirmativa*. All that exists, exists fully and over-fully; there is always more, it is always flowing, and this undulating embrace of all being elicits in us a kind of euphoria, the ecstasy of being. One always has faith in something more, perhaps because this something more is, at the end of the day, always some more for us as human subjects. But this rather romantic, vitalistic image of the flow of being also inadvertently evokes the enigmatic negation—the negation that is not negative—evoked by mystics such as Dionysius. Is there a *via negativa* that would not simply be recuperated into the vitalistic and romantic *via affirmativa* of saturated phenomenon? To Marion's "saturated phenomena" we could suggest the "desaturated phenomena" of negative theology; to Marion's ontology of generosity we could offer a paradoxical ontology of nothingness or emptiness, even inviting a comparative approach with non-Western philosophies. But all this would simply recapitulate a game of logic already at work within the texts of Augustine and Dionysius themselves. The real question is what is it that seems to necessitate, within the philosophical stance, a proposition concerning either the givenness or the withdrawal of mediation. In philosophy, mediation is constantly slipping away, either saturated or subtracted, either ebullient flow or the void of specters and traces. What is that philosophical blind spot that a priori commits philosophy to a metaphysics of either generosity or of poverty? To ask such questions is, in short, to inquire into the non-philosophical boundaries of philosophy.

This is precisely the question taken up by François Laruelle near the end of his essay "The Truth According to Hermes." There Laruelle points out the fundamental link between philosophy and media. All philosophy, says Laruelle, subscribes to the "communicational decision," the idea that everything that exists can be communicated or mediated. In this self-inscribed world, all secrets exist only to be communicated, all that is not-said is simply that which is not-yet-said. The communicational decision presumes that everything that exists, exists *in order to be mediated and communicated*. One senses that, for Laruelle, the communicational decision is even more insidious than the philosophical decision (the idea that everything is philosophizable). It is one thing to claim that everything that exists, exists for a reason. It is quite another to claim that that everything-that-exists-for-a-reason is immediately and transparently communicable, in its reason for existing. If the philosophical decision is a variant on the principle of sufficient reason, then the communicational decision adds on top of it the fidelity of any media theory to the communicability of meaning.

But this is all speculation—there is no *reason* per se to presume this is the case. Perhaps this is why Laruelle criticizes philosophers for simply being "mailmen of the truth," these academic "civil servants of the Postal and Telecommunication Ministry." When one presumes the communicational decision on top of the philosophical decision, what results, according to Laruelle, is a compounded fidelity to the communicability of anything that exists, indeed of being itself. Laruelle mimes (and mocks) the hermeneutic presupposition of any philosophy of media: "Meaning, always more meaning! Information, always more information!" The logical conclusion of this position is encapsulated by Laruelle: "the real is communicational, the communicational is real."[57]

Communication is inherently ambiguous; it connects at the same time that it separates, unifies at the same time that it differentiates. Arguably, the communicational decision reaches a point of crisis, not in the postmodern architectonics of semiotics, information theory, cybernetics, or language games, but in the premodern context of mysticism. Nearly every account of mystical experience relies in some way on a union between the mystical subject and an enigmatic, inaccessible, and mysterious "outside" that is variously called God, Godhead, or the divine.

As we've seen, the dominant paradigm for this is established by Augustine, who describes the divine as an "Unchangeable Light" that is beyond human vision, beyond anything that can be seen, and ultimately beyond human comprehension. This duplicity—accessible manifestation and inaccessible source— is especially marked in those mystical texts where the divine is almost paradoxically described in terms of darkness, shadows, or the abyss. We've seen this in Dionysius the Areopagite, who notes how the divine is in itself absolutely inaccessible, and is therefore an enigmatic "ray of divine darkness."

This sort of duplicity is addressed by Laruelle in his own non-philosophical vernacular. In his *Principes de la non-philosophie*, Laruelle distinguishes between "la mystique" and "le mystique." Let us call "la mystique" *mystical* and "le mystique" *mystique*. A single article distinguishes them, but the differences are significant. As Laruelle notes, "the mystical is an experience of identity between the soul and the transcendent."[58] But the soul—the divine part existing within the earthly subject—can only experience the transcendent "outside" of itself, and thereby attain a union with the divine, so long as there is a baseline immanence that can serve as the backdrop for the union of the soul with the transcendent. Thus, for Laruelle, this identity of transcendence and the soul takes place within a certain immanence. The mystical "makes of this immanence a property or an attribute of a relation between the soul and God, more than an essence in and of itself." Immanence is the mystical launching pad for transcendence.

By contrast, Laruelle calls mystique "a real and actual essence, something already-formed-without-formation, as it were, an absolutely autonomous instance more than an attribute, property, event, or relation." The stakes of mystique are high; mystique "absolutely excludes transcendence." The reduced and residual aspect of the divine that is the soul begins to confuse itself with this absolute immanence. There is no mystical subject that goes out of itself (*ec-stasis*) to meet the divine or the great beyond. There is no religious subject that discovers the divine spark within itself, bolstering and reaffirming the coherence of the subject. As Laurelle notes, "mystique is never a *below* or an *above*, and not a phenomenon of the frontier or the limit." Instead, "mystique is 'subject' in the most rigorous sense . . . [it is] that which determines the subject in-the-last-instance." The finite and the infinite, the temporal and eternal, the relative and the absolute—all these "confuse" themselves into an immanence that can only be immanent "with" or "in" itself.

But the immanence of mystique is, arguably, different from the fecund and saturated immanence of Gilles Deleuze, Henri Bergson, or Alfred North Whitehead, those continental beacons of the metaphysics of generosity. Laruelle's brand of mysticism looks askance to Meister Eckhart, for whom there was an important distinction between "God" and "Godhead," the latter in itself a "nothing" or "nothingness" that immanently pervades everything. Insofar as this is immanence, it is a *negative immanence*, moving not toward proliferation but indistinction. It is, in Laruelle's phrasing, an affect prior to all affection, a given prior to all givenness, a manifest prior to all manifestation. There is no First Cause because there has never been causality; but this also does not mean that what is real is simply what exists, a tautology that would simply bring us back to the Kantian problematic. When contingency becomes immanent in this way, it also becomes boundless, and this boundlessness, far from being a great beyond, is nevertheless something inaccessible that Laruelle terms "the One" or "the Real." As Laruelle comments, in his own specialized grammar, "mystique is in-us or better it is us who are actually in it, in-mystique or in-One as the One itself."

From the vantage point of philosophy, Laruelle's treatment of immanence here is complicated. On the one hand, he places himself "on the side of" immanence, and in particular on the side of an immanence that is not subordinate to transcendence. But Laruelle is also careful to distinguish immanence of this type from that of Deleuze and Michel Henry, both of whom remain committed to a dynamic and fecund notion of immanence. Laruelle also remains committed to a notion of the Real that is absolute, and which is not apparent (that is, not manifest, not given, not a becoming). Again, from the philosophical point of view, the only remaining option is a notion of immanence that is pervasive (immanent with/to itself) and yet that is absolutely inaccessible. In Laruelle's terms, it is as if immanence is all-pervasive and all-withdrawn.

This brings us back to Laruelle's discussion of the two decisions: the philosophical decision and the communicational decision. Historically speaking, mysticism is interesting because, on the one hand, it subscribes to the communicational decision—in this case, that an experience of the divine or the supernatural can be communicated via earthly or natural means. While the actual forms of this communication may vary (from scholastic treatises to mystical poetry), what they have in common is this commitment to the communicability of experience. Except that, in the case of mysticism, what it is that is being communicated is itself, by definition, beyond all comprehension and beyond language. Mysticism is interesting because it finds itself in the position of having to communicate the incommunicable. Even those who assert a generative, fecund notion of the divine—as outpouring, radiating Light—must at some point resort to a paradoxical language beyond language in order to hint at the absolute inaccessibility of the divine. Others in the darkness mysticism tradition utilize a hyperbolic language of darkness, nothingness, and the "wayless abyss" to indicate that which cannot be adequately thought or put into language. All roads of light, it seems, lead to darkness—but a darkness of which light is only a shadow.

With mysticism generally (including Laruelle's "mystical" and "mystique"), what we see is a sort of perversion of philosophy's dual fidelity to the philosophical decision and the communicational decision. Philosophy believes in both, that existence is meaningful (by virtue of existing) and thus communicable. At one level, mysticism retains the philosophical decision, but it subtracts the communicational decision. The divine is manifest, and therefore filled with meaning—and yet we as human beings cannot comprehend this manifestation and its meaning. Mysticism is thus the inability to communicate what is manifest in the inaccessibility of the divine (that is, the inaccessibility that "is" the divine). Further, this opens onto a subsidiary form, in which mysticism inverts its prior position, retaining the communicational decision and subtracting the philosophical decision. Here the divine can indeed be communicated—in its incommunicability. Both of these movements redescribe, through the language of mysticism, the passage from "object" to "thing" that we derived from the Kantian framework.

DARK MEDIA—AN ABBREVIATED TYPOLOGY

At this point, we can pause and offer an abbreviated typology of media based on this basic distinction between objects and things, incorporating this motif into the mediation of the inaccessible (the supernatural) that we've been calling dark media. Such a typology will not only help elucidate the concept of dark media, but it will also allow us to make distinctions within dark media, for, as we will see, the mediation of the supernatural doesn't always occur in the same way. In particular, we will distinguish three variants within dark media—"dead media," "haunted media," and finally "weird media." All of these variants can be grouped under the larger umbrella of dark media, insofar as they each grapple with the inaccessible as that which is ambivalently mediated. In all cases, the primary rule is that the media are not "broken," but are working "too well," so well in fact that mediation functions at a level beyond that of traditional forms of human mediation.

To begin with, we can distinguish dead media from haunted media. With dead media, the object is no longer in use, but the form of the object remains active.[59] For example, while we no longer use magic lanterns, one could argue that the idea of image projection remains very alive today with digital projectors and the like. With haunted media, the object is still in use, but in a non-normative way. An example is the complex interplay between the photographic camera and spirit photography in the late nineteenth century. The camera normally used to take pictures of people or places was also the privileged medium for revealing the spirits of the dead. Both dead media and haunted media involve a temporal disjunction, but in different ways: with dead media the disjunction is between an outmoded or outdated artifact and its still-active technical principle; with haunted media the disjunction is between a contemporary artifact and its connection to adjacent fields such as religion and spirituality. There are functional differences between them as well: with dead media, objects oscillate between being activated and inactivated, whereas with haunted media, the object becomes more than an object, endowed as it is with almost divine (or divining) powers—something like a "divine object."

While there are many examples of haunted media in history, the horror genre again gives us the most instructive case studies. Consider the genre of the "occult detective" story, popular in the late nineteen and early twentieth centuries, and exemplified by books such as Sheridan Le Fanu's *In a Glass Darkly* (1872), Algernon Blackwood's *John Silence, Physician Extraordinary* (1908), and William Hope Hodgson's *Carnacki the Ghost-Finder* (1913). In these and other like stories, one often finds a protagonist schooled both in modern science and the ancient occult arts. The occult detective must use a combination of scientific ratiocination and practical magic to solve a given mystery. In some cases the mystery turns out to be a hoax, and the apparently supernatural phenomena simply a bit of trickery. But in other cases we actually see an affirmation of the supernatural, ironically affirmed through scientific rationality (or its failure).

In the occult detective genre, the supernatural is always mediated—in fact, the supernatural can only be mediated. In Hodgson's stories, published together as *Carnacki the Ghost-Finder*, we see detective Thomas Carnacki employ an array of means for revealing the supernatural. Sometimes Carnacki uses media as a means of documentation—a camera used to take a snapshot of a haunted room, sound equipment to record the strange sounds of a haunted house, even candle wax seals on windows and threads across doors to indicate an entrance. At other times Carnacki must actually build his own media to continue the investigation—a shining example of this is the "electric pentacle," a vacuum-tube, steampunk variant on the magic circle, that Carnacki uses both as a protection and as a conduit. Still other moments move beyond media artifacts altogether into another dimension that Carnacki can only describe as "Outer Monstrosities"—a haunted room turns into a giant, fleshy mouth, emitting an eerie whistling sound; a man is possessed by a horde of cosmic pigs emerging from a black hole; a derelict ship encounters a menacing, sentient, nocturnal mist.

The occult detective genre gives us two types of haunted media. First there is the *artifact*, in which a media object in itself is haunted or endowed with supernatural powers.[60] With the artifact we witness the strange animation of inanimate objects—dolls begin to talk, haunted houses seem to have intentions of their own, and an ancient relic at a distant archaeological dig calls up malefic "Old Ones." Along with the artifact, there is also the *portal*, in which a media object, while not in itself haunted, serves as a passageway or conduit between the natural and supernatural.[61] Here it is not the object itself but the act of mediation that is haunted. The spiritual medium, the séance, and necromancy all fall into this category. In some cases the mediation of media objects may appear to function normally (e.g., the white noise on the TV set that is actually transmitting messages from the dead), while in other instances the mediation may take place through ancient or premodern means (e.g., a magic circle drawn on the floor).

Haunted media, then, may express themselves as artifacts or as portals, and sometimes as both.[62] Here we come to a key characteristic of haunted media, whether it be an artifact or a portal: with haunted media, the "divine object" establishes a connection between two different ontological orders (natural-supernatural, earthly-divine, life-afterlife). This is quite different in principle from the modern view of mediation given by cybernetics and information theory. There one has a mediation between two points within a single, shared, consensual reality. While there may also be messages, channels, senders, and receivers, haunted media have one important difference: the mediation is not between two points in a single reality, but between two realities.[63] More often than not, haunted media mediate the supernatural in a positive sense, in that the mediation process brings that which cannot itself be understood within the am-bit of human sense and knowledge—cameras reveal images of ghosts, sound recording devices capture the sounds of spirits, and video images depict the invisible presence of the dead.

There are also stories in the supernatural horror tradition that move beyond even this paradigm. Tales of supernatural horror from the late nineteenth and early twentieth centuries offer examples, engaged as they are both in the developments of modern science as well as in the tradition of mysticism and the occult. Fitz-James O'Brien's 1859 story "What Was It?" takes up the monster motif, but puts a spin on it—the creature in the story is, strictly speaking, non-existent. It can neither be seen nor heard, and its only manifestations are negative ones—an impression in a bed, the shifting of a curtain, the creak of a floorboard, and so on. Physical yet non-empirical, the creature can only be verified by forcing it to become a body; eventually it is trapped and the characters make a cast mold of it, in effect creating a monstrous sculpture. The same theme is dealt with in Ambrose Bierce's 1893 story "The Damned Thing," in which a menacing, predatory creature stalks a village, invisible except for the large claw marks it leaves on its victims. A lesson in optics and the fourth dimension enables the characters to catch fleeting, shadowy glimpses of the creature, as its movement blackens out the stars of the night sky. Just as there are sounds outside the range of human hearing, so there is light and color beyond the range of human vision (and, as one of the characters horrifically concludes, "God help me, the Damned Thing is of such a color!"). In Bierce's story, the characters encounter the same challenge, both philosophical and practical—first they must verify the existence of "the damned thing" (drawing on knowledge from science and religion), and then they must figure out how to either ward it off or evade its threat.

That the human sensorium is a medium, and at best an imperfect medium, serves as the premise for many instances of haunted media. But, that the human sensorium can be augmented, transformed, or, in some instances, "see" more than a human subject is prepared to see—this is the premise of what we can term "weird media." Many examples of weird media are given in the subgenre of "weird fiction," published in early-twentieth-century pulp magazines such as *Weird Tales* and *Amazing Stories*. One type of story involves what we might call the other-dimensional creature, found in stories such as H. P. Lovecraft's "From Beyond" (1920), Frank Belknap Long's "The Hounds of Tindalos" (1929), and Clark Ashton Smith's "Ubbo-Sathla" (1933). In Lovecraft's story, a crazed scientist has invented a device that enables the average human being to see the invisible, menacing, amphibious creatures that swim about us in the air every day. In Long's story, a heady combination of drugs and quantum physics leads to the discovery of a portal in the strange angles of a room, through which predatory, bodiless creatures enter. And in Smith's story, a modern-day sorcerer uses a crystal—the medium of all mediums perhaps—to make contact with the first, primordial ooze of life on the planet.[64] In each case mediation comes up against an absolute limit, while also mediating beyond what is normally expected.

In weird tales such as these, one again finds the mediation of the supernatural that is expressed in haunted media stories, but with a crucial difference: the mediation only results in an absolute impasse, in the strange non-knowledge of the impossibility of mediation, in the way that all communication collapses back into a prior excommunication. Whereas haunted media expressed the mediation of the supernatural in positive terms, with weird media mediation only indicates a gulf or abyss between two ontological orders. Sometimes the supernatural is present but not apparent (e.g., an invisible creature that nevertheless exists within our same reality, but outside the visible spectrum). At other times the supernatural is apparent but not present (e.g., unnamable entities from other dimensions). With weird media, all objects inevitably withdraw into things. What results is a negative mediation, the paradoxical assertion and verification of the gulf between two ontological orders. Table 1 provides a comparison.

To summarize: media are "haunted" when they affirmatively

TABLE 1. HAUNTED VERSUS WEIRD MEDIA

Haunted Media	*Weird Media*
Connection	Disconnection
Communication	Silence
Transparency	Opacity
Phenomenal presence	Noumenal "nothing"
Transcendence	Immanence
Recapitulates the human	Limit of the human
Reciprocity	Indifference

mediate between two different ontological orders, and by transforming the object into a divine object (the artifact or the portal). By contrast, media are "weird" when they negatively mediate between two ontological orders, whereby the object recedes into a thing.

Between the object "for us" and the thing "in itself," there is at once the smallest interval and the greatest void. As we've noted, the media objects that populate supernatural horror are not broken—in fact, they are working quite well, perhaps too well. When ordinary objects become extraordinary, are we witness to this secret passage from object to thing? In supernatural horror, relations of subject-object and object-object are the by-products of a more fundamental relation between object and thing. Given this, let us put forth a hypothesis: in supernatural horror, *the mediation of the supernatural takes place via the ambivalent transition from object to thing.*

MYSTICISM AND MEDIATION

In spite of the fact that dark media (inclusive of our typology above—dead media, haunted media, weird media) are replete with objects of all kinds, at the core of dark media is the idea of the mediation of what cannot be mediated. As we've suggested, this has the structure of the *via negativa* in mysticism, which we can summarize as follows: first, an originary decision regarding the fundamental distinction between the human and the divine (even if the divine is "in" the human); second, the philosophical assumption of a commonality between human and divine that is prior to their distinction, and that serves as the condition for their possibly being mediated; third, the assertion that this mediation between human and divine is of a different order than human-human mediation; fourth, that divine mediation involves a union with a "something" that is by definition contradictory, lying as it does beyond the senses, beyond language, beyond thought, and beyond the subject-object distinction altogether; and finally, the proposition that any comprehension of this divine mediation can only proceed through negation, ultimately the negation of the human subject that is mediated in this way.

If we're willing to take an expanded view of media, and consider media not just as devices, tools, or even objects, but as a form of mediation that is operative in this passage between objects and things, then the question is the following: at what point do media and mediation end up negating themselves, resulting in a kind of pure continuum or "communication"—or even, with what an earlier age would call mystical experience? This is a question posed by Georges Bataille, who, in his own critique of and reinvention of mystical theology, makes frequent use of the terms "communication" and "mediation."

As Bataille notes, in case of mystical experience, "knowledge is still mediation—between me and the world—but negative: it is the rejection of knowledge, the night, the annihilation of all middle terms, which constitutes this negative mediation (*médiation négative*)."[65] What Bataille calls negative mediation names this paradoxical mediation of non-mediation. It is precisely this type of negation that Bataille, in an early text called *The Anti-Christian Manual*, regards as being regulated within institutional religion: "In fact, the intimate and blood-stained aspects of Christian divinity are nothing more than aspects of *mediation*, which are *intermediary* between the real world of living bodies and the movements of the transcendent world of the 'God

of the philosophers.'"[66] Whenever Bataille speaks of communication or mediation, his reference is always that of the mystical
tradition of the *via negativa*; for him mediation and communication always imply the dissolution of sender and receiver, leaving perhaps only the message that is the gulf or abyss between
them. "These movements flow out into an external existence:
there they lose themselves, they 'communicate,' it would appear,
with the outside (*le dehors*), without the latter taking a determined shape and being perceived as such."[67]

For Bataille, negative mediation involves a threefold process:
a minimal connection between two ontologically distinct and incompatible orders; the production of an absolute gulf or abyss
between these two orders; and finally, the effacing of this mediation altogether, in part due to this gulf or abyss. Bataille provides
one of many descriptions of what such inner experience entails:

> It is the annihilation of everything which is not the ultimate "un-
> known," the abyss into which one has sunk. . . . Understood in
> this way, the full communication which is experience leading to
> the extreme limit is accessible to the extent that existence succes-
> sively strips itself of its middle terms.[68]

Bataille here isolates something that is central to dark media and
its preoccupation with the mediation of what cannot be mediated—the annihilation of "middle terms," conceived not as the
result of a saturated and overflowing divinity, but as the no less
ecstatic outcome of a mediation that has delimited itself.

In addition, Bataille's comments lead to a question: Given
the way that dark media arbitrate between the natural and supernatural, would it be going too far to consider the premodern
cases of divine ecstasy and demonic possession as instances of
mediation? If so, then another question poses itself: Could one
then consider the governance of the boundary separating divine
ecstasy and demonic possession as an act of political theology?
The discourse surrounding demonic possession in early modern

Christianity is especially instructive in this case. Given that the realm of the supernatural (divine and demonic) was, by definition, absolutely beyond the earthly and the human, by what living signs or activities (*opera vitae*) could this inaccessible domain become accessible? Philosopher of religion Maaike van der Lugt summarizes these dilemmas:

> In the theological discourse, the concept of the possessed body presupposes and is opposed to the notion of life and the human person. The Scholastics . . . asked themselves to what degree angels and demons could take advantage of the possessed body. Were they capable of feeling, of moving, of speaking, or eating, or, finally, of generating life? Could they, according to the expression of Saint Thomas, exercise the *opera vitae?*"[69]

In Scholastic theology, the human body comes to be conceived as the primary medium upon which and through which the signs of the divine or demonic are evident. However, divine theophanies are different in this regard from the manifestations of the demonic; while theophanies are resplendent in their spectacular presence, in Scholastic demonology the manifestation of the demon is given only in negative signs, only as aberrations, only as the error of the body. Indeed, it becomes difficult to even speak of the mediation of the demon, since, according to the demonologists, the demon is rarely present as such, only manifest negatively, obliquely, and opaquely. In Scholastic demonology, the demon and its manifestation are always a horizon. Such a theory required an entire discursive and hermeneutic apparatus for allowing the demon to be manifest and present. Armando Maggi, writing about the role of language in early modern demonology, notes the following:

> By reading natural signs (winds, clouds, animals' expressions), devils are able to bring about storms, plagues, and floods. Moreover, by reading a human being's gestures, facial expressions, lin-

guistic intonation, a devil can produce a "discourse" able to erase
that human being's soul and body. . . . The devil constructs his
nonlanguage by interpreting nature's and human being's signs
and turning them against creation itself.[70]

Perhaps, then, dark media are really demonic media, the mediation of that which recedes beyond an always-moving horizon.
Of course, this may be taking things too far, widening the scope
of the terms "media" and "mediation" beyond the point where
they cease to have any reliable meaning at all. But it can also
be argued that the world in which we find ourselves today constantly challenges our conventional ideas about media and mediation. In the midst of planetary disasters both human-made
and nonhuman-oriented, we find we are in the position of recording and documenting events that increasingly slip from
our comprehension, events that we can only define using vast
phrases like "global climate change" or "planetary extinction."
We are living in the very world that we stand apart from in order
that we may record, document, and mediate it. If there is a lesson to be learned from Scholastic demonology or medieval mysticism, it is that our ideas of media and mediation are, perhaps,
all-too-human.

CONCLUSION — ON WHAT CANNOT BE SAID (CON'T)

In the opening pages of his book *Deep Time of the Media*, Siegfried Zielinski notes the need for an expanded view of media
and media studies today:

> The history of the media is not the product of a predictable and
> necessary advance from primitive to complex apparatus. . . . In-
> stead of looking for obligatory trends, master media, or impera-
> tive vanishing points, one should be able to discover individual
> variations. Possibly, one will discover fractures or turning points
> in historical master plans that provide useful ideas for navigating
> the labyrinth of what is currently firmly established.[71]

For a thinker like Zielinski, what matters is less the academic founding of new fields or subfields, and more the variations that allow one to move across fields, or even to abandon them altogether. It is this that Zielinski refers to as "variantology." In *Deep Time of the Media* Zielinski appropriates the geological concept of deep time, with all its connotations of nonhuman and material fluxes and flows, and asks us to consider what a deep time of media might look like. For Zielinski, this gesture is necessarily experimental. It means that sometimes one will end up not going far enough, perhaps recuperating a novel artifact or event into the deeply entrenched histories of technology—by humans, for humans. At other times, one will go too far, opening up the terms "media" and "mediation" so much that one ends up simply talking about life or being in the abstract. Zielinski seems aware of this; but he is also equally aware of the need to not settle for institutionally calcified boundaries:

> It is our hope that media experts will see their research areas in a broader light than before, and that disciplines which have so far not participated in these discourses (such as theology, classical studies, many areas of the history of science and technology) will develop an openness for media questions.[72]

The concept of dark media offered here is just one example that asks us to bring approaches from philosophy, genre horror, and mysticism to a kind of occult variantology of media. Magic circles, grimoires, dowsing devices, spirit photography, ectoplasmic images, ghostly static on the radio, the possessed TV, the cursed videotape, and the webcam of the dead—in supernatural horror all these "really" exist in that they are not mere figments of the imagination, symptoms of mental illness, or the by-product of drug abuse. Their artifactuality is expressed in their pragmatic and material use as media objects. At the same time, the mediation of the supernatural allows such objects to recede from the familiar and the everyday, often to the point that the object itself becomes vitalistically lifelike and animate. There is, perhaps, a strange life of media that is equivalent to the slippage from "objects" to "things." In a way, then, media are the most alive precisely at the moment that they are the least accessible . . .

NOTES

1. I derive this phrase "communicational imperative" from an essay by François Laruelle, "The Truth According to Hermes," translated by Alexander R. Galloway and published in *Parrhesia* 9 (2010).

2. This is an issue that has been taken up by recent work in media studies, to which I am indebted: Erik Davis, *TechGnosis: Myth, Magic, and Mysticism in the Age of Information* (New York: Three Rivers, 1998); Tom Gunning, "To Scan a Ghost: An Ontology of Mediated Vision," *Grey Room* 26 (Winter 2007): 94–127; Akira Mizuta Lippit, *Atomic Light (Shadow Optics)* (Minneapolis: University of Minnesota Press, 2005); Joe Milutis, *Ether: The Nothing That Connects Everything* (Minneapolis: University of Minnesota Press, 2006); Jeffrey Sconce, *Haunted Media: Electronic Presence from Telegraphy to Television* (Durham, NC: Duke University Press, 2006); Art Symons, "Divine Decadence: Towards a Degradation of the Senses," *Literary History* 49.2 (2004): 23–44; and Siegfried Zielinski, *Deep Time of the Media: Toward an Archaeology of Seeing and Hearing by Technical Means*, trans. Gloria Custance (Cambridge, MA: MIT Press, 2008).

3. William James, *The Varieties of Religious Experience* (New York: Modern Library, 1902), 58.

4. Ibid., 71.

5. Shannon's ideas are elaborated in his 1948 paper "On the Mathematical Theory of Communication," published in *Bell System Technical Journal*, vol. 27. This research was expanded into his book with Weaver, published as *The Mathematical Theory of Communication* (Urbana: University of Illinois Press, 1949).

6. Baran's 1962 paper is titled "On Distributed Communciations," published in *RAND Corporation Papers*, P-2626.

7. This film, like others in the J-horror style, features media as

"portals," much in line with earlier horror films, except whereas in earlier films it is the architecture of the house that is the portal, in J-horror it is the media device. Kurosawa's film also shows the webcam images as eerie interior shots of other rooms, shrouded in darkness, without any human beings—an aesthetic that seems to evoke Ozu's films, with their many long takes of empty, domestic interiors. (In fact, it is tempting to imagine Kiyoshi Kurosawa as the Ozu of horror . . .)

8. John Durham Peters, *Speaking into the Air: A History of the Idea of Communication* (Durham, NC: Duke University Press, 2001), 71.

9. Augustine, *Confessions*, bk. 7, ch. 10, trans. William Watts (Cambridge, MA: Harvard University Press/Loeb Classical Library, 2006), vol. 1, 371.

10. Ibid., bk. 10, ch. 6 (vol. 2, 87ff).

11. This is dramatized later on in the same passage, where Augustine asks "where" God is, posing the question to the lowly beasts as well as to the heavenly stars, all of whom reply "I am not God." Interestingly, Augustine's own corporeality becomes a sort of mediator between the horizontal plane of earthly creatures and the vertical plane of divine transcendence.

12. Peters, *Speaking*, 71.

13. Pseudo-Dionysius, *The Mystical Theology*, III 1033B, in *The Complete Works*, trans. Colm Luibheid (New York: Paulist Press, 1987), 139.

14. Ibid., I 1000A, 135.

15. Ibid., I 1000B, 136.

16. Denys Turner, *The Darkness of God: Negativity in Christian Mysticism* (Cambridge: Cambridge University Press, 1995), 34–35.

17. Ibid., 35.

18. Tzvetan Todorov, *The Fantastic: A Structural Approach to a Literary Genre*, trans. Richard Howard (Ithaca, NY: Cornell University Press, 1975), 25. Todorov's structuralist study remains one of the most important sources for the analysis of supernatural horror. Other, later, studies that both draw upon his work and extend it include Noël Carroll's *The Philosophy of Horror: Or, Paradoxes of the Heart* (New York: Routledge, 1990), Istvan Csiceray-Ronay's *The*

Seven Beauties of Science Fiction (Middletown, CT: Wesleyan University Press, 2008), and Rosemary Jackson's *The Fantastic: The Literature of Subversion* (New York: Routledge, 1981).

19. Todorov, *The Fantastic*, 25.

20. H. P. Lovecraft, *At the Mountains of Madness*, ed. S.T. Joshi (New York: Penguin, 2001), 331.

21. Ibid., 334.

22. Ibid., 334–35.

23. It is also worth noting that, while for Todorov the fantastic proper belongs to the horror genre (in particular, supernatural horror), the marvelous takes one into the genre of fantasy, whereas the uncanny takes one into the genre of science fiction.

24. As Todorov notes, the uncertainty of the fantastic applies both to the characters in a story as well to the readers of the story—though they do not necessarily overlap. We as readers may have knowledge of events that characters do not, and vice versa. Thus the fantastic may characterize what occurs in the story as well as the story itself (the most common technique used in the latter case is the "dossier" or documentary approach found in authors such as H. P. Lovecraft—"these are the papers of X, found at a distant archaeological dig," etc.).

25. Meister Eckhart, Sermon 19, in *The Complete Mystical Works of Meister Eckhart*, ed. and trans. Maurice O'C. Walshe (New York: Herder and Herder, 2009), 137.

26. Ibid., Sermon 97, p. 469, and Sermon 96, p. 465.

27. We have outlined two general usages of the term "nothing" in Eckhart. But even this division ultimately breaks down. The nothing of creatures immediately opens onto the nothing of the Godhead, collapsing the division into what Eckhart describes as the nothing of that which is, the nothing of "letting be."

28. But Eckhart too runs into problems, and any careful reading of Eckhart must acknowledge that all this talk about God as nothing is always attenuated by an equal commitment to the Trinity, the *kenōsis* or self-emptying of Christ, and a Person-oriented mysticism of Father, Son, and Human. Put simply, the "philosophical" Eckhart is always doubled by the "theological" Eckhart. Both are, perhaps,

brought into an uneasy relation, and it is this assemblage that constitutes the "mystical" Eckhart. Eckhart at once shores up the limits of the human while at the same time asserting a profound commitment to the human—but a human that is also a "living without a why."

29. The role of "nothing" or "nothingness" in Eckhart is elaborated in my essay "Wayless Abyss: Mysticism, Mediation, and Divine Nothingness," *Postmedieval* 3, no. 1 (2012): 80–96. On the concept of nothing/nothingness in Eckhart with respect to continental philosophy, see John Caputo, *The Mystical Element in Heidegger's Thought* (New York: Fordham University Press, 1986), 97–139; Beverly Lanzetta, "Three Categories of Nothingness in Eckhart," *Journal of Religion* 72, no. 2 (1992): 248–68; Reiner Schürmann, *Meister Eckhart, Mystic and Philosopher* (Bloomington: Indiana University Press, 1978), 135–68.

30. Presumably the camera is being remotely moved by the ghosts, suggesting that even the dead desire their fifteen minutes of fame (and it is comforting to note that even ghosts have a sense of *mise-en-scène*).

31. But if one looks closely, there is a slippage even in this scene (as there is in Méliès), for the actual ghost and the recorded ghost on the monitor are different, even though they are placed side-by-side, and even though the human characters appear to react in the same way to both the event and its recording.

32. The sequel to *Demons* updates this motif—in *Demons 2* (1986; again a Bava/Argento production) the break-through comes through the TV in a high-rise apartment building.

33. Of course, more recent horror films do experiment with narrative linearity and continuity; the *Saw* franchise often adopts the structure of a puzzle, whereas the onslaught of zombie films frequently uses a video game logic. Films such as *Devil* and *Cabin in the Woods* build on viewers' knowledge of the horror genre to push self-reflexivity to new extremes. Arguably, however, all these techniques are already evident in earlier films, such as the 1960 William Castle production *Thirteen Ghosts*.

34. The term "art horror" is explored in Joan Hawkins, *Cutting Edge: Art-Horror and the Horrific Avant-Garde* (Minneapolis: Univer-

sity of Minnesota Press, 2000). Here one could also include many of Stan Brakhage's films, as well as those by the Vienna Actionists. This would invite a further exploration of the linkages between the horror genre, avant-garde film, and performance art.

35. Georges Bataille, *Erotism*, trans. Mary Dalwood (San Francisco: City Lights, 1986), 63, 69.

36. "If we let the thing be present in its thinging from out of the worlding world, then we are thinking of the thing as a thing." "The Thing," in Martin Heidegger, *Poetry, Language, Thought*, trans. Albert Hofstadter (New York: Perennial, 1975), 181.

37. Bruno Latour, "From Realpolitik to Dingpolitik," in *Making Things Public: Atmospheres of Democracy*, ed. Bruno Latour and Peter Weibel (Cambridge, MA: MIT Press, 2005), 5, 13. This essay builds upon Latour's earlier work in such books as *We Have Never Been Modern*, trans. Catherine Porter (Cambridge, MA: Harvard University Press, 1993).

38. Recent examples include the work of Bill Brown on what he terms "thing theory," and the work coming out of science studies on objects and objectivity in the history of science. See Bill Brown, "Thing Theory," *Critical Inquiry* 28, no. 1 (2001): 1–22, as well as Elaine Daston and Peter Galison, *Objectivity* (New York: Zone, 2010). Brown borrows from Heideggerian distinction between objects and things, which is different from that of Kant. Suffice it to say that for Heidegger the thing is that which presences, whereas for Kant the thing is that which "absences" (indeed, the thing is an absencing integral to all objects).

39. Graham Harman, *Guerrilla Metaphysics* (Chicago: Open Court, 2005), 20.

40. Ibid., 19.

41. Ibid. Suffice it to say that, when all is said and done, the main insight of OOO is to have inadvertently shown us the limitations of philosophical phenomenology.

42. Immanuel Kant, *Prolegomena to Any Future Metaphysics*, §49, trans. Paul Carus, revised James Ellington (Indianapolis, IN: Hackett, 1977), 77.

43. "[O]bjects in themselves are not known to us at all, and that what we call outer objects are nothing other than mere representations of our sensibility . . . whose true correlate, i.e. the thing in itself (*Ding an sich*), is not and cannot be cognized through them, but is also never asked after in experience." Immanuel Kant, *Critique of Pure Reason*, A30, trans. Paul Guyer and Allen Wood (Cambridge: Cambridge University Press, 1998), 178.

44. "[T]he purity of the categories from all admixture of sensuous determinations may mislead reason into extending their use beyond all experience to things in themselves. . . . Such hyperbolic objects are distinguished by the appellation of *noumena*, or pure beings of the understanding (or better, beings of thought)." Kant, *Prolegomena*, §45 (74).

45. The principle of sufficient reason is commonly traced back to Aristotle's logical treatises, such as *The Categories*. It was later expanded by Leibniz, who agreed that anything that exists must have a reason for existing, but added that such reasons may be infinite and/or only known by God (that is, such a reason may exist, but may not be comprehended within the human framework of cognition). Schopenhauer, deeply influenced by Kant, undertook an extensive critical examination of the principle in his early work *On the Fourfold Root of the Principle of Sufficient Reason* (1813; originally written as his doctoral dissertation). There Schopenhauer offered a more pessimistic Kantianism; he analyzed the principle in more detail, outlining its four major aspects and suggesting that what Kant called the noumena or the thing-in-itself was forever blocked from our understanding—except in this comprehension itself of an absolute limit. For Schopenhauer, every form of human knowledge—including the sciences—assumed some prior principle of this type, and thus relied on some unquestioned, purely speculative *qualitas occulta*, whether or not it recognized it as such.

46. Arthur Schopenhauer, *On the Fourfold Root of the Principle of Sufficient Reason*, trans. E. F. J. Payne (La Salle, IL: Open Court, 1974), 213.

47. Arthur Schopenhauer, *The World as Will and Representation*,

vol. 1, trans. and ed. Judith Norman, Alistair Welchman, and Christopher Janaway (Cambridge: Cambridge University Press, 2010), 107.

48. Jean-Luc Marion, "What Do We Mean by 'Mystic'?," trans. Gareth Gollrad, in *Mystics: Presence and Aporia*, ed. Michael Kessler and Christian Sheppard (Chicago: University of Chicago Press, 2003), 2.

49. As Marion notes, "[n]o phenomenon can be given to knowing, or be admitted into the limited field of knowledge, if it does not accept being made into an object—in other words, if it does not assume as its own the conditions of phenomenality that the limits of our mind assign to it in advance" (ibid.).

50. Ibid., 3.

51. Ibid.

52. The idea of saturated phenomenon is developed in Marion's book *Being Given: Towards a Phenomenology of Givenness*, trans. Jeffrey Kosky (Stanford, CA: Stanford University Press, 2002).

53. Ibid., 199.

54. Marion, "What Do We Mean by 'Mystic'?," 4.

55. Marion, *Being Given*, 197.

56. Ibid., 206.

57. Laruelle, "The Truth According to Hermes," 22.

58. François Laruelle, *Principes de la non-philosophie* (Paris: PUF, 1996), 66. All translations from this text are my own, and the following quotations are all from this page.

59. "Dead media" was a term employed by science fiction author Bruce Sterling in the 1990s, in his proposal for a Dead Media Project that would collect outmoded or outdated communications technologies. The term has been taken up and theorized in media studies in works such as Matthew Kirshenbaum's *Mechanisms: New Media and the Forensic Imagination* (Cambridge, MA: MIT Press, 2012) and the collections *Media Archaeology: Approaches, Applications, and Implications*, ed. Erkki Huhtamo and Jussi Parikka (Berkeley: University of California Press, 2011), and *New Media, 1740–1915*, ed. Lisa Gitelman and Geoffrey B. Pingree (Cambridge, MA: MIT Press, 2004).

60. The supernatural horror tradition is replete with artifacts of this type. They often appear as everyday objects that become extraordinary, from a painting or sculpture, to furniture, to the corpse itself (cf. Edgar Allan Poe's "The Facts in the Case of M. Valdemar"; Charlotte Perkins Gilman's "The Yellow Wall-Paper"; M. R. James's "The Mezzotint"; Edogawa Rampo's "The Human Chair"; up through the stories of Richard Matheson, Ray Bradbury, and Ramsey Campbell). Haunted artifacts may also appear as unique charms, objects endowed with a possibly supernatural power—one finds many objects of this type in the stories of M. R. James and Sheridan Le Fanu. Or they may appear as religious objects at the same time rendered highly technological, as we see in Fritz Leiber's novels *Gather, Darkness!* and *Our Lady of Darkness*. In addition, postwar TV programs such as *One Step Beyond*, *The Veil*, *Twilight Zone*, and *Outer Limits* often feature artifacts of this kind—the 1964 *Twilight Zone* episode "Night Call" (written by Richard Matheson, and directed by Jacques Tourneur), features a telephone that gradually shifts from being an annoyance to an object of horror; in the final scene, it becomes both haunted and an object of love. The *Twilight Zone* episode "Nick of Time" (also written by Matheson, and starring William Shatner), features a "Mystic Seer" napkin holder at a diner that has the uncanny ability—or so it seems—to predict the future. In other shows, the artifact is at once quotidian and archetypal—the 1964 *Outer Limits* episode "Don't Open 'Till Doomsday" features an enigmatic, tiny box with a strange creature inside, possibly from another dimension, foretelling of a future apocalypse. Anyone who looks into the box instantly goes insane. The episode closes with uncertainty as to whether or not the world had ended.

61. The portal is also a recurrent feature in supernatural horror, perhaps finding its origins in Christopher Marlowe's *The Tragicall History of the Life and Death of Doctor Faustus* (1602), with its dramatic scenes depicting the magic circle and necromantic rite. Hodgson would recast the motif in his Carnacki occult detective stories, and Dennis Wheatley would reference both Marlowe and Hodgson in his occult page-turner *The Devil Rides Out* (1934). The

Hammer Studios production of the film version in 1968 (starring Christopher Lee) features an extended, detailed scene of the magic circle. This motif is elaborated in my book *In The Dust of This Planet* (Hants, UK: Zero Books, 2011), 49ff.

62. The artifact and the portal come together in horror stories that feature objects loaded with symbolic meaning. Consider the case of mirrors and mirroring: Edgar Allen Poe's "The Oval Portrait"; Oscar Wilde's *The Picture of Dorian Gray*; Robert Chambers's "The Mask"; Edogawa Rampo's "Hell of Mirrors"; and, though it is not, strictly speaking, part of the horror genre, Maya Deren's 1943 avant-garde film *Meshes in the Afternoon*. The culmination of the artifact and the portal is also evident in the haunted house story. In some instances the house itself, as architectural object, becomes an artifact, while in others the house or parts of the house serve as portals. The former describes much of the gothic novel tradition, exemplified in Horace Walpole's *The Castle of Otranto*, and extended in earlier horror films such as *The Haunting*, and in contemporary examples such as the TV series *American Horror Story*. The latter case might include films such as *The Sentinel*, *The Legend of Hell House*, and *The Amityville Horror*. The 1960s TV series *Thriller* (hosted by Boris Karloff) often featured haunted houses of this kind. The episode "The Hungry Glass" features haunted mirrors in a haunted house—or a house haunted by mirrors. Again playing on the mirror/mirroring motif, Alejandro Aménabar's 2001 film *The Others* features a haunted house in which memorial photography serves as a medium. Finally, the 1959 William Castle film *The House on Haunted Hill*, while it ultimately dispels the supernatural, is one of the few horror films to openly meditate on horror cinema and illusion (much in line with the spirit of Méliès).

63. A more rigorous, Lovecraftian way of writing this last sentence would be: " . . . the mediation is not between two points in a single reality, *but between two realities*."

64. This idea of the crystal as the ultimate medium is further explored in Dominic Pettman, "A Dream of Crystal Ships," in *Illuminations: A Journal of Critical and Cultural Theory* 2, no. 3 (forthcoming

2014). Pettman's text draws on the Baudrillardian notion of "the revenge of the crystal" and the J. G. Ballard novel *The Crystal World*.

65. Georges Bataille, *Inner Experience*, trans. Leslie Anne Boldt (Albany, NY: SUNY Press, 1988), 115.

66. Georges Bataille, *Oeuvres complètes*, vol. 2 (Paris: Gallimard, 1973), 456, translation mine.

67. Bataille, *Inner Experience*, 117.

68. Ibid., 115–16.

69. Maaike van der Lugt, *La Ver, La Démon, et la Vièrge* (Paris: Belles Lettres, 2004), 238, translation mine.

70. Armando Maggi, *Satan's Rhetoric* (Chicago: University of Chicago Press, 2001), 41, 54.

71. Zielinski, *Deep Time of the Media*, 7.

72. Siegfried Zielinski and Silvia Wagnermaier, eds., *Variantology 1: On Deep Time Relations of Arts, Sciences, and Technologies* (Cologne: Walther König, 2007), 11.

FURIOUS MEDIA

A QUEER HISTORY OF HERESY

McKenzie Wark

It is curious to note how much more lenient society is to the cheat than to the spoil-sport. This is because the spoil-sport shatters the play world itself. . . . In the world of high seriousness too, the cheat and the hypocrite have always had an easier time of it than the spoil-sports, here called apostates, heretics, innovators, prophets, conscientious objectors, etc. It sometimes happens, however, that the spoil-sports in their turn make a new community of their own.   *Johan Huizinga*

TOTALLY WIRED

You can fill in the salacious details for yourself. This is just the outline of a certain kind of *constructed situation*.[1] Let's begin with our characters, and let's call them the wild boys, in honor of William Burroughs, who certainly had their number. (They may of course not be boys, or may be boys in different senses.) The wild boys are getting ready. They try on outfits, do their makeup, get a little loaded, and gossip. This happens in many private rooms, all over the big city, and well after the sun has retired for the day.

There is the business of admission. There may be passwords or tokens, knowledgeable glances, a scrutinizing of the codes of dress and demeanor, and then entry to a foreign land. Foreign at least to the rest of the city. The wild boys call it home. It may be a place outside the law, or they may not be of legal age, and certainly the drugs are not legal. There is a sense of being on the outside and unobserved.

There's a science to the next part. There will be too much sound and too little light. Both will pulse to the same repetitive rhythms. Light will blare in the dark; sound will strobe bass notes. The bodies of the wild boys are stripped of their borders. There may be glimpses of strange skins or snatches of conversation, but it isn't possible to stay separate for long. Seen from above, from the DJ booth, it's a swarm of particles, close but not quite touching.

There is also a labyrinth, of darker rooms, some quieter, some louder, each with its own textures of sounds and surfaces, variable dimensions for more intimate and intense situations. Wild boys filter from the big room into them. There's the smell of leather, sweat, santorum, and of cracked and bleached wooden floors. A cluster-fuck starts, stops, merges with another. Spent bodies languish like used condoms.

The sun is up, and wild boys slink away, trying to make it back to some private space, unmolested. The industrial tools for delivering music and liquor are crated up and shipped away from the scene. Certain sober-minded people count their money over black coffee. A cleaning crew gets to work. The city goes back to its daytime labors. In some quiet place, some wild boys gossip about who did what with who, while in another some others marvel at the incontrovertible truth that some time last night they touched the infinite. The situation yields both unremarkable and unutterable signs, and sometimes to the same wild boys.

Some might even try to write about it. How are these signs to be read? How are these flickering images to be experienced? How is this knot of bodies to be untangled? And how can making sense of such situations contribute to making other situations? Can there be a theory and practice of situations, of the objects and subjects who come together, not to mention the part-objects or part-subjects?[2] Could there be a pedagogy of how to construct situations that enable particular desires to be communicable and which make desirable certain kinds of communication? Could there even be, not a knowledge, but perhaps a sensibility, of what is and isn't communicable, of how communication at the limit can remain free from centralized control?

Can we, in short, rewire the world? Marx: "The philosophers have only interpreted the world. The point, however, is to change it."[3] The passage from interpreting to changing, however, might pass through the velvet rope from a one-dimensional model of mediation to one with three dimensions, or perhaps four—or more—and even beyond mediation itself. What follows is something of an adventure, a slightly queer history rather than in any sense an orthodox one, which aims solely to get us near to that place where such questions could be asked, and even answered.

HERMES, IRIS, AND THE FURIES

Alexander Galloway proposes three kinds of mediation, each of which has its classical figure: Hermes, Iris, and the Furies. Hermes stands for the hermeneutics of interpretation, Iris for the iridescence of immediacy, and the Furies for the swarm of the distributed network. I want to restate and modify his three categories, not so much in the spirit of a hermeneutic reading as a constructivist retooling, which is one of the things I take the third mode really to be about.

Hermes is the divine messenger. He guards the door against ghosts. He is the market god, but also the god of promiscuity, seduction, travel, trickery, and informing. Hermes gets around. He is the slayer of Argus the all-seeing, whom he lulled to sleep with his talk. He shuts down the immediacy of the image with an exegesis without end.

Hermes stands for the middle part of a three-part process of textual trafficking: *exegesis, hermeneutics, symptomatics*. In the Hermetic mode, the text is assumed to be a foreign land, to which the reader must travel with a guide. The text is not itself to be read without first being rewritten—the exegesis—which wheedles the goods of interest from this foreign land for our own.

Exegesis is just the first step, however. Like all things foreign, it is not to be trusted. The second stage, the hermeneutic, inspects the goods carefully, looking for cracks in the merch. It is assumed to be false, a gyp. The hermeneutic looks past the surface to hidden depths.

Such was the hermeneutic procedure, but lately a third stage has become more important, the symptomatic. Hermeneutics at least imagines the exegesis to be a fair trade for the original text, and gets to work on the exegesis. Symptomatics ignores the exegesis and works instead as a second-order strategy on the hermeneutic reading. It reads not for what is there, in the depths. It reads for what isn't there at all, but "should" be. Thus the three stages of the hermeneutic evolve over time to explicate, denaturalize, and then complicate the text, which, far from becoming familiar to us, becomes all the stranger.

It is always worth bearing in mind that historically exegesis and hermeneutics did not function without agencies of law enforcement. The boundaries of legitimate communication were—like markets—not really self-regulating, but bound by censure, torture, and excommunication. When Nietzsche announced that God is dead, perhaps not the least sign of this is that straying from a correct hermeneutic was ceasing to be a life or death matter. You could no longer read as if your life depended on it. This is the other side of the now perennial cries of the decline of reading, of the humanities, of literary culture, and all that. What the psychoanalysts call the decline in symbolic efficiency is more about the decline of the repressive function that excommunicated those who read the wrong way.[4] The rise of the various schools of symptomatology really take advantage of the absence of a police function to advance reading onto more fanciful terrains.

Another reaction, as Galloway notes, was a revival of the appeal of a second mode of mediation, *iridescence*, which works in a quite different way.[5] Iris is a less storied figure than Hermes. Her sign is the rainbow, the dazzling arc. She is the bright goddess, daughter of wonder. She is a pure relay, simultaneously here and there, but she does not merely copy and repeat. There is always a difference. She shimmies and she shimmers.

Iris differs but she doesn't defer. Unlike Hermes, she does not traffic in the foreign. She is a goddess of nearness. Hers is an unmotivated expressive surplus of expression. There is never anything lacking in what she communicates. On the contrary, there's always a little too much. Where with Hermes representation always falls short; with Iris expression always exceeds. The iridescent is the too-real.[6]

If the privileged mode for Hermes is the text; for Iris it is the image. Where Hermeneutics is troubled by the *fetish* and its blockage of the full relation; Iridescence is troubled by the *graphic*, by the experience of too much information. Sometimes she seems more contemporary than Hermes. She is the goddess of the spectacle. Telesthesia, or perception at a distance, via the telegraph, telephone, television, and now digital telecommunications, keeps arcing the "too-much" toward us.

The too much can be celebratory. It is fitting that Iris's rainbow flag is the mark of Gay Pride and its insistence on visibility—usually "too much" visibility for homophobes.[7] Nor is it surprising that paranoid reactions to iridescence sometimes take a sexualized form: fear of an internet that is nothing but sexual predation. In any case, the internet really does turn out to be iridescent in that so much of it is porn, the contemporary mark of iridescent plenitude.[8] If the hermeneutic entails excommunication, iridescence entails *hypercommunication*; it is not an excluding but an exceeding or overloading. Jean Baudrillard's anxieties about the obscene ecstasy of communication are a pretty good marker of the valence of Iris in recent times.[9] If Hermes is obsessed with qualities of communication; Iris is more about the quantities.

Perhaps the years in which Iris was the prevailing goddess were a short-lived era in media history. Perhaps the attempt to celebrate the iridescent side of mediation comes too late. Perhaps there is already a third kind of mediation at work, which Galloway names after the *Furies*. The sign for this stage is not a Hermes or Iris, not a humaniod man or woman, but the pack of beasts. They are a flock of indefinable number, a multiplicity or a complexity. They are an incontinence of form.

Rather than the equivocation of Hermes or the relentless "yes!" of Iris, the Furies cry "never!" But maybe it is the case that they don't speak at all. At least not in a way that is recognizable to Hermes or Iris. They utter an inhuman speech. They can't be communicated with; they do it to us, not with us. The Furies generally get a bad rap. But perhaps that is because we are used to seeing them from the point of view of an Iris or a Hermes, to which they can only ever be a monstrous, inhuman other.

GRAN FURY

In a beautiful passage, the Comte de Lautréamont writes:

> Flights of starlings have a way of flying which is theirs alone and seems as governed by uniform and regular tactics as a disciplined regiment would be, obeying a single leader's voice with precision. The starlings obey the voice of instinct, and their instinct leads them to bunch into the center of the squad, while the speed of their flight bears them constantly beyond it; so that this multitude of birds thus united by a common tendency toward the same magnetic point, unceasingly coming and going, circulating and crisscrossing in all directions, forms a sort of agitated whirlpool whose whole mass, without following a fixed course seems to have a general wheeling movement round itself resulting from the particular circulatory motions appropriate to each of its parts, and whose center, perpetually tending to expand but continually compressed, pushed back by the contrary stress of the surrounding lines bearing upon it, is constantly denser than any of those lines, which are themselves the denser the nearer they are to the center.[10]

Lautréamont is here describing his own swarming poetics, only these lines are lifted straight out of the natural history writings of the Comte de Buffon.[11] Perhaps the Furies can get their due only when conceived from a point of view that attempts to be inhuman itself, as can happen at the discursive extremes of science and poetry, those twin attempts to expunge the reciprocal and human point of view from communication. The Furies keep surfacing and diverging in work which takes Hermes or Iris to be the governing deity. Perhaps they have not yet had their day.

Deleuze pits both iridescence and infuriation against hermeneutics, and Galloway does us a great favor by disentangling these two modes somewhat. But perhaps the Furies are not well captured by either political or military thought, for which infuriation tends toward a swarm of disorder, to be recognized and contained. In Clausewitz, for example, the swarm is both a force subject to command, but also the indeterminacy of fog and friction. In Marx the swarm is both the proletariat coming to consciousness of its historical mission, but also the misplaced enthusiasms in the dreaded lumpen proletariat. The Furies are always not what we bargained for and not to be bargained with.

The language of the Furies in and of themselves, unmediated by Hermes or Iris, is not a common one. Even Buffon and Lautréamont have to imagine a commander's voice, when what they are really describing with their starlings is a flocking algorithm, a kind of distributed protocol for a network of communicating bodies, each following simple procedures but which in the aggregate produces a complex, heterogeneous totality.

Mark C. Taylor notes in a similar vein that there are three theologies: the immanent, the transcendent, and the networked, which is not merely a return to immanence, but something else.[12] Meanwhile, in the Western Marxist subspecies of continental thought, it seems that what we have are turns toward theologies of immanence or transcendence, but not toward a networked one. The path not taken might then be this: not to refuse but to accept the strange theological turn descending from

Western Marxism, but firstly to see it as a turn really to questions of mediation, and to pose above all the question of a third
mode of mediation, beyond Hermes and Iris, if the Furies' game
can still be called mediation.

The project, at least in part, is one of overcoming the hermeneutic turn in Marxism, and its very strange habit of substitut-
ing the practice of reading the hidden text of the world for that
of collectively making a new one. For Galloway, Fredric Jameson stands for a hermeneutic Marxism at its finest. His slogan—
"always historicize!"—provides the code word to the crypt of
capital, its base modes of meaning-making.[13] But perhaps there
is still work to do to construct not only a critical theory but also
a *critical practice* of constructing situations for communicating
otherwise.

In theory at least Michael Hardt and Antonio Negri are close
to one of the figures of the Furies, the proletariat, or as they
quite openly rename it—the multitude—a concept which heals
the split between mass and swarm.[14] But like Deleuze, theirs is
a practice of immanence and excess, the pure productive, dif-
ferentiating power, in which Iris and the Furies are mixed. Lyotard's less well known *Libidinal Economy* perhaps comes closest
to a pure Irenic (post)Marxism, where libidinal affects arc across
pure surfaces without depth.[15]

One could write a whole genealogy based on variants within
the threefold space of mediation whose sign for Galloway is
Aphrodite. I shall limit myself to a few pertinent instances, all
from the orbit of the Situationist International. The Situationists (1957–1972) were perhaps the last of the historic avant-
gardes.[16] As such, they are something of a heretical formation
within modernist culture, cross-pollinated with Marxism, and
who proposed innovations not only in critical theory but in
organization, everyday life, and communication as well.

Not the least reason to highlight the Situationists in this context is that this organization was a conscious practitioner of the
art of excommunication. In the end, everybody was either ex-

communicated or resigned under the threat of excommunication. This practice, more characteristic in the twentieth century of communist parties than the church, became for the Situationist International something of an art form. They pose the question of the extent to which the coherence of the communications of a group presupposes some means of exclusion even outside of strictly theocratic communications.

Guy Debord's *Society of the Spectacle*, perhaps the central text in the Situationist "canon," starts out as a hermeneutics of negation, but by the end has moved on to its own peculiar iridescence. After reading through the fetish of the spectacle to the fetish of the commodity, and beyond it to the productive apparatus that produces it, the book moves to a celebration of *détournement*, or the practice of making a new culture out of a past culture that is taken as always and already a commons.

To quote Debord's 207th thesis: "Ideas improve. The meaning of words plays a role in that improvement. Plagiarism is necessary. Progress implies it. It sticks close to an author's phrasing, exploits his expressions, deletes a false idea, replaces it with the right one."[17] This is of course plagiarized—détourned—straight out of Lautréamont. Détournement is an appropriation of past into present, an Irenic arc of excess, to be trimmed only as the exigencies of the present situation and its struggles demand.

The work of Debord's Situationist comrade Asger Jorn hews closer to the temperament of the Furies. He was a great constructor of avant-garde networks, and a painter of entangled, swarming works that express the forms and forces of nature by further ornamenting their pathways. In his writings he warned against taking the classical Greeks at face value. Their distaste for anything too furious or too monstrous was the product of slave-owning merchant society.[18] The Greeks were more at home with Hermes, who parsed the barbarous language of strangers and parted them from their goods, although they could dally with the Irenic in their off days.

Of particular help to us in beginning the task of a Marxism

of the swarm might be the work of Raoul Vaneigem. Even more than Debord and Jorn, he championed the idea of a philosophy not of the sedentary hermenaut but of the delinquent pack. But in his mature writings there is a more subtle differentiation between kinds of swarms, and the beginnings of a theory and practice of *infuriating media*.

Like Jorn, Vaneigem did it by opening new communicating passages between past and present, new détournements and detours off the official canon of received ideas. In Vaneigem's case, the new passages through the labyrinth were those of the heretics excommunicated by the Christians, and indeed whose excommunication is what constitutes the church as such.

This is a key methodological point. Escaping from hermeneutic Marxism might take, among other things, finding alternate pathways through the archive to the canonic successions and obsessions that came to characterize not only Western Marxism but continental and post-continental thought in general. It's a question of moving from the suspicious reading of the authorized text to the drift through the network of protocols by which texts come to be texts as such in the first place.

Questions need be asked, not about the meaning of texts but about their control, and in a quite particular sense. This inquiry will start not with who or what authorizes a text in this world, but with its relation to the impossible, or rather with the control of the *portals* which appear to govern the relation between what is possible and that which lays claim to command them.

XENOCOMMUNICATION

The most sensitive point for any practice of media, let alone a theory, is its communication with the incommunicable. One could present this via a refashioning of Bataille's theory of the sacred.[19] Communication always seems to happen in the shadow of a lost immediacy with the totality. Communication is always a bringing together of a this with a that. Each this is connected to another that, and each that to another this. There's no beginning or end, and there is always either an excess or a lack to any particular communication, a more-than or less-than. But for there to be connections there have to be disconnections—excommunication. Something or someone is excluded, be it heresy or noise or spam.[20]

At moments of particularly fragile traffic around such a network, there are appeals to another kind of communication which can either legitimate these paltry linkages or at least cast them in some sort of perspective. If regular communication sometimes seems impossible, then it doesn't seem all that ridiculous to imagine it possible to communicate with the impossible, with the infinite, with the great outdoors—the totality.

I call this *xenocommunication*, and it can take two forms. It can be the irruption within a mundane communication of something inhuman. Or, it can take the form of an alien mode of communication itself, which nevertheless seems legible, at least to someone within the sphere of communication. A working hypothesis at this point might be that what is excommunicated to make communication possible are forms of xenocommunication that point to something other than communication as ordered by the powers of the day.

In the story "Hinterlands" by William Gibson, contact with some ineffable other has indeed happened, at some remote coordinates out there somewhere in the night sky.[21] The story presents the problem of xenocommunication in space drag. Spaceships are sent to these coordinates in the heavens, and some time later they come back. Almost invariably, contact has happened, but the hermenauts who have traveled to the limit are unable to communicate anything about the experience. They bring back some tiny artifact with them that turns out to be weapons-grade higher technology, so hermenauts keep getting rocketed off to meet their maker, or whoever, or whatever—it is. The returnees are not just mute and withdrawn, they are suicidal. Of the experience that so overwhelms them, nothing can be said, and yet some queer trinket of its existence returns.

Our narrator is the "surrogate" who tries, and fails, to get the returnees to communicate, and also to save them. The twist is that this surrogate once was thrust out there to this rendezvous, but the other didn't appear. From the other to us then is not one link but two: the hermenaut and the hermenaut's failed, sedentary double, the surrogate. A double moreover who knows their real service is to the military industrial complex that weaponizes the returning artifacts.

While "Hinterlands" presents the problem of xenocommunication as a space opera story, Eugene Thacker shows how one of its primary domains is horror fiction. His interest is in what he calls *dark media*, which embody exactly this paradox of communicating with or as the incommunicable. Interestingly, many such stories are of xenocommunication as a kind of iridescent arc in negative, an immediate experience of a kind of radical (in)difference, which is so excessive that its effect is traumatic on mere human receivers. Xenocommunication appears at the outer limit to both hypercommunication and excommunication. It is both the Irenic too, too much as well as the Hermetic too, too little.

Also of interest is the common role of media tech as either *artifact* or *portal* to other-worldliness. Sometimes xenocommunication takes the form of a mundane object like a camera acting as a portal for images from elsewhere, and becoming animate in this world; sometimes it's the presence of an artifact, a trinket which is itself of strange origins entering the world.

Dark media are mediations to that which is inaccessible, to a different ontology. Perhaps it's a property of all media, although the form this "darkness" takes might be contingent on the historical form of media in a given time. Media communicate between humans, but can sometimes also bind the human to the nonhuman. In spite of Heidegger's claim to the contrary, media do not always picture a world as if it were for us.[22]

Simon Critchley argues that a political theology is unavoidable: For there to be politics requires some structure of belief.[23] But perhaps this problem is reducible to a prior one. For there to be politics there has to be communication, and for there to be communication there has to be xenocommunication. There has to be an outside, an other space or time, with which communication is not actually possible, but whose impossibility must somehow still be communicated. This may once have been a theological problem, or rather a problem subject to theological control, but at the start of the twenty-first century it sprawls across genres, from J-horror to science fiction to psychedelic raves to s&m practices.

A good index of the languages of xenocommunication close to our time might be the *Exegesis of Philip K. Dick*, where the science fiction author throws every possible kind of writing at his disposal at the problem of accounting for his own experience of xenocommunication. He knows he may be experiencing a schizophrenic break, but he also knows it as a gnostic experience, contact with aliens, "dialectical materialistic mysticism," and many other things besides.[24] He struggled to give a positive account of his experience with unearthly information.

From among the available languages, Thacker has a preference for the *via negativa* as the means by which xenocommunication might be signaled. Any representation of what it is will always fall short. What's out there is beyond description. But perhaps it can be described by what it is not. It is striking that xenocommunication always hovers on the edge of describing (or not describing) something swarming. Iris communicates an outside that exceeds us; Hermes communicates one that is in the silences between what is said. Either way there is often something furious about it: patterns of both presence and absence, pluses and minuses, a code—more or less—of more and less. A code which nevertheless cannot be entirely known.

Tim Watts's novel *Blindsight* offers a particularly detailed description of xenocommunication, or rather of its failure. This science fiction novelist draws on his background as a biologist to come up with seemingly credible descriptions of alien life. His alien thing quickly discovers how to exploit a flaw in human optics to remain invisible. What is detected of it is only sensed via technology, all tentacular and seething, a "hydra of human backbones, scorched and fleshless."[25] Whatever it is, it has a terrible power over us, yet refuses all communication with us.

It is a commonplace now to think that as a subject we are internally divided. Part of the subject remains inaccessible, that part we call the unconscious. It is also a commonplace to think of the object, as it were, as externally divided. There is the object that can be perceived, but then there is the imperceptible thing-in-itself. Freud and Kant: perhaps what they achieve is an excommunication of the ineffable swarm so as to make possible a hypercommunciation just "this" side of if, which can then have a whole series of readerly protocols applied to decoding it— by those who make it their business to claim control over these portals.

The portal between unconscious and subject is that controlled by psychoanalysis. The portal between subject and object is that controlled by phenomenology. The portal between object and object is that which object-oriented ontology, which holds that objects withdraw from each other as objects withdraw from subjects, would like to control.[26] The portal between object and thing is that of Thacker's dark media, or weird realism. It is where philosophy, even on its ambitious days, knows it hasn't the passwords. It is the domain formerly of mystical thought, now up for grabs. Thacker shows how J-horror and the weird horror genre more generally, stake a claim to it.

Like Galloway, Thacker is interested in François Laruelle's critique of philosophy—even the philosophy of difference—as merely an abstract version of the world of exchange and communication, the surface world of capitalism itself.[27] The real is communicable; the communicable is real: That might be the desiderata of philosophy so understood. Laruelle rather raises to the philosophical plane the non-communicability of the real, a *via negativa* which admits no possibility of xenocommunication at all—but more on that later.

It is interesting that, in the J-horror movies Thacker studies, it is contemporary communication devices that are the portals (or artifacts) through which the horror enters. It is as if it weren't bad enough that these devices enable a hypercommunication within this reality, they also open portals to xenocommunications from another reality. The era of digital hypercommunication raises again the question of what can't be communicated. The excess of the Irenic arc, its strobing plenitude, gives evidence of both a desire that communication extend to other realities, and a fear of this very possibility. But it is not the Godhead, it's the swarm that always seems to lurk outside. Dabbling in dark media seems always to be tipping over into a dark pantheism in which far more than one portal to another world might open and can no longer be controlled by known protocols. Or worse: where access to such portals might become common.

It might help to put this-worldly communication, and in particular excommunication, back into the picture to understand just what is at stake. Is it an accident that H. P. Lovecraft, a central figure to weird horror, has such a problem with race? In Lovecraft, it's the excommunication of part of what is human that is the step toward the xenocommunication with the nonhuman.[28]

The novels of China Miéville tend to be good on this: xenocommunication is always caught in the struggle between communication and excommunication. Taking a leaf from Henri Lefebvre, Miéville gives new energy to that tendency that descends through the fringe romantics and the Surrealists, which puts the weird on the outside of a hierarchical order of communication, and also makes it the sources of a struggle for new life.[29]

In this Miéville inherits, perhaps unwittingly, a certain heretical strand. It is not an accident that Raoul Vaneigem's best work is about Christian and proto-Christian heresies. That was the labyrinth in which he found the precursors to exactly this tradition of fringe romantic, surrealist, and situationist works in whose shadow he cast his own.

THE SPLEEN OF A SPLENETIC WORLD

Communication appears to work on the basis of a prior excommunication. There is always a *protocol* in place for determining what is a legitimate communication, and the illegitimate ones are not merely excluded.[30] Their adherents are to be exterminated, and their utterances to be subject to the additional violence of a reading. The rationale given for an excommunication is often a textual error, but perhaps the real threat that has to be excluded is any challenge to the control of xenocommunication itself.

Where once what one challenged was the xenocommunicaton that anchors the faith, now it is the spectacle. Vaneigem: "God has been abolished but the pillars which supported him still rise towards an empty sky."[31] The Situationists had long thought that the precursor to the critique of the spectacle lay in the critique of religion. Debord called the spectacle "a permanent opium war waged to make it impossible to distinguish goods from commodities, or true satisfaction from a survival that increases according to its own logic."[32] Debord here appropriates and varies Marx's famous remark that religion is "the opium of the people."[33] Calling the spectacle an opium *war* rather shifts the emphasis. Just as the British fought two wars to impose the opium trade on China, so too capital keeps offering an unequal treaty to its subjects, in which it forces them to work to survive, but also obliges them to take the opium of the spectacle as compensation, from which capital also profits.

Marx's understanding of religion had a dialectical edge. Religion was also the "heart of a heartless world." Religion presented, in alienated form, the desires and needs of an oppressed and exploited people. Religion was in turn exploited and channeled as a support for the ruling powers. This double-sided quality to religion had sometimes come back to bite the ruling powers on the ass. A long line of Marxists, starting with Engels, noted the way that all through the Middle Ages popular uprisings of peasants and artisans turned their faith against the church. The emphasis in Marxist readings was generally on either the origins of faith in ancient class struggles, or faith as revolutionary ideology— the Anabaptists, for example.[34]

Starting with Ernst Bloch, some Marxists began to find the roots of Marxist thought itself in Jewish and Christian sacred texts. This opened the door for a host of post-Marxist readings in which sacred texts eventually replace Marx. Following Bloch, Antonio Negri offers a reading of the *Book of Job* as the testament of labor.[35] One could be forgiven for forgetting that Marx himself found the roots of his materialism not in Platonism or the Gospels but in Democritus and Epicurus.[36]

Both Vaneigem and Debord were more critical of the limits to faith as revolutionary ideology. Vaneigem: "As for the God of the Anabaptists of Münster and of the revolutionary peasants of 1525, he is a primitive expression of the irrepressible thrust of the masses towards a society of whole men."[37] For Debord the Anabaptists put their faith in God as the agent of change, believing that a cyclical time was about to turn full circle, and return them to Eden, to the promise of a life in which there was no masters, and in which property would be held in common. This was a critique of alienation in alienated form. The break into a genuinely revolutionary theory required a turning of revolutionary religion back on its feet. The power of God had to be brought down to earth.

Vaneigem will diverge from Debord in finding many more resources in spiritual communities—and communications—for the transformation of everyday life. The Situationist program was to abolish the separation of labor from desire and abolish the spectacle in which all that could be desired returned in the form of mere images of commodities. To *spectacle* and *separation*, Vaneigem offered a third object of critique: *sacrifice*. If Debord's critique was of political economy in the era of the reign of the image, then Vaneigem's was a critique of general economy—of mythical as well as real mediations—in the era of a generalized

political economy. It is also a critique of how control of the protocols of xenocommunication function to extract a surplus from
very this-worldly forms of labor and exchange. The problem of
the thing-in-itself is thus not a theoretical or theological problem, and not even a political one, but one of communication as
itself a form of control.

To everything there is a place and to everything there is a
time under heaven. There is a time and a place to be born, to die;
to build, to destroy; to weep, to laugh; to get, to lose; to give, to
take; to buy, to sell; to work, to rest—and to sacrifice. Each is
particular and separate, fragmenting time and space into dis-
parate, disconnected moments. There is a time and a place for
everything. But "everything" in the sense of the totality, the
unity of time and space—what of that? It too has its separate
time and space, that of the sacred. The sacred is a separate time
and space with the paradoxical quality of being that of the totality. It is the separate moment for what is not separate. The sacred
is the place and time for a very particular kind of sacrifice, for
the xenocommunication of something from this world of particular things, communicated toward the world of the totality,
of what is universal and eternal.

For Georges Bataille, the sacred persists as a problem for
the modern world, which has excommunicated itself from this
other realm of totality, to which it no longer knows how to offer
itself. The desire for immediacy with the totality persists, however, and other means have to be found to xenocommunicate
toward it.[38] For Raoul Vaneigem, it's a question of discovering
what kinds of gift could be freely given that might break with the
whole logic of sacrifice. "The urge to play is incompatible with
self sacrifice," but once the rules of the game become the rites of
a ritual, it becomes an offering in exchange for something else.[39]
Vaneigem extends the Marxist critique of mediation from the
secular to the spiritual economy.

For the Marxist hermeneutic, an exchange between owners
and non-owners of property is always suspect. It is a mediation

whose protocol is always an unequal exchange. With nothing to exchange but labor power, the non-owner of property does not get the full value of labor returned in the form of wages. For Vaneigem, the labor of the non-owner is also a sacrifice, a real giving up of time, effort, not to mention a renunciation of desires. In exchange for this material sacrifice, the owners of property offer imaginary ones. "To the sacrifice of the nonowner . . . the owner replies by appearing to sacrifice his nature as owner and exploiter; he excludes himself mythically, he puts himself at the service of everyone and of myth."[40] The protocol of the mediation is asymmetrical. Real sacrifices flow one way; the image of imaginary ones flows the other.

Vaneigem identifies what one might call three modes of sacrifice: ancient slavery, medieval feudalism, and modern capitalism. Rather than modes of production, they are perhaps modes of destruction. Vaneigem is not interested in the social product; he is interested in what is destroyed in its making. He is not interested in the objects extruding from an economy; he is interested in the subjective potential sacrificed to it. He is interested in what is sacrificed in this world by the alibi of a xenocommunication with another. His three modes differ only in how the sacrifice of free agency is extracted from their subjects.

In slavery, the sacrifice of the non-owner was in the last resort to be compelled by force. The slave sacrifices everything and the owner nothing. In the face of slave revolts, Vaneigem states, Christianity proffered an ingenious solution. It created a reason for the non-owner to offer a voluntary sacrifice. The sacrifice of particular labors and desires in the temporal world could be returned in the form of eternal salvation. This requires command over the portals of xenocommunication to another world from whence that return might come.

But wait! There's more! As if that offer wasn't enough, Christianity throws in a free set of steak knives: at the end of times the just will be resurrected and the golden age return. The nonowner will be the closest to God—eventually. For the moment,

however, the non-owner is furthest from God, at the bottom of a
hierarchy, underneath the priests and overseers, who in turn are
underneath the lords and cardinals, who in turn are underneath
the kings and popes. The non-owner makes a modest, particular
sacrifice of time and effort. The owner—whether of temporal
or spiritual power—makes a symbolic sacrifice to the totality
itself. The non-owner is given over to the particular task; the
owner is given over to that which orders all particular labors. We
all have to make sacrifices, but some sacrifices are more equal
than others.

Vaneigem's human trinity expresses the mythic unity of the
Christian world. Man's soul belongs to God and can be saved,
the body belongs to temporal power, while the spirit remains
free and belongs to nobody. The non-owner sacrifices the actual
body to the master; the master sacrifices his spirit to the good
of the whole. Both kinds of sacrifice, one actual, one mythical,
are validated by a third, the sacrifice to God. "God is the principle of submission."[41] Under the sign of God, the non-owner
makes a voluntary sacrifice to the master (the emblem of which
is Christ's suffering), the master makes an imaginary sacrifice to
God (while playing the part of the Father to the Son of the non-
owner). The ectoplasm that mediates them all is the Holy Spirit.

For Vaneigem, faith is not Marx's "heart of a heartless
world"—it is the spleen of a splenetic world. Far from being a
point of resistance or alternative to this-worldly unequal mediation, religion is an integral part of it. Christianity triumphed
over paganism but then had to confront the commodity
economy. It did so by becoming its spiritual accomplice. "The
Gods are the mythic form of the exchange economy. . . . They
are the supreme expression of the domination of use value by
exchange value."[42]

The church labored for centuries to make all of philosophy
and myth into a machine with which it could command all of
time and space. It created a standardized theological language,
with Latin as its universal medium of exchange, the gold standard of the spiritual market. This whole superstructure was dedi-

cated to the triumph of death over life. Vaneigem: "Death stares at our passions and we mute them; we mesh our desires with what is inimical to life."[43] If desire is nowadays intertwingled with spectacle, before that its entanglements were with sacrifice. Birth, death, sex, pleasure, pain—in the church's world it all had to be paid for. The church is not so much a political-economy as a media-economy of death, taxing every appearance of life to sustain it. It is "a kind of death that does not want to die."[44]

Atheists sometimes insist on the historical Christ as opposed to the spiritual one. Vaneigem wants to cast doubt on his very existence. "The creature whose crucified body and spirit of sacrifice have dominated two thousand years of an inhuman civilization pushed abstinence and abnegation so completely that he left no traces of his passage through history." Not only Christ, but the apostles are *characters*. "Around the end of the second century, the reassembling of the apostles would put together a team of heroes on which only Joshua/Jesus has no existence outside of Hebreaic mythology." The profusion of messiahs, saints, and sects was the material out of which the myth of Jesus was eventually synthesized, perhaps as late as the fifth century. The trinity caps it in the fourth century. To Vaneigem, the *New Testament* is "the *effervescence* of three centuries."[45] Orthodoxy invented its own past, choosing what it wanted from past texts, purged and rewritten. Through the labyrinth of détournement, it insists on the splendid arc of canonic texts, subject in turn to a stringent hermeneutic—and excommunicates the rest.

It is striking how contemporary post-Marxist writers think not only that something good can still come of a veneration of Saint Paul, but that his very existence is not a matter for serious doubt. Giorgio Agamben's brilliant hermeneutic of Saint Paul finds it the quintessential messianic text. Slavoj Žižek thinks Saint Paul is to Jesus as Lacan is to Freud and Lenin is to Marx (and perhaps for that matter Žižek is to Hegel), the one who gives form to a structure of belief. Simon Critchley finds in Saint Paul the living commitment to the infinite demand. And then there's Alain Badiou, but more on him later.[46]

For Vaneigem, on the other hand, the construction of the fictional character of Paul is not to be so easily erased. "Catholics, Byzantines, Protestants and Christians of all kinds have erected Paul and his Christic theology as a pillar of the church. His biography offers fewer lacunae than that of Hölderlin. . . . On what is such striking certitude based? On a composite novel that redactors from the end of the second century compiled from moral fables and Jewish midrashim, the meaning of which escaped them."[47]

Agamben treats Saint Paul as a site for demonstrating hermeneutic skill with perfect professional vanity, accompanied by a quiet forgetting of the traditional purpose of such forensic procedures. For Vaneigem, the textual residues of the church are not a scholarly archive. They are *police records*. "Here was born—in the daily interpretations of the infernal and paradisiac universes, which were rhythmed by riots, pogroms and social struggles—a theology that successive pruning, rational readjustments and polemical reasoning would transform into a dogmatic edifice shakily built upon murky assizes, which the church would not cease to shore up through the combined action of hired thinkers and state terrorism."[48]

Like the spectacle, Christianity had to be all things to all people. It had to incorporate even the meek as representation, if not as will.[49] It had to transcend class conflict and spiritualize it. It had to be at once a refined thing of intellectual loveliness that could seduce the aristocracy of the Roman world, but also a popular cult that could validate the poverty of the poor as Christ-like, as a sacrifice, whether voluntary or not, redeemable in some other world beyond this one.

And it would have to excommunicate at least four sources of heresy to achieve this. Among the ruling class, it would need to guard against excesses of purely intellectual pleasure, as well as against a taking too seriously of the ascetic nature of Christ. Among the oppressed, it would need to remind the faithful that only the *next* world belongs to them, not this one. But it would also have to guard against renunciations of the very doctrine of sacrifice itself.

Communication defines itself negatively, by the noise the communicants struggle to exclude.[50] In the act of exclusion, quite heterogeneous things can be excommunicated together. In the twenty-first century, putting a bomb in your underpants and putting diplomatic cables on the internet are both acts that might get their authors labeled *terrorists*. In earlier times, quite different kinds of deviants might all be labeled *heretics*. What power excludes, those opposed to power may well embrace willy-nilly. A characteristic of the aftermath of May '68 is that otherwise quite different kinds of dissent from spectacular power all acquired positive value for those for whom spectacular legitimacy had collapsed.

By carefully picking through past heresies, Vaneigem pointed forward as well, to protocols for distinguishing between lively heresies and dead—or deadly—ones. The control practices of Christianity turn up so often in those who would reject it. Such control practices are evident, for Vaneigem, in the cult of sacrifice, guilt, hatred of amorous desire, obsession with the spirit, disinterest in the body and nature, obedience to the masters of the portal and the keepers of the artifacts. Some kinds of heresies are just tributes in reverse to orthodoxy. How then could one distinguish not only heresy from orthodoxy, but distinguish among heresies, and on what basis? Vaneigem's peregrinations are in the end a natural history of everyday human gestures, one that is as remote as humanly possible from the terrain of the enemy, but which enable a selecting of pathways through the labyrinths of the excluded.

SIMON OF SAMARIA AND HELEN OF TROY

The first systematic worldview to come in conflict with emerging Christianities of which there is documentation is that of Simon of Samaria.[51] It grew into a legendary heresy among the

early church fathers. Sometimes called the father of all heresies, it is perhaps better described as the heresy of all fathers, or
at least of those who took the time to rebuke it. It reads exactly
like queer science fiction.

According to legend, Simon liberated a prostitute in the Pho-
encian city of Tyre by buying her freedom. Her name was Helen,
and she was, perhaps allegorically, also Helen of Troy. In Simonism, Helen represents *thought* and Simon represents *mind*, who
between them conceived of all things. She descended to the
world and made the angels and the earth, but was imprisoned
by the angels out of envy.

The angels mismanage the world, since each of them desires
to be sovereign. They will not permit her to return to union
with mind. Her spirit was obliged to transmigrate only among
human female bodies, which is how she came to be a prostitute
in Tyre. The world was made by thought, but not to the design
of mind, and the two are alienated. And so mind descended to
earth to reconcile with thought and save humanity.

Simon declared that the prophets were inspired by the angels
who made *this* world, and so should be ignored. The followers
of Simon and Helen should heed their own desires, as they are
free. Those who follow them can be free from the rules of those
who made this infernal world. The portals of xenocommunication are open both ways.

What remains of Simonism is its aberrant hermeneutic. Simon offered an allegorical reading of the first five books of what
would become the *Old Testament*. Or perhaps a reverse allegorical reading, one which returns an allegory back toward that
of which it is a palimpsest. It's a procedure that Vaneigem elsewhere calls, following Brecht's Herr Keuner, a "reversal of perspective."[52]

In Simon's reading, *Genesis* is, as the name implies, about
how life is born into the world. His *Genesis* is not so much about
the law of Moses as the fire of Heraclitus. Fire is the universal
principle, the uncreated creator. It is thought, logos, the great

and boundless power. While man is born below, this boundless power is still within him, or at least it can be.

The boundless power has two stems. One is *manifest*; one is *manifold*. One can be sensed; one cannot be sensed and is concealed. The concealed is hidden in the manifest; the manifest is produced by the concealed. These two stems of the boundless power are respectively what is sensible and what is intelligible. (They are in our terms: Iris and Hermes.) Both are real: the manifest can be sensed; the concealed can be thought. The fire is all things that are visible and invisible, all things named aloud and all things named in silence, all things that can be numbered and all things that are numbered. It is everything that can be thought an infinite number of times in an infinite number of ways.

The fire, the boundless power, is above the heavens, as if it were a great tree from which all flesh is nourished. What is manifest about this tree of life is its bark and leaves, and fire consumes them. The fruit of the tree, if its imagining is perfected, and in its imagining takes on its perfect form, is a fruit that can be placed in the storehouse and not cast into the fire. All aspects of the fire possess perception and intelligence. They are not uniquely human qualities. The task of the adept is to align her or himself with the way of fire, far away from any unequal sacrifice.

From the boundless power, and the branching stems of the sensible and the intelligible, come the six roots that the cosmos took from it. They are mind and thought; voice and name; reason and reflection. The first pair, mind and thought, is also heaven and earth, and male and female. Earth receives the seed of mind from the heavens. The second pair, voice and name, is also sun and moon. The third pair, reason and reflection, is also air and water. And in these six roots is the boundless power, in virtual but not actual form. One has to become in actuality what one is virtually, uniting the two aspects of the boundless power. If this power is not perfected in oneself, it perishes when one perishes. Simon reasons by analogy: it is just like grammar and geometry, which are virtual achievements in the mind but not actual unless one practices them. When the virtual acquires an art it becomes the light of all generated things, but without becoming actual it disappears as if it never existed at all.

There is a seventh power beyond the six roots. It can be figured as God or Word or Logos, but it is really the boundless power actualized. The seventh power subsists in the first power, the incorruptible form. The six roots, and the seventh that they can give rise to, are the seven days of creation described in *Genesis*. Humans are made from earth, made doubly in the image or form of the two stems of the boundless power.

Simon interprets *Genesis* by reversal of perspective. Eden is the womb and the garden of Eden the placenta. The river going forth from Eden is the umbilical cord. The cord divides into four channels, two of which send air to the infant, and the other two blood. These correspond to the four senses of the fetus. The book is called *Genesis*, after all, so that's what it has to be about! It is an inverse hermeneutic which converts the metaphoric back to the literal.

The following books of what would become the *Old Testament* are also read through the reversal of perspective. The second book, *Exodus*, is the difficult path of knowledge. It is about the sense of taste. Moses makes the bitter waters of exile sweet. The various sacrifices mentioned throughout *Leviticus* are only there to stimulate the sense of smell that one inhales with the breath, and so *Leviticus* is, by extension, about respiration. *Numbers* is about hearing and speech. The word energizes if the names of all things are uttered in their proper order, by the numbers, as it were. *Deuteronomy* is the touch that can confirm what another sense suggests. The deuteronomic law code, in this fifth book, is the synthesis of all the senses.

All of the six roots are in us virtually, but not in actuality. If people follow the Samarian teachings, then swords can become plowshares, and the fire of the unbounded power will not bear just husks but also fruit. But the fruit has to be shaped after the perfect form of the boundless power itself. Every tree that does not give good fruit is cut down and consigned to the flames. All generated and generating things have their beginnings in fire, which is the color of blood, and which is also the mark of desire. For desire to be generative, blood has to become two other fluids: sperm and milk, which disseminate and sustain life, respectively. Desire is the flaming sword that turns and turns to keep the way of the tree of life. The tree is the seventh power, the virtual image of the six powers together.

It is hard to know how much to credit in the legends of Simon and Helen, the vagabond magicians. It could just be a fantasy of the church fathers that the followers of Simon and Helen practiced what they considered a perfect love of promiscuity. The church fathers were certainly alarmed by Simon's playing of roles. Depending on local customs, he could claim to be the Son of God, or the Holy Spirit, or the Father Himself, or whatever else people wanted to call him.

Nor were they fond of the antinomianism of the Samarians. Since the laws were made by jealous angels and not by the boundless power, they need not really be followed. They also practiced magic and rituals, used love potions, and could send dreams arcing into the sleep of others, apparently. Some of this could be no more than the gossip of spies, police, and prosecutors. In Vaneigems's eyes, it does not capture Simon's challenge: to be done with the unequal mediation of sacrifice.

Vaneigem: "The rare fragments of his last work suffice to suggest a radical will in the precise sense of the term: that which attaches itself to the root of being and things." It is crucial at this point not to erect either a philosophy or a counter-theology on the bones of Simon of Samaria. Vaneigem's interest is in heresy as more or less well documented instances of the reversal of perspective, of the détournement of the reigning world view, be it religion or spectacle. "Simon of Samaria evokes the thinkers who, as much as Heraclitus and Lucretius, have irresistibly inscribed themselves in the modernity of each epoch."[53]

What distinguishes Simon from religious or hermetic gnostics is the nature of the amorous relation. It isn't burdened with guilt in Simon. There's no asceticism. "Surpassing the monstrous couple, formed by man and his gods, the man of the Great Power invents a universe that belongs to him without reserve."[54] There is nevertheless an instability, a tendency for hermeneutic text-grubbing to overwhelm the pure Irenic plenitude. Simon's is an experiment in the construction of situations from which to learn but not to venerate.

THE CULT OF BARBELO

If the error to which Simon could lead is forsaking the somatic for the semiotic, or rather the Irenic for the hermetic, the cult of Barbelo offers a different space of possibilities, and different limitations. Simon was bad enough, but the orthodox church fathers reported of the Barbelites: "these despicable, erring founders of the sects come at us and assault us like *a swarm of insects*, infecting us with diseases, smelly eruptions, and sores through a storyteller's imposture."[55] Not for the first or the last time, what has to be excommunicated is the swarm, the plurality of protocols, the free openings and closings of portals for xenocommunication outside of central control.

The Barbelites had their own reversals and détournements of the then circulating sacred texts. For instance, they held that Noah's wife was called Noria. While Noah was obedient to the malign angels, Noria knew of the goddess-mother Barbelo. When Noah forbade her to come aboard the ark, she burned it down—three times! The whole style of the Barbelites is that of Irenic excess.

According to this story, Barbelo is the goddess-mother who reveals herself not as spirit but as sensual power. She dwells in the eighth heaven. Her son is tyrant of the seventh heaven, who presides over the bad world. She decided to save humanity from her despot son by seduction. She presented herself to his servants and having made them ejaculate, used their sperm to

restore her power. The faithful to Barbelo "with the good conscience of an offering, abandoned themselves to making flow —
in the place of the blood that so many religions shed — the sperm
and the cyprine whose emission revives the energy of the Natura Magna."[56]

The Barbelite sign of recognition was a tickling of the palm.
This could lead to feasting and fucking, but the sperm is to be
received into the hand so it can be offered to Barbelo and then
eaten. Menstrual blood was also an artifact of Barbelo, to be
xenocommunicated back to her. Such beliefs and practices could
be hidden in the language of more or less Christian observance.
Sperm was referred to as the body of Christ, menstrual blood as
the blood of Christ.

Like the Samarians they had their own anti-allegorical readings. "In the midst of the street of it, and on either side of the
river, was there the tree of life, which bare twelve manner of
fruits, and yielded her fruit every month: and the leaves of the
tree *were* for the healing of the nations" (Rev 22:2). The fruit offered more or less every month they read as menstruation. If all
this wasn't enough, they also anoint their bodies day and night,
devote themselves to indolence and drink, and abstain from
fasting, or so their enemies allege.

The Barbelites turn the language of transcendence against
itself. The offering to Barbelo up above is only to affirm earthly
powers and sensations. Vaneigem: "the body is that earth whose
creative power merits the exclusive attention of men. The goal
is the fusion of self and world, but, whereas Simon identified
the consciousness of pleasure and the consciousness of self-
creation, the Barbelites, obeying the religious solicitation,
ended in a mystical vision of pleasure that, in the end, is a hom-
age to the soma of the Spirit and the divine."[57]

There is a danger in this, however. Rather than affirm the
free play of pleasures, they are caught in an otherworldly net.
"Barbelo, orgiastic Goddess and sucker of the universal sperm,
turns — as in Tantrism — the pleasures of life into a heavenly
duty, voluptuousness into a ritual obligation." Language im-

poses itself on sensation, and "the amorous exaltation is travestied as an ejaculation of the sacred." As in Wilhelm Reich, the trap that opens here is making pleasure compulsory, making it a form of work, and thus a sacrifice.[58]

Vaneigem's attention to the Samarian and Barbelite heresies points both toward ancient possibilities and contemporary ideologies. The church created itself by excommunicating such heresies. They were anathema to the sacred purpose of controlling the portals of xenocommunication which legitimate the unequal mediation between the voluntary sacrifice of non-owners with the imaginary ones of their masters. The pleasures of thought and life, of embodied sensation, of free enjoyment, flickered briefly in such cults. Such heresies undo the protocols of xenocommunication, letting rogue-portals and unregistered artifacts traffic back and forth.

As capitalism sheds its sacred shell, it inspires in its devotees cults which unknowingly repeat Samarian and Barbelite beliefs in all their limitations. The fascination with esoteric philosophies, from Lacanian psychoanalysis to Speculative Realism, no matter how liberal-minded, is still for Vaneigem as an overcoding of sensual experience. Yoga, the cult of the functional orgasm, making sex into a workout, and such practices likewise turn the labile and voluptuous morays of the body against the body itself.

TEEMING EPIPHANES

Still, the free play of mind and body implicit in Samarian and Barbelite practices can be instances of an ongoing heretical life, if compounded (under the effervescing sign of Aphrodite) with a third kind of heresy, which likewise recurs again and again in different guises, adapting itself to different historical circumstances. Its key character is Epiphanes, the "Gnostic Rimbaud," although whether he actually existed or not is another question.[59]

Preserved in Clement of Alexandria's *Stromates* is a fragment of Epiphanes's teachings on justice, in which justice means a community of equality. The sun shines equally on all, and so the creator can only have intended that all of creation belongs to everyone. The sun makes the pastures grow for the common enjoyment of all without the benefit of laws. Even concerning reproduction there are no laws. The sun shines on men and women and all their desires—and nothing is owed in return.

Property only enters the world through its man-made laws. The world had been in communion with universal and divine law; particular, man-made, laws fragment that communion. It is the law that produces the thief. Epiphanes mocked the biblical commandments on sin and guilt. The living perpetuates itself by changing form. Epiphanes links social equality to the free use of desire, self-regulating and without law, making and breaking its own protocols, gathering and dispersing. It is an affinity theory of social organization that anticipates Charles Fourier.

The heresies of the Samarians, of the Barbelites, and of Epiphanes produce distinctive ways of thinking about communion, sexuality, and property, but ways which can also be recuperated and turned into legitimations for new kinds of sacrifice. Latterday Samarians may stray into sacrificing mind, and Barbelites into sacrificing body, to a transcendent power. From Epiphanes too can come a politics of the resentment of the owners of property, a revolutionary violence that—ironically enough—usually does not abolish property so much as modernize it. From Epiphanes can come the cult of the sacrifice of the leader of the oppressed, the sad militant, the grim ascetic, from the Anabaptists to the Jacobins to Lenin and Mao.[60] It is a question then of extracting practices from the maze of heresies that bypass the controls of both heresy and orthodoxy.

THE MOVEMENT OF THE FREE SPIRIT

When slavery was the mode of production, various sects and movements competed with each other, some of which would be retrospectively cast as heresies once Christianity emerged as a centralized power. Once that power was consolidated, heresy becomes something internal to the space and time of feudal order, rather than an external challenge to it.

Norman Cohn wrote a famous book that saw only childish fantasies in feudal millenarian movements like the Anabaptists, something which postwar liberal democracy had outgrown. His *Pursuit of the Millennium* was a Cold War tract, a simple allegory that saw revolutionary heresies as the intellectual antecedents of both Fascism and Communism.[61] The analogy did not extend very far, however: those who tortured and butchered heretics were somehow not to be compared to the murderous friends of the free world in Asia, Latin America, and elsewhere. Or as Vaneigem once noted: "The state is the bad conscience of the liberal, the instrument of necessary repression for which deep in his heart he denies responsibility."[62] What distinguished Cohn's book was its detailed research into several centuries of heretical thought. The Situationists rather approved of it, although for reasons that would be anathema to Cohn.[63]

Vaneigem, when he came to write about some of the same heretical movements as Cohn, comes surprisingly close to some of Cohn's view of them. Vaneigem is not so interested, for example, in the Christ of the resentful poor, the "Zorro for the edification and salvation of the working masses." Or in apocalyptic and messianic faith: "It is the song of an immobile history, stuck in its glaciation, that can only break free in a total explosion. Born in the rupture of archaic Judaism with history, it reappears every time that hopeless oppression explodes under the blows of a hopeless revolution."[64] By then Vaneigem was fully taking his distance from what he saw as the negative consequences of modern heresy: "the frog in the revolutionary stoup swells with bile, eager to play the bull of theory on the commons [champ libre] of business."[65] The frog may very well be his former Situationist comrade Guy Debord, whose flirtations with the Jacobin style in the end proved too much for Vaneigem.

What particularly attracts Vaneigem is the Movement of the

Free Spirit, a heresy that lasted, in one form or another, for five centuries, across a fair swathe of Europe. While a few of their texts survive, they are known mostly because of the confessions extracted by "those executioners who perpetuated their victim's memories."[66] The Catholic Church denounced The Free Spirit, as did Martin Luther. Calvin's accusation was that they "confound all order" and "mingle heaven and earth." Worst of all, the Free Spirit gives "the name of spiritual impulse to the *raging impetuosity* that inflames a man like a bull and a woman like a bitch in heat."[67] Peering back through Calvin's misogyny, he seems buzzed by something that sounds quite marvelous.

Vaneigem's reading of the surviving evidence follows a threefold strategy. One tactic is to remember that most of the documents are confessions extracted under torture, offered in plea bargains, or are memos from spies and informants. The second is to trace an evolving line of thought through these often compromised, partial, and contradictory documents. The third strategy is more subtle: to realize that the Movement of the Free Spirit is never entirely free. It has to use a language that shapes its desires only negatively, and it constantly runs into the traps such language sets for it. "Beneath the name Free Spirit were concealed the most unfathomable parts of life, those parts of living that could not be expressed in either economic or religious terms."[68] This other *via negativa* is a way of (not) saying what can (not) be said of *this* world.

This reading strategy is not hermetic or symptomatic, so much as homeopathic.[69] Vanegeim reads against writing itself: "life has nothing in common with the language imposed on it." He reads, and writes, in the name of an Irenic "will to live, which speaks no recognized language." His interest is in a writing which gestures to the life that exceeds it. Some lightless, inarticulate thing lurks just beyond its ken. "Around the black holes of current language, power's pronouncements dance wildly."[70]

The Movement of the Free Spirit, in breaking with the authorized communications of the church, oscillates between two options. One is replacing the communication of power with the power of communication. The other is lovingly tending the teeming perimeter of the black hole where communication ends. Or, to vary the metaphor: "Signs are thus the vanishing points from which diverge the antagonistic perspectives which carve up the world and define it: the perspective of power and the perspective of the will to live."[71] The *via negativa* of this world and its censors are thus connected to the *via negativa* of xenocommunication as well.

The power of communication and excommunication of the church appears to emanate from its authority to speak of, and speak with, God. In declaring that anyone can have unmediated access to God, the Free Spirit bypasses the constraints of both religious and secular power. But then it is obliged to choose between identifying with the despotic powers of the Christian God, or of absorbing his grace into a genuinely human practice of being. Vaneigem: "Through the emancipation of sexual pleasure and the nurturing of love, it expressed a desire to transcend a life turned against itself, and to annihilate the pitiful pairing of oppressive God and oppressed nature."[72]

Within the necrophilic language of the church could always be found the red trace of another way of life. It can even be found in Paul: "Now the Lord is that Spirit: and where the Spirit of the Lord is, there is liberty" (2 Cor 3:17).[73] As one commentator notes: "Taken to its logical conclusion in an individualistic vein this came to have the connotation that where freedom is, everything is permitted."[74] This was probably not something Paul meant to recommend. This famous line can either be read more narrowly, or the whole of Corinthians can be read more as a warning against the free spirit. But 2 Cor 3:17 is there, on the page, and its significance is not just a matter of textual exegesis.

On the one hand there are the institutions of the church, in which various authorities are themselves authorized to interpret the verse. But on the other, there are less overt, more clandestine practices, not so much of reading as of détournement, which might make of scripture quite something else, much more in the spirit of Irenic bounty. Regardless of what he intended, Paul points toward the black hole of language, to that around which communications thrumb but cannot sting.

If there was a most troubling doctrine for the church, it was the poverty of Christ. How is so vast an enterprise as the church to reconcile its rent-seeking behavior with the renunciation of wealth by the Son? This is the contradiction upon which Vaneigem brings his Marxian critique of general economy. "The church despised all sin that was not profitable. It hated nature, that sewer of all temptations, but could not hate sinful nature, the source of its revenue."[75] Vaneigem remarks that far more troubling to the church than sinful behavior, greed, gluttony, and fornication, is their voluntary renunciation. "Christianity was very careful not to encourage any virtues that might cause its profits to dry up" (71).

Unlike his contemporary Michel Foucault, Vaneigem thinks there is a place for class analysis here.[76] The church is the bouncer at the door to xenocommunication, taking its cut from all who went—and came. Vaneigem sees the church's struggle as twofold: On the one hand, it had to exert its authority over all of space and time through control of a textual apparatus and all its appurtenances, through images, symbols, built form, costume, and so forth. On the other hand, it had to extract a rent from its subject populations through the management of as many of the portals in and out of life as it could manage. It had to keep a grip on the communicative superstructure of not one but two worlds.

BEGHARDS AND BEGUINES

The doctrines which legitimated the church's communication had the tendency to slip out of its grasp and become the support for more or less autonomous practices of life. The Beghards and Beguines, for example, created their own networks of vagabond spirits and communal ways of living. This milieu was a fertile one for heresies. Or so the church was inclined to imagine, and not least because these lay communities tended to look askance at the church's supposed monopoly on xenocommunucation and the rents it extracted for its services.

This was the everyday life within which the Amalricians, influential among some Beghards and Beguines, brought back the solution of an immediate relation to God. God is everywhere, and produces both the good and the evil things. Christ was not resurrected. God is a being of goodness, not a judge. The Amalricians recognized "the stark but banal truth: that there was already so much hell on earth that it would be better for people to stop tormenting themselves and to learn to enjoy pleasure" (97).

Their project was a powerful one, and unwittingly Epicurian: "the pulverization of God in the crucible of nature" (109). To make matters worse for the church, its own enclosed orders could foster the rediscovery of a life outside of its grasp, including this discovery: "Whoever is united with God can assuage his carnal desire with impunity and in any way, with either sex, and even by inverting the roles" (118). There have, it seems, always been wild boys, and wild girls.

A rare text which offers something close to the doctrine of the Movement of the Free Spirit, in its own words, and not extracted by torture, is *The Mirror of Simple Souls*, written in Old French by Marguerite Porete.[77] She was burned at the stake in 1310 after an extensive trial, in which twenty-one theologians read the *Mirror of Simple Souls* for heresy. She refused to recant. The crowd at her execution were moved to tears by how calmly she went to her death. While her writings were supposedly destroyed, some copies survived.

Her book takes the form of a dialogue between the Soul, Reason, and other abstract characters. It charts seven stages of mystical initiation. The early stages are fairly conventional. The soul's progress starts with three stages of asceticism, which gradually bare the soul to God's radiant love in the fourth stage.

The fifth stage is where the soul recognizes its sinfulness, but is subsumed within God. The sixth stage is where Porete's text diverges. Here the soul is annihilated in God.

Only God now exists. Finally, in the seventh stage, the soul rejoices permanently in God while still on earth. It regains primal innocence and cannot sin, indeed is liberated from original sin. The soul now has no will but God's will. It cannot be perfected until it does what it pleases, since what it wills is the will of God. The soul passes to a state of indifference. It no longer cares for the sacraments, the lives of the saints, or for the asceticism of the earlier stages of its progress to perfection.

After the seventh stage, even God is no longer necessary. The soul touched by grace is without sin. Once the soul is annihilated in Irenic xenocommunication with God it loses its will, desires, and essence. It becomes subsumed within God. This unification of the soul with the totality that is God is the way to freedom. It can take from the world what it needs without restraint. Porete: "Who should scruple to take what he needs from the four elements?" Vaneigem: "There is nothing base in the service of love. We must risk everything for it, and be able to renounce self-love and vanities in order to be purified in it and by it" (123). The sacred task is to create a nature in which God is reincarnated, by rehabilitating the nature that existed before the fall, before unequal mediation, before obedience to the landlords of the portal.

It isn't clear how closely connected Porete is with the Movement of the Free Spirit. Critchley is keen to separate the spiritual exercises of Porete from the sexual practices attributed to them. It is the case that the main evidence for their sexual practices are confessions made under torture. To the confessors any deviation from church strictures is immediately taken as a sign of pure wild sexual excess. Still, it seems artificial to separate Porete's theory from everyday practices, even if we have no reliable guide to what those practices actually were. It does not seem unreasonable to imagine that while they were not the libertines of the confessors' imagination, they did practice sexuality differently, outside of the prescribed economy of guilt and shame. As the wild boys know, such other protocols are one of the conditions of possibility of a discreet, and discrete, network.

John of Brünn, for example, claimed intimate knowledge of the practices of the Movement over twenty years, even if what we know from him comes from his betrayal of the movement and collaboration with the authorities. He describes an ascetic initiation, in which he was instructed never to confess to priests. He was taught that it was right to mislead people, to take money from others and spend it freely, to "send it into eternity" (165). He was taught to have no fear of the devil or purgatory, as these are just inventions of priests. Hell is torturing oneself. The adept, as in Porete, recognizes that "I am not master of myself; I am utterly dissolved in the flux of eternity," and "I belong to the freedom of nature" (167). It is right to seek "free satisfaction in the works of nature." For "all things that god created are for everyone" (169).

John recounts the secret signs of amorous conduct among adepts of the Movement: "If a sister places a finger on her nose, she invites a brother to come to her house. If she touches her head, then the brother enters her room and prepares the bed. If she touches her breast, he climbs into the bed and performs the task of nature and of love as many times as he is able" (168). Vaneigem remarks that these are the signs of the trinity, but where the nose (sex) aligns with head and heart: détournement at work in the heart of the everyday.

LIBERALISM'S HERETIC: FOURIER

Vaneigem contrasts the Free Spirit favorably with atheism, which brings the Holy Spirit down to earth as Reason. Atheism doesn't really depose God. It preserves him as the separation of intellect from life. Reason communicates to the body and the social body in the place of God, and just as with God, from without. The portals between reason and life become the renovated sites of controlled xenocommunication.

The Free Spirit, on the other hand, brings God down to earth not exclusively as intellect but also as passion, body, nature (195). A free spirit, being God, is part of the eternity of life, whereas atheism disposes of God by placing eternity in the world as nature. Asger Jorn called this the distinction between the materialist worldview and the materialist attitude to life.[78] The enlightenment of the Free Spirit democratizes the portals between the sensuous body and nature with a materialist attitude to life that is compatible with the materialist worldview of the sciences but is neither identical nor reducible to it.

Vaneigem: "Philosophy shattered theology only to perpetuate it in a different form" (44). The church used selected elements of Greek rationalism against the pagans, but such rationalism was used against the church in turn by the philosophy that overturned it. Vaneigem: "When philosophy took the absolutely abstract and life denying qualities of God and brought them to bear on an abstract image of man, the result was a humanized reverse-image of nature: self alienation brought on by economic necessity" (60).

There are dangers to severing the materialist worldview of the sciences from the materialist attitude to life as everyday practices. For Vaneigem, the temptation of the materialist worldview is to make oneself a God and take over his authoritarian personality, not least toward nature. To aspire to become ruler of all creatures is to proclaim a thoroughly denatured nature. "This sort of behavior—which Sade and Nietzsche would justify as they did all strategies of revolution—is to the project of the fulfillment of life what the charlatanism of the gold blowers was to the alchemical magnum opus" (264). Like Jorn, Vaneigem advocates an alchemy of everyday life, understood as a materialist poetics of constructing situations.

Vaneigem: "the followers of the movement of the Free Spirit identified, with remarkable lucidity, all that is negative: work, constraint, guilt, fear, money and possession, keeping up appearances, exchange and the striving for power" (250). However, there are tendencies inherent in it which call for a critique:

Sometimes, he says, it identifies too strongly with the Father (power) and sometimes with the Son (asceticism); sometimes it is too much, and sometimes too little. In either case, the error lies in an insistence on a privileged portal to eternity. It is not the portal of the church, but it is still a claim to possess exclusive access.

Vaneigem holds out little hope for the Movement of the Free Spirit in modern times. "If a spirit of revolt once existed within Christianity, I defy anybody who still calls himself Christian to understand that spirit. Such people have neither the right nor the capacity to inherit the heretical tradition."[79] The heretical tradition, within and against Christianity, continued rather through such works as Jean Meslier's remarkable excoriation of church doctrine and authority in his *Testament*.[80] Just as Marx grasped the necessity to move critique along from religion to political economy; so too heresy has to make its move in and against the portals of power of its time.

Vaneigem: "History has been the twilight of the Gods."[81] When the French Revolution lopped off the king's head, it cut the social body off from its spiritual head as well. "By directly attacking the mythical organization of appearances, the bourgeois revolutions unintentionally attacked the weak point not only of unitary power but of any hierarchical power whatsoever."[82] The bourgeois revolutions kicked God from his throne, one way or another. Nietzsche declared him dead; his contemporary Lautréamont revealed the golden throne itself to be mixed with shit. Before them Nerval had declared that "Christ is no more! . . . And they do not know it yet."[83] By denying this divine providence, the enlightenment sent civilization on a course of political revolution that did not result in a harmony below to match the—now abolished—heaven above. God is dead, but in his place, the Fraternity that founds the modern state still require sacrifices, and sometimes human sacrifices.

More than one sensitive soul discovered that with the head removed, the unitary social body was in a slow motion fall. Vaneigem: "The death of God democratizes the consciousness of separation."[84] Henceforth the Trinitarian unity devolved into irreconcilable binaries: body and soul, public and private, being and consciousness, self and society. Various opiates proffered to replace the third term of the old Trinity proved only temporary expedients, the most dangerous of them being the 'spirit' of nationalism. A new superstructure of mediation, a network of both communication and xenocommunication, is a work (and play) in progress.

Vaneigem: "This mission can only be accomplished by the new proletariat, which must forcibly wrest the third force (spontaneity, creation, poetry) from the Gods, and keep it alive in everyday life for all."[85] But rather than cut down already fallen Gods, Vaneigem gleans from what remains something of value for unpicking the rest of the unitary social order. Vaneigem revives certain other species of heresy, such as that of Fourier.[86]

Bourgeois liberal theology has its heretics, no less than the Christian. One of its first heretics was Charles Fourier, the provincial traveling salesman, who took a bleak view of the so-called *civilization* that the French Revolution had supposedly inaugurated.[87] For all his visionary nuttiness, Fourier's insistence that the revolution was not progress, that a quite different path to leaving the eighteenth century was called for, is an astonishing insight.

Bourgeois thought would get along fine without the one God. It would substitute for it one Law, one Nature, one Reason, and would insist on holding onto the one Family of the Christian order. (It now becomes more flexible about the gender of its founding couple, and that is a blessing, but bourgeois order still blanches at wild boys and their chosen familiars.) Against all this, Fourier's world is a pantheist universe of the passions, rather than of reason alone. If all cosmologies are analogical, then his is built on that of harmony: planetary, mathematical, and musical. God lives on in Fourier's cosmos, but requires no sacrifices to maintain his providence. Xenocommunication is all one way in Fourier, from God, or the One, to the world.

Fourier takes Newton's celestial mechanics to be the only

major scientific discovery, and boldly offers to fill in what it lacks. In the absence of a science of energy, growth, and life, he adds to Newton an alchemical poetics of that which the science of his time was incapable of systematically thinking. For Fourier the planets themselves are animate. Like humans, they have twelve passions, and communicate with twelve aromas. Planets, like humans, can have one or more dominant passions. Some, for example are Monogynes (one dominant passion). Some are Digynes (two dominant passions), and so on. The universe is dynamic and alive. There is "copulation between the planets."[88] Unlike humans (or perhaps not so unlike), planets each have a male north pole and a female south pole. They are androgynous and bisexual.

For all his Irenic surplus, Fourier's remains the most original heretical passage-work out of bourgeois recomposition of the powers of sacrifice to nation and economy. What Fourier's heresy was to the revolutionary stage of bourgeois ideology, Vaneigem's heresy is to the stage of restoration in the form of spectacle. Vaneigem traces a double path. The dominant path is the succession of the three modes of sacrifice, those of the slave, feudal, and capitalist modes. Each is legitimated after the fact by doctrines maintained by rigorous hermeneutic practices, backed by force.

Vaneigem's other path is a wandering, labyrinthine one. What is excommunicated is a heterogeneous body of both readings of texts and everyday practices. What these all have in common is a challenge to authorized control over the portals of xenocommunication. Among the excommunicated swarm are those who challenge control over xenocommunication, not to make a more authentic claim to the portals to sacrifice but to give up all such claims, to the portal and even to the necessity of sacrifice at all.

This, at its best, is the Movement of the Free Spirit and its precursors and successors. It does not install another controlling externality in the place of God. It does not legitimate a new claim to control the portal. Nor is it the pure Irenic solar plenitude of Bataille.[89] Rather, it is a plethora of protocols, an everyday poetics, a materialist attitude to life which does not foreclose or claim to command its mysteries: *furious media.*

THE RETURN OF THE WILD BOYS

Vaneigem's sensibility about the good life has a rather gentle side to it. Imagine young Belgians in love. They take a hunk of the local cheese and a good cheap wine and picnic on a hill. They gently caress each other's breasts or asses while declaiming surrealist poetry. It's a version of pastoral.[90] And so I call on the wild boys to stand in for a rather more experimental and plural conception of the construction of situations that deploy both the three modes of communication (Hermes, Iris, and the Furies) and the three protocols which can operate within each (Communication, Excommunication, and Xenocommunication). A critical theory and practice of communication for the twenty-first century can do no less—and may need to do a little bit more: One more effort, wild boys, if you would become heretics![91]

For anyone who wants to continue critical thought in the Marxist tradition, Vaneigem's thought has a lot to recommend it. He stays true to the heretical instincts of Marx, in congress with Fourier. The domains of everyday life, technology, the economy, and sexuality are surely the ones that critical theory and practice ought to be both within and against, for these are the domains within which capital itself appears as a historical and transformative power.

On the other hand, Alain Badiou prefers the world of art to everyday life, of politics to economy, of love to sexuality, of mathematics to science, particularly the nitty gritty of applied sciences and technologies. In each case, he abandons the field of particular historical struggles for what he imagines to be universals. He declares the attempt to oppose these bourgeois universals with concrete struggles to have been defeated, and decides that if one can't beat the bourgeoisie at its universalizing game, one might as well join it. Against the universal theology of the market he wants a universal theology of politics. His avatar of this struggle will be Saint Paul.[92]

For Badiou, Paul creates a universal singularity, a subjective truth, imposed on the world, and against the particulars of community. Badiou goes looking for a new Lenin or a new Mao, and finds him even further in the past. It is like the return to the Pauline purity of the Anabaptists, but not understood historically, as in Engels, but spiritually. Badiou preaches fidelity to a founder rather than Ernst Bloch's coming utopia. He pits a universalist politics against the universal of bourgeois liberalism—the market. This is the Jacobin idea rejected by Fourier—who lived through its consequences.

Vaneigem reads Paul against himself: if one is with God one cannot sin. Given that Paul was castigating Corinthian heretics, it is hardly a likely reading. It isn't meant to be. It is a détournement, a reversal of perspective. It is a recourse to the inverted, alienated world of God to find means of restoring life to the everyday and the everyday to life. Rather than a new universalism, Vaneigem offers the stories of particular attempts to wrest life back from its sacrifice, all contingent, but with a maze of recurring patterns. They might have failed, and might have had certain limitations, but at least these heresies have the merit of not installing a new control over mediation.

The problematic category here is "life." Eugene Thacker: "Every ontology of life thinks of life in terms of something other than life."[93] The thing other than life through which life is thought can take one of three forms. Number one: Life is spirit. It is interiority and exteriority. It is an incorporeal essence that remains the same or immaterial essence common to all living, that which is common to all forms and moments of life. Number two: Life is time. It is affirmation and negation, movement and change, it is process and self-organization. It is dynamic and self-organizing. Number three: Life is form. It is additive and subtractive. It is boundaries and transgressions. Vaneigem points perhaps to a fourth option: life as self-organizing matter. As we shall see, François Laruelle points instead to another way of thinking, of life as immanent to The One.

Heresies, at their best, are *tactical media theories*.[94] They are quick and dirty means of exposing the control of the portals and artifacts of xenocommunication, of underscoring the protocols of unequal mediation, and of routing around them by mobilizing other pathways through the labyrinth, ways which are to be found by tapping into the flocking algorithms of the swarm.

Henri Lefebvre and the Situationists moved the site of Marxist critique from the factory to everyday life, and in the process the conceptual object of critique changes also, from political economy to its quotidian articles of faith, against which heresies are a helpful resource.[95] Not the least of which is their legacy as tactical media theories, which can be used not only against the official *doxa* of the day, but also against some of its pretenders which appear as its mirror image.

Hence it doesn't take much to see in Badiou a rival claim to control the portals, the genius of which is to have them all covered. The artist, the mathematician, the philosopher and the dead tyrant are all celebrated as holding the power to xenocommunicate with the infinite. It may lay claim to control of another totality to that of bourgeois liberalism, or its so-called neo-liberal inheritor, but it is the same controlling gambit. Thus the special brand of heresy Vaneigem favors has the capacity of pointing out the limits of at least some of the others—of how critical theory becomes *hypocritical theory.*

VERONICAS OF THE FACELESS

A third stage of heresy within bourgeois thought, after Fourier and Vaneigem, might be that of François Laruelle. His is a work of prolonged heresy, in and against philosophy, in that he rebels against philosophy's claim that everything can be subject to philosophy: that logos (world) can be divvied up by logos (reason) and expressed as logos (word). He renounces the unthinking principle of sufficient philosophy: its faith in its powers over the portals that communicate between the apparent world and the Real. Like the gnostic heresies, his work is in a certain sense ascetic, a renouncing of philosophy's desire to *know* the totality.

The totality, or in Laruelle's terms the Real, or the One, is closed to thought. It cannot even act as a regulatory other for the thinkable. Philosophy keeps playing the same game, splitting the Real between terms, one transcendent, one more or less immanent, and playing out the game of the Two. First the transcendent concept—Being, Alterity, Difference—which tries to negate the radical immanence of the Real; and then the partially immanent term which claims to be its communicant. Laruelle: "the One is only the One, even with the Two, and the Two forms a Two with the One only from its point of view as Two."[96] If there's a portal, it opens one way; while we may finger the artifacts and imagine where they came from, only a hallucinated control of xenocommuncation can be installed there.

Laruelle picks up the scarlet banner of the heretics vis-à-vis the Christians and the Marxists vis-à-vis the philosophers. "We thus pose the decisive question to gnosis rather than to dominant Christianity, to Marxism rather than to philosophy, in front of this question they are cleared only because they have tried to respond to it: what is the real cause of human struggle?"[97] Heresy is a name for a myriad of struggles against all evil, but which need not take evil as primary. Laruelle: "How to make of rebellion something other than a reaction of auto-protection against aggression?" (7). Heresy thinks rebellion as such, not as a reaction, or at least it might. Heretics are rebels without a cause. What are we rebelling against? What have you got?

As in Vaneigem, there's a disentangling of certain strands of heresy in Laruelle. Both think it tended to get stuck in resentment, in damning this world in the name of another. They do not favor the same strands, however, or offer the same remedy, although like Vaneigem, Laruelle wants to "appropriate religion and adapt the divine mysteries to our humanity rather than to our understanding" (15). They are in accord that Christianity is a religion of the dead. Heresy can stand for a life that can excommunicate the phantom of other-worldliness. This is not unlike what Vaneigem tries to reconstruct out of the Movement of the Free Spirit and some of its precursors: that heresy whose special practice is of that One that exceeds the everyday but is not governed by rules of consistency or the persistency of rules.

Laruelle's tactics are very different, and for Vaneigem would partake of a certain gnostic intellectualism, even though Laruelle turns his considerable talent for axiomatic presentation toward key elements of gnostic heretical theory. Laruelle: "So you will not find here any exegesis of historical gnosis and its prejudices, which are those of a heavily transcendent imagination, something mythological, but rather an attempt at unloosing the original nucleus, as it were, its specific difference in relation to a sufficient Christianity and philosophy" (35).

Vaneigem and Laruelle both draw resources from both heresy and Marxism, for they both understand rebellion as primary, but for Laruelle, Marxism subordinates rebellion to salvation through class struggle, and heretical gnosis subordinates it to the struggle for salvation through knowledge. Nevertheless both are preferable to philosophy and Christianity in practicing revolt as reason and reason as revolt. Laruelle: "It is the revolt that commences, and does not cease to commence in each instant, proletariat or not, exploitation or not." (8). There is a nucleus to both heretical faith and (heretical) Marxism that sets aside claims to control the portals.

If Vaneigem's target was popular bourgeois sensibility and its theological ruins, Laruelle takes aim at their residues within the most recondite philosophy. This tactic is only apparently detached from a wider rebellion. "Philosophy and war are the secular arms of the purism of transcendence" (15). Laruelle wants to press beyond the renewal of philosophy by means of its critique to a heretical break in and against it. "The critical analysis of power, the innumerable political doctrines—of the State, of sovereignty—we know are among the exquisite pleasures where philosophy reassures itself of its existence and its usefulness. Philosophy would be more credible if it *considerably* extended that analysis to itself and, among other things, to Reason as auto-conquest and auto-defense which integrates all possible differences" (8). Laruelle holds out the promise of a ninety-degree arc from the plane of consistency upon which philosophy claimed to mediate between its dueling worlds, toward a critical questioning of the phantasmal media upon which such claims are tabled.

As he says in a mock-gnostic tone: "As there is a bad demiurge there is a bad theoretician, the Philosopher or the Theologian, who created a failed knowledge such that we must begin again completely differently, by avoiding the infernal circles to which they have doomed themselves" (41). But there is good news, of course: "Philosophy, form of the World, is our prison but the prison has the form of a hallucination and a transcendental illusion, not the form of flesh—it is itself knowable" (41). Laruelle's non-philosophy is a practice of relentless critique of philosophy.

Non-philosophy is a practice of struggle, a syntactic tactics. "Non-philosophy is not even the continuation of philosophy by other means, the way of alterity, but by the 'means' devoid of their war-form or philosophy. Unilateral struggle where axioms and theorems are turned once each time rather than once and for all against their original philosophical expositions" (14). It is—on a very refined plane—a tactical media theory that cuts through the claims to xenocommunication of otherwise rival theories.

What philosophy and Christianity have in common is that they claim to control the portal between worlds, or in Laruelle's terms between aspects of World: heaven and earth, spirit and flesh, beings and Being, and so forth. As Vaneigem notes in a quite different register, philosophy is far from leaving behind theology's powers of xenocommunication. Laruelle: "Yet it is the role of religion, from which philosophy is effectively inseparable, to bring about the affect of the Real. Monotheism in particular benefits from a special privilege of grafting itself to this claim, over-determining it and bringing it that which it lacks. It thus extenuates that structure, which is in other respects a creator of indefinitely hollow fantasies, purified of their dross. How does it come to live in this medium?" (15).

Philosophy lives in the shadow of Christianity's control of xenocommunication. By claiming to control the portal, it authorized that thought in which it is the (unequal, asymmetric) passage through the portal of reciprocal sacrifices that calls the totality into being, whether in the form of heaven and earth, Being and beings, Being and nothingness, Being and event, etc. The thought of what Laruelle calls the One, but which could have other first names, might install itself in the "and," as that from which such dueling terms issue but which is indifferent to them.

Rather like Vaneigem, Laruelle claims that what is recoverable from heresy is its gospel of the living. "Heresy presupposed that Life is a first name of the Real" (19-20). The Living are outside the controlled exchanges of Heaven and Earth (which together Laruelle calls World). They are testimony to another Life, one that is identical to the non-consistent, non-communicable Real. It is the heretical acknowledgement of the noncommunication with the Real that "protects against auto-specular fantasies" (17). The Real is that which the spectacle claims to call into being but which is actually indifferent to it.

A religion is an orthodoxy cleaving from (and to) multiple heresies. The Furies are on the side of heresy, or rather of *heresies*. Laruelle does not want to make a new orthodoxy of any given heresy, thereby "maintaining the religious exploitation of man under another form" (26). Rather, it's a matter of making the ninety-degree arc, of being done with the violence of one to the other, and showing the incommunicability between worlds. It is not that God is dead; it is that *media is dead*. If the Gods can be said to exist, then as with Epicurus, they have no interest in communicating with us at all: such might be the path toward a radical heresy.[98]

The portal to xenocommunicaton is always secured by fiat (if not by outright violence). "In gnosis it goes from man and no longer from the World, . . . no longer from Being or the Other. The human Real revealed by heresy in an original way and the heretical practice of thought which it reveals, exclude the authority of the ontological and philosophical apparatus" (35). Or as Debord once put it, "obedience is dead."[99]

Mark of the bourgeois leftist: like all leftists, he picks the disreputable side; but he instinctively prefers the more reputable among the disreputable. He prefers Althusser to Debord; Debord to Vaneigem. He prefers Lenin to Bogdanov; Bogdanov to Victor Serge. He prefers Marx to Engels; Engels to Paul Lafargue. He prefers Saint Paul to the heretics. Usually he (and it is usually a he . . .) *does not even mention* the heretics. Laruelle, like Vaneigem, restores them, but in this case not their names, not even their doctrines. He does them the courtesy of taking them as collaborators in thought. "Yet we will ask, for lack of anything better, that the philosophers, theologians and historians reconsider the 'heretic question' and examine to what extent it is instead heresy which questions their traditional posture and their good conscience, their authority and their prejudices" (33).

Heresy is the essence of thought's *rigorous* non-consistency, but heresy must be defined by heretical means, and here Laruelle steps beyond Vaneigem's practice of treating so carefully the evidence for heresy embedded in orthodoxy's anathemas. Laruelle: "As for the 'decisions' of language and thought by which we formulate and define heresy, we know that they themselves must be heretical and not philosophical and theological orthodoxies" (45). Here the path opens to that garden of forked paths that is the real history of the revolt into everyday life.

From the side of orthodoxy, heretics are separated, excommunicated. "The non-consistency of human Living that says it is separated from the consistency of an essence or from Being, this is what the heretics have revealed to us and it challenges philosophy and theology" (46). At its best, heresy lives *in* an immanent Real, whereas philosophy dwells in the *and* between a Real and some other. Heresy is within the *and* that refuses to mediate any terms. It remains prior to xenocommunication as separation and control. Heresy, as Laruelle practices it, is détourne-ment at the level of syntax, correcting *and* to *in*.

If heretics claim a separate orthodoxy, a compromise is possible. In the end, the Catholics will open diplomatic relations with the Protestants, the Leninists with the Maoists, and so forth. They come to care more about such "frenemies" than about anyone else. The true heretics care nothing for that. They preach instead "to the multitude *and in the most theoretical language*," as indeed did Fourier and the Situationist International (46). Heresy is a low theory, and always an everyday theory; high theory is always institutional, and communicates beyond that realm via public relations.

Laruelle, like Vaneigem, remembers the murdered, but as the living. "The contempt the victorious have for the intelligence of heretics and minorities is unfathomable in its naiveté" (47). Certain pages in certain "canonic" texts cannot really be read without being viewed first and last as veronicas of the faceless. "Those Murdered in the cause of heresy are not dormant in memory and buried in history. The murder of human beings reveals, in trying to fill it, the gap within the World that is Man-in-person" (20). They stand for an everyday life lived directly in The Real with which there is no xenocommunication, like the sun of Epiphanes. For the real heretic, as for the real Marxist, there is no general economy surmounting this world and another.

Laruelle pursues the direction of Marx's critique on a broader and deeper front. It is not just that the supposedly equal exchange of capitalism masks unequal exchange. It is that it masks a non-exchange, a *noncommunication*. This requires a freeing of Marxism, not just from Hegel but from philosophy, as philosophy for Laruelle always implies that the Real is in communication and that communication is real.

Laruelle takes very literally Marx's assigning of causal priority to *infrastructure* over superstructure. The Real—the One, the infrastructural—communicates its effects upon superstructure, which shows up perhaps something like the artifact. But there is no way to reverse the portal. There is no exchange of sacrifices, actual for imaginary. From the point of view of the super-structure, it appears to have a relative autonomy, to communicate both from and to the infrastructure. But from the point of view of infrastructure—the point of view of Laruelle's (non) Marxism—there is no such two-way communication. The infrastructural is determinate *in the last instance*, says Laruelle, in a phrase détourned from Althusser, in the sense that it is copied from him but also corrected.[100] If for Althusser the last instance never arrives, thereby giving license to set up superstructural portals within Marxist thought itself, for Laruelle the last instance always comes, and unilaterally.

Capitalism is a communicable disease in the form of a disease of communication. It puts everything into communication with everything else. It universalizes the "and" in the form of (apparently) equal exchange. As such, it is philosophy made concrete—or almost concrete—as the endless separation of the world into exchange values, all equivalent to, and competing with, each other. Capitalism is a realization of the practice of philosophy itself.

Against exchange value, Laruelle hews to use value and its incommensurability, its immanence. Labor-power makes, in and with infrastructure, a plethora of use values, but communication works only one way. There is no return. Labor-power makes out of the totality something else, which imagines itself to be always and already separate, and indeed to be what makes the totality out of a dialectic or a difference between itself and its other. But it is already just inconsistent parts of the One, the Real, the infrastructure, the "given without given-ness." Whatever one calls it, and whatever it is, it isn't exchangeable, by either capitalism or philosophy.

Where Marx critiqued the nineteenth-century ideologies of capitalism, Laruelle sets his sights on its philosophies, both its most ancient and its most contemporary. This spoil-sport might be particularly useful for retrieving the Furies from capitalism, from the now widespread belief that the network is a swarm of benign communicants, of happy busy worker bees. Through their distributed protocols of decision, it is supposedly possible to communicate between worlds, and through multiple portals. This pet swarm that capital hallucinates to replace the spectacle can supposedly reconcile capital and its other, be it nature, God, or whatever: That which is good, networks; that which networks is good.

Something like J-horror might point to how capitalism seeks to capitalize on and contain a more wild version of the Furies. The culture industry becomes the vulture industry, preying on the carcass of Christianity and philosophy, making a business of peddling portals. You too can xenocommunicate for a low monthly fee, no money down! The snaking path from Epiphanes to Laruelle might rather remind us: no deal. The immanent sense of the Real belongs always and already to anyone. Even heresies and Marxisms are in the end just fragments of The One become Two, which simply evidence The One unilaterally without pretending to be negotiating with it.

Of course it is yet to be seen whether Laruelle might not merely renovate the temple of bourgeois philosophy, but perhaps that's no less honorable a fate than the attempts by Fourier or Vaneigem to escape it. And it is yet to be seen whether there can be a connection between that heretical thought which declares that media is dead, that there is no xenocommunication, and certain practices of that everyday life—the wild boys are my witness—which knows it instinctively. It is yet to be seen whether the age of the Furies has really come, where there are portals without end to other worlds without end—precisely because they don't really work as advertised.

NOTES

1. In McKenzie Wark, *The Beach beneath the Street* (Brooklyn, NY: Verso, 2011), I develop some themes only touched on here, such as: the situation (ch. 11), the Situationists and Bataille (ch. 2),

détournement as method (ch. 3), Asger Jorn's radical monism (chs. 4 and 7), excommunication and the Situationists (ch. 5), Lefebvre on everyday life (ch. 8). In *The Spectacle of Disintegration* (Brooklyn, NY: Verso 2013) I develop further the connection between Vaneigem and Fourier (chs. 6–8).

2. Brian Massumi, *Parables of the Virtual* (Durham, NC: Duke University Press, 2002).

3. Karl Marx, "Concerning Feuerbach," *Early Writings*, translated by Rodney Livingstone and Gregor Benton (Harmondsworth, UK: Penguin, 1973), 421–23.

4. On the psychoanalytic concept of the decline in symbolic efficiency, see Jodi Dean, *Žižek's Politics* (London: Routledge, 2006), 42ff.

5. For a quite different take on the Irenic, see Mihai Spariosu, *Wreath of Wild Olive: Play, Liminality, and the Study of Literature* (Albany, NY: SUNY Press, 1997).

6. See McKenzie Wark, "Too Real," in *Prefiguring Cyberspace: An Intellectual History*, ed. Annmarie Jonson and Darren Tofts (Cambridge, MA: MIT Press, 2003), 154ff.

7. A connection could be made here to Eve Kosovsky Sedgwick, *Epistemology of the Closet* (Berkeley: University of California Press, 2008).

8. See for example Katrien Jacobs, *People's Pornography: Sex and Surveillance on the Chinese Internet* (Bristol: Intellect, 2012).

9. Jean Baudrillard, *The Ecstasy of Communication*, trans. Bernard Schütze and Caroline Schütze (New York: Semiotext(e), 1988).

10. Comte de Lautréamont, *Maldoror and the Complete Works*, trans. Alexis Lykiard (Boston: Exact Change, 1994), 159.

11. On Lautréamont and détournement, see Tom McDonough, *The Beautiful Language of My Century* (Cambridge, MA: MIT Press, 2008), ch. 1.

12. Mark C. Taylor, *Confidence Games: Money and Markets in a World without Redemption* (Chicago: University of Chicago Press, 2008).

13. Fredric Jameson, *The Political Unconscious: Narrative as a Socially Symbolic Act* (Ithaca, NY: Cornell University Press, 1982), 9.

14. Michael Hardt and Antonio Negri, *Multitude: War and Democracy in the Age of Empire* (London: Penguin, 2004), 91ff.

15. Jean-François Lyotard, *Libidinal Economy*, trans. Iain Hamilton Grant (Bloomington: Indiana University, 1993).

16. Patrick Marcolini, *Le Mouvement Situationiste: Une Histoire Intellectuelle* (Paris: L'Échappée, 2012).

17. Guy Debord, *Society of the Spectacle*, trans. Donald Nicholson-Smith (New York: Zone Books, 1994), 145; Lautréamont, *Maldoror and the Complete Works*, 240.

18. Ruth Baumeister, ed., *Fraternite Avant Tout! Asger Jorn's Writings on Art and Architecture 1938-1957* (Rotterdam: 010 Publishers, 2011), 153-65.

19. Georges Bataille, *Theory of Religion*, trans. Robert Hurley (New York: Zone Books, 1992).

20. On spam, see Graham Parker, *Fair Use: Notes from Spam* (London: Bookworks, 2009).

21. William Gibson, 'Hinterlands', in *Burning Chrome* (New York: Harper, 2003), 61-83. It is a variation on Stanislaw Lem, *Solaris* (New York: Haughton Mifflin, 2002), and Arkady and Boris Strugatsky, *Roadside Picnic* (Chicago: Chicago Review Press, 2012). Perhaps not surprisingly, these inquiring minds from what was then the Soviet sphere of influence had a very interesting take on orthodoxy, the control of portals, and xenocommunication.

22. Martin Heidegger, "The Age of the World Picture," in *The Question Concerning Technology and Other Essays*, translated by William Lovitt (New York: Harper Torchbooks, 1982).

23. Simon Critchley, *Faith of the Faithless* (Brooklyn, NY: Verso Books, 2012).

24. Pamela Jackson and Jonathan Lethem, eds., *The Exegesis of Philip K Dick* (New York: Houghton Mifflin, 2011), 506.

25. Tim Watts, *Blindsight* (New York: Tor Books, 2008), 220. My thanks to Ed Keller for introducing me to this book.

26. Graham Harman, *Towards Speculative Realism* (Winchester: Zero Books, 2010).

27. François Laruelle, *Philosophies of Difference*, trans. Rocco Gangle (London: Continuum, 2011); see also François Laruelle,

From Decision to Heresy: Introduction to Non-Philosophy, edited and translated by Robin Mackay (New York: Sequence, 2013).

28. Michel Houellebecq, *H. P. Lovecraft: Against the World, Against Life*, trans. Dorna Khazeni (London: Gollancz, 2008).

29. See for example, China Miéville, *Perdido Street Station* (New York: Ballantine, 2003). On the everyday, see Henri Lefebvre, *Introduction to Modernity*, trans. John Moore (London: Verso, 2012).

30. Alexander Galloway, *Protocol: How Control Exists after Decentralization* (Cambridge, MA: MIT Press, 2006).

31. Raoul Vaneigem, *Revolution of Everyday Life,* trans. Donald Nicholson-Smith (London: Rebel Press, 2001), 187.

32. Guy Debord, *Society of the Spectacle*, trans. Donald Nicholson-Smith (New York: Zone Books, 1994), 44. The video *About a Theological Situation in the Society of the Spectacle* (2003) by Masayuki Kawai brings out this dimension in Debord quite nicely.

33. Karl Marx, "Introduction to the Critique of Hegel's Philosophy of Right," in *Early Writings*, trans. Gregor Benton and Rodney Livingstone (Harmondsworth, UK: Penguin Books, 1973), 244.

34. Friedrich Engels, "The Peasant War in Germany," in Karl Marx and Friedrich Engels, *Collected Works*, vol. 10 (London: Lawrence and Wishart, 1975); Karl Kautsky, *Foundations of Christianity* (London: Socialist Resistance, 2007).

35. Antonio Negri, *The Labor of Job: The Biblical Text as a Parable of Human Labor*, trans. Matteo Mandarini (Durham, NC: Duke University Press, 2009).

36. Karl Marx, "Difference between the Democritian and Epicurian Philosophy of Nature," in Marx and Engels, *Collected Works*, vol. 1 (London: Lawrence and Wishart, 1975)

37. Vaneigem, *Revolution of Everyday Life*, 120.

38. Georges Bataille, *Theory of Religion* (New York: Zone Books), 17–25.

39. Vaneigem, *Revolution of Everyday Life*, 258.

40. Raoul Vaneigem, "Basic Banalities," in *Situationist International Anthology*, edited and translated by Ken Knabb (Berkeley, CA: Bureau of Public Secrets, 2005), 123.

41. Vaneigem, *Revolution of Everyday Life*, 119.

42. Raoul Vaneigem, *Movement of the Free Spirit*, trans. Randall Cherry and Ian Patterson (New York: Zone Books, 1994), 33. See also David Graeber, *Debt: The First 5,000 Years* (Brooklyn, NY: Melville House, 2011), which on my reading is at least slightly inspired by Vaneigem.

43. Raoul Vaneigem, *Book of Pleasures*, trans. John Fullerton (London: Pending Press, 1983), 1.

44. Vaneigem, *Movement of the Free Spirit*, 54.

45. Raoul Vaneigem, *La Résistance au Christianisme: Les heresies des origines au XVIII Siècle* (Paris: Fayard, 1993), 103, 45, 112, emphasis added. Translations from this text are mine, but I have also consulted those of Bill Brown.

46. Giorgio Agamben, *The Time That Remains: A Commentary on the Letter to the Romans*, trans. Patricia Dailey (Stanford, CA: Stanford University Press, 2005); Slavoj Žižek, *Repeating Lenin* (Zagreb: Arkzin, 2001), 32; Simon Critchley, *Faith of the Faithless* (Brooklyn, NY: Verso Books, 2012).

47. Vaneigem, *Résistance*, 131.

48. Ibid., 147.

49. See Debord, *Society of the Spectacle*, ch. 4: "The Proletariat as Subject and Representation."

50. A line of thought that could also be developed from Michel Serres, *The Parasite*, trans. Lawrence Schehr (Minneapolis: University of Minnesota Press, 2007). Also of interest to our present line of inquiry: Michel Serres, *Hermes: Literature, Science, Philosophy* (Baltimore: Johns Hopkins University Press, 1983).

51. Also known as Simon of Gittha and Simon the Magus or Magician. G. R. S. Mead, *Simon Magus* (San Diego: Book Tree, 2003), has the virtue of marshaling all of the textual sources on Simon in one place, even if one resists his annexing of Simon to theosophy.

52. Vaneigem, *Revolution of Everyday Life*, 185. Based on Brecht's Herr Keuner stories. Bertold Brecht, *Stories of Mr. Keuner* (San Francisco: City Lights, 2001).

53. Vaneigem, *Résistance*, 67.

54. Ibid., 71.

55. *Panarion* of Epiphanius, vol. 1 (Leiden: Brill, 1994), ch. 26. Emphasis added. Compare this to the opening pages of Michael Leigh, *The Velvet Underground* (New York: Wet Angel Books, 2011).

56. Vaneigem, *Résistance*, 92.

57. Ibid., 95.

58. Ibid. For Vaneigem on Reich, see *Book of Pleasures*, 10, 16.

59. Vaneigem, *Résistance*, 171.

60. For a fictional parable that further develops a similar point, see Luther Blissett, *Q* (London: Heinemann, 2005).

61. Norman Cohn, *Pursuit of the Millennium* (Oxford: Oxford University Press, 1970).

62. Vaneigem, *Revolution of Everyday Life*, 170.

63. Cohn is quoted in *Internationale Situationiste* 11 (October 1967): 25. See also Greil Marcus, *Lipstick Traces* (Cambridge, MA: Harvard University Press, 1989), 322. Vaneigem refers to Cohn in *Revolution of Everyday Life*, 167. See Debord, *Society of the Spectacle*, 138.

64. Vaneigem, *Résistance*, 12, 25.

65. Vaneigem, *Book of Pleasures*, 86. Champ Libre was the name of the publishing house set up by Debord's patron Gerard Lebovici, which published a number of works of a Debordian sensibility.

66. Vaneigem, *Movement of the Free Spirit*, 196.

67. Ibid., 228–32, emphasis added.

68. Ibid., 93.

69. On symptomatic reading, see Louis Althusser and Étienne Balibar, *Reading Capital*, trans. Ben Brewster (London: Verso, 1997), 28.

70. Vaneigem, *Book of Pleasures*, 48, 50, 47.

71. Vaneigem, *Revolution of Everyday Life*, 102.

72. Vaneigem, *Movement of the Free Spirit*, 93.

73. Ibid., 68. See also 1 Cor 6:12 and 10:23.

74. Raymond Pickett, *The Cross in Corinth: The Social Significance of the Death of Jesus* (Sheffield, UK: Sheffield Academic Press, 1997), 98.

75. Vaneigem, *Movement of the Free Spirit*, 85. Page numbers of

subsequent citations to *Movement of the Free Spirit* will be given in the text throughout this and the next two sections.

76. Michel Foucault, *Security, Territory, Population*, trans. Graham Burchell (New York: Picador, 2007), 191ff.

77. Margaret Porette, *The Mirror of Simple Souls*, trans. E. Colledge et al. (Notre Dame, IN: University of Notre Dame Press, 1999). While this translation gives her as Margaret Porette, she is more widely known as Marguerite Porete.

78. On Jorn's distinction between the materialist worldview and materialist attitude to life, see Graham Birtwhistle, *Living Art: Asger Jorn's Comprehensive Theory of Art* (Amsterdam: Reflex, 1986), 55–60.

79. Vaneigem, *Revolution of Everyday Life*, 168.

80. Jean Meslier, *Testament*, trans Michael Shreve (Amherst, NY: Prometheus Books, 2009).

81. Vaneigem, *Revolution of Everyday Life*, 186.

82. Vaneigem, "Basic Banalities," 155.

83. Gerard de Nerval, *Aurélia* (Boston: Exact Change, 1996), 50.

84. Vaneigem, *Revolution of Everyday Life*, 121.

85. Ibid., 119.

86. See Charles Fourier, *Des Harmonies Polygames en Amour*, edited and with a preface by Raoul Vaneigem (Paris: Rivages 2003).

87. Jonathan Beecher, *Charles Fourier: The Visionary and His World* (Berkeley: University of California Press, 1986).

88. Charles Fourier, *Harmonian Man: Selected Writings of Charles Fourier*, ed. Mark Poster trans. Susan Hanson (New York: Anchor Books, 1971), 51.

89. Georges Bataille, *The Accursed Share*, vol. 1, trans. Robert Hurley (New York: Zone Books, 1991).

90. See his Fourieresque pastoral utopia: Raoul Vaneigem, *Voyage a Oarystis* (Brussels: Estuaire, 2005). The title comes from Theocritus.

91. See for example, Harry Hay, *Radically Gay* (Boston: Beacon, 1997).

92. Alain Badiou, *Saint Paul: The Foundation of Universalism*, trans. Ray Brassier (Stanford, CA: Stanford University Press, 2003).

See François Laruelle, *Anti-Badiou: Sur l'introduction du Maoïsme dans la Philosophie* (Paris: Kimé 2011).

93. Eugene Thacker, *After Life* (Chicago: University of Chicago Press, 2010), x.

94. See Rita Raley, *Tactical Media* (Minneapolis: University of Minnesota Press, 2009).

95. Henri Lefebvre, *Critique of Everyday Life*, vol. 1, trans. John Moore (London: Verso, 1991). If early Vaneigem tried to radicalize Lefebvre's tending of the resources of Rimbaud and the Surrealists for everyday life, later Vaneigem traces them back to their heretical precursors.

96. François Laruelle, *Introduction au Non-Marxism* (Paris: PUF, 2000), 39. My thanks to Taylor Adkins for his translation of ch. 3 of this book.

97. François Laruelle, *Future Christ: A Lesson in Heresy*, trans. Anthony Paul Smith (London: Continuum, 2010), 5. Page numbers of subsequent citations to *Future Christ* will be given in the text throughout the rest of this section.

98. On the history of the reception of Epicurus, via the discovery of Lucretius, see Stephen Grennblatt, *The Swerve: How the World Became Modern* (New York: Norton, 2011).

99. Guy Debord, *Complete Cinematic Works*, trans. Ken Knabb (Oakland, CA: AK Press, 2005), 168–69.

100. See Louis Althusser and Étienne Balibar, *Reading* Capital (Brooklyn, NY: Verso Books, 2009), 216–18.

94392621R00121

Made in the USA
Lexington, KY
28 July 2018